African Women, Religion, and Health

WOMEN FROM THE MARGINS

An Orbis Series Highlighting Women's Theological Voices

Women from the Margins introduces a series of books that present women's theological voices from around the world. As has long been recognized, women have shaped and continue to shape theology in distinctive ways that recognize both the particular challenges and the particular gifts that women bring to the world of theology and to ministry within the church. Their theological voices reflect the culture in which they live and the religious practices that permeate their lives.

Also in the Series:

Grant Me Justice! HIV/AIDS & Gender Readings of the Bible,
    Musa W. Dube and Musimbi Kanyoro, editors
*Korean Women and God: Experiencing God in a Multi-religious
    Colonial Context*, Choi Hee An
Feminist Ecology in Latin America, Mary Judith Ress

African Women, Religion, and Health

Essays in Honor of
Mercy Amba Ewudziwa Oduyoye

Isabel Apawo Phiri and Sarojini Nadar,
editors

ORBIS BOOKS

Maryknoll, New York 10545

Founded in 1970, Orbis Books endeavors to publish works that enlighten the mind, nourish the spirit, and challenge the conscience. The publishing arm of the Maryknoll Fathers and Brothers, Orbis seeks to explore the global dimensions of the Christian faith and mission, to invite dialogue with diverse cultures and religious traditions, and to serve the cause of reconciliation and peace. The books published reflect the views of their authors and do not represent the official position of the Maryknoll Society. To learn more about Maryknoll and Orbis Books, please visit our website at www.maryknoll.org.

Copyright © 2006 The Circle of Concerned African Women Theologians.

Published by Orbis Books, Maryknoll, New York 10545–0308.
Manufactured in the United States of America.
Typesetting by Joan Weber Laflamme.

Library of Congress Cataloging-in-Publication Data

African women, religion, and health : essays in honor of Mercy Amba
    Ewudziwa Oduyoye / Isabel Apawo Phiri & Sarojini Nadar, editors.
    p. cm. — (Women from the margins series)
    ISBN-13: 978-1-57075-635-1 (pbk.)
    1. Feminist theology—Africa. 2. Women in Christianity—Africa.
3. Women and religion—Africa. 4. Women—Health and hygiene—
Africa.   I. Oduyoye, Mercy Amba. II. Phiri, Isabel Apawo.
III. Nadar, Sarojini. IV. Series.
BT83.55.A295 2006
276.0082—dc22

                                        2005033121

Mercy Amba Ewudziwa Oduyoye

Contents

Acknowledgments

The editors wish to express their grateful thanks to the following:

Cluster Publications, Pietermaritzburg, KwaZulu-Natal, South Africa, for permission to re-publish the following: Musimbi R. A. Kanyoro, "Beads and Strands: Threading More Beads in the Story of the Circle" and Letty M. Russell, "Mercy Amba Oduyoye: Wise Woman Bearing Gifts."

The Journal of Constructive Theology, December 2004 © Centre for Constructive Theology, Durban, KwaZulu-Natal, South Africa to re-publish the following: Sarojini Nadar, "'Texts of Terror,' The Conspiracy of Rape in the Bible, Church, and Society: The Case of Esther 2:1-18"; Isabel Apawo Phiri, "Dealing with the Trauma of Sexual Abuse: A Gender-based Analysis of the Testimonies of Female Traditional Healers in KwaZulu-Natal"; Susan Rakoczy, "Women and Peacemaking: The Challenge of a Non-Violent Life"; Denise M. Ackermann, "From Mere Existence to Tenacious Endurance: Stigma, HIV/AIDS and a Feminist Theology of Praxis."

Rev. Gary S. D. Leonard for his excellent work in copyediting our articles. He truly makes our papers "read better than we can write."

To all those Circle members who responded so positively to our call for papers, even though space precluded our publishing all of them within this book.

We are grateful to the Women's Desk of the World Council of Churches, for its financial support in subsidizing this publication.

Akoma Ntoso
"Linked Hearts"
The *Adinkra* Symbol of Understanding
and Agreement from West Africa

Preface

Elizabeth Amoah

This collection of essays celebrates and honors the life of Professor Mercy Amba Ewudziwa Oduyoye. She is indeed a pioneering and a wise African woman theologian who has contributed tremendously in the area of theology, the study of religion and culture, missiology, and to academic life in general. All of these areas of study have been framed and undergirded by a deep commitment to the wholeness of life for all African women. Mercy has researched, written, and published several books and articles on a variety of themes in these areas. She has been a great teacher, having trained and mentored several scholars in and outside the African continent. Having successfully worked in the ecumenical movement since her youth, she has also initiated movements that continue to nurture African women in theology and the study of religion in general. By initiating, for example, the Circle of Concerned African Women Theologians, Mercy has created an important space in which many African women theologians can undertake theological reflection. As a Methodist, she has remained in the church and has positively contributed to its life, growth, and work.

Mercy is a wise and creative person, with many sides and talents, who treads softly but firmly through the field of theology. This book reaffirms Mercy's approach in confronting difficult situations, which could be based on Matthew 10:16 to "be wise as serpents and innocent as doves." Mercy's contribution to the academy and to society in general has been recognized and honored by several individuals and institutions. This collection of essays is a further celebration of her life.

Notwithstanding what nature endows upon us, the circumstances of a child's birth and the historical context in which she or he grows up shape and direct to a large extent what that child ultimately becomes. This is abundantly true of the life of Mercy Oduyoye. Mercy is endowed as the palm tree, useful from its expansive roots through to its verdant branches. Born to Charles Kwaw Yamoah and Mercy Yaa Dakwaa Yamoah on her paternal grandfather's cocoa farm in Amoana near Asamankese in the eastern region of Ghana, her life was not only to be marked by being first among her siblings, but also by a bumper yield of yams, which followed the planting of seed together with her placenta and umbilical cord upon the Yamoah farmstead.

The act of planting the umbilical cord and the afterbirth of a newly born baby together with a food crop continues to be a cultural and religious practice of some rural Akan who continue to deliver babies under the supervision of traditional birth attendants. This ritual act symbolically links and spiritually identifies individuals with the land, the family, and the entire community.

By this act, nature in its infinite wisdom was already carving a path for Mercy Oduyoye's role in religion and society. It is not surprising, therefore, that one of her principal academic pursuits and fields of research was that of women, religion, and culture, an arena where her footprints remain forever in the sands of time.

A brief glance at her family tree reveals many golden threads, both past and current, that weave together into a beautiful tapestry. Mercy's maternal lineage is to the royal Asene family originating in Amakom near Kumasi, that later migrated to Akyem during one of the Ashanti wars. Eventually settling in Asamankese, many were to become rich cocoa farmers. They converted to the Presbyterian faith, which was the predominant Christian church in that part of Ghana. Her grandmother was given in marriage to Ampofo Amenano from Nkroanza in the Brong Ahafo region. Ampofo lived in Buronikrom, Asamankese (a Basel mission station) until the Presbyterians enforced a regulation that all who had not converted to Christianity should move out. Having strong roots in the traditional religion of his hometown, Mercy's maternal grandfather could not easily turn to this new religion and opted to move to another part of the town. This determination to hold on to traditional belief systems was later to be carried down to his granddaughter. It was only after further and careful consideration that he converted to Christianity, but he did not move to the Basel mission ghetto. Mercy too has refused to become a ghettoed Methodist.

Mercy's paternal lineage is also of a royal line. Coming from Apam and Ekwamkrom on the coast of the central region of Ghana, the Yamoah family consisted of Methodist farmers and traders who migrated and settled in Asamankese, where they established a Methodist church. Mercy's paternal grandmother Martha, rich in African beads, became a prosperous trader dealing in fish and crockery. She was also a renowned baker. Both grandparents were active and prominent church people, with Maame, as her grandmother was popularly known, contributing immensely to traditional music known as *Ebibindwom* in the Methodist church. It is little wonder that Mercy's father, Charles Kwaw Yamoah, a trained teacher, later became a Methodist minister who rose to the office of presidency in the Methodist Church of Ghana.

The first-born of a teacher, who later became a clergyperson, and an educated mother whose schooling took place in the prestigious Wesley Girls' High School, Mercy had to live up to the high expectations of Christians of that time. She was expected to become exemplary, first to her siblings and then to her entire community. From the art of cooking to modes of dressing, gait, manner of speaking and thinking, as well as by general demeanor, she had to conform to certain standards set by the church and society. Her training at home and school made her very diligent and industrious, a meticulous and modest person with an extraordinary sense of excellence. Mercy was also a most versatile child. At the tender age of eleven, she got stage fright during preparations for her first formal and public speech; I say formal because she was already involved in the church as a chorister and a Sunday school teacher.

Synergized by this background, Mercy's perception on life is one of harmony in diversity, whether it is with respect to ethnicity or religion. This equipped her with the tools necessary for her later ecumenical experiences and life. It is not surprising, therefore, that Mercy eventually married the renowned Nigerian, Adedoyin Modupe Oduyoye, a linguist, publisher, and writer and an Anglican and Yoruba of patrilineal descent.

Another experience that cannot be denied and that is closely related to this preparation for diversity is her secondary school life from 1949 to 1952 in Achimota, a primarily non-denominational institution whose motto, symbolized by the piano keyboard, is "That all may be one." The Achimota experience taught her that people of varying cultural, economic, religious, and social backgrounds can live together in harmony in the way that individual colors overlap and blend imperceptively into one another to form a rainbow.

From Achimota, where Mercy successfully sat for the Cambridge School Certificate Examination, at the prompting of her father she attended the Teachers' Training College in Kumasi College of Technology, now the Kwame Nkrumah University of Science and Technology, Kumasi. Upon graduation, she obtained a teaching post at Asawase Methodist Girls' School near Kumasi.

In addition to her teaching duties, she was assigned the filial responsibility of caring for three of her siblings when her parents traveled abroad. Caring, mentoring, and nurturing others had already become an indelible part of Mercy's nature. She was now twenty-one. At this early age she juggled the custody of her younger siblings with her profession as a teacher, while furthering her education through self-tuition, taking "A-level" high school examinations in geography, economics, and British Constitution. This was to culminate in her admission to the University College of Ghana, Legon, in 1959.

Mercy's interest was initially in geography. However, Noel King, a professor in the then Department of Divinity at the University College of Ghana, aware of her background as the daughter of a clergyperson, convinced her to study theology. Propelled by her care and nurture of others, a routine visit to an ailing colleague eventually crystallized into a university prayer group, an earlier forerunner to the current University Christian Fellowship.

Additionally, at the university her taste for music and an excellent singing voice drew her into the famous Dr. Ephraim Amos's choir. Such was the influence of Dr. Amos's music and message that to this day Mercy uses some of the music texts as sources for her reflections and poetry.

Excelling in her studies, Mercy was rewarded with the opportunity to study further at Cambridge University as part of the department's staff development program. At Cambridge, motivated by a desire to understand the development of Christian theology, Mercy studied for the Tripos Part III in dogmatics and was taught by such prominent professors as Alec Vidler and Maurice Wiles.

Upon completion of her theological studies at Cambridge, she returned to Ghana to teach religious knowledge at Wesley Girls' High School, Cape Coast, the same school her mother and three of her siblings attended. At this school the students were so impressed by Mercy's outstanding teaching skills and academic performance that some went on to study Christian theology and the study of world religions. Mercy has never stopped mentoring and nurturing these students.

The life and academic work of Mercy Oduyoye have inspired and influenced the theological work of not only Ghanaian women, but also significant numbers of African women theologians, many of whom she nurtured through the creation of the Circle and the Institute of African Women in Religion and Culture. Mercy Oduyoye's concerns expressed in her earlier works such as *Hearing and Knowing* and *Daughters of Anowa* have, to a large extent, influenced many of the Circle members.

Mercy's rich and varied experiences gained through many years of experience continue to contribute to the main foci of her theological work. This is clearly seen in the three leading themes that emerge from one of her recent books, *Beads and Strands*: 1) reflections on post-colonial Christianity in Africa; 2) women, tradition and the gospel in Africa; and 3) global issues from African perspectives. These themes form the pivot around which many current African women theologians do their theologizing.

In summarizing the importance of Mercy Oduyoye for the Circle, mention can be made of three important facets of her life and work:

- The first is her background in dogmatic theology, which gave her the tools necessary to interpret the gospel within the African context in ways that meet the spiritual needs of the continent in the postcolonial era. These concerns are reflected in the theological work of other Circle members such as Musimbi Kanyoro and Musa Dube.
- A second facet is her commitment and participation in the ecumenical movement. Looking at the ecumenical and missionary movements through the eyes of women has made Mercy very conscious of their participation in the church and society. This concern is reflected in the works of Nyambura Njoroge and Isabel Phiri.
- An important third facet is her rootedness in African culture. Mercy continues to be deeply rooted in African religion and culture, both of which have shaped her concerns about global issues such as HIV/AIDS and other sociocultural issues in an African perspective. Many of these concerns form the current focus of Circle discussion.

This collection of essays follows in the footprints of Mercy Oduyoye, who has gone ahead. Keenly aware of the many issues and challenges that confront the African continent in this new century, the present work seeks to address those concerns that impact women's health within the broader paradigms of African religion and culture. Utilizing, to a large extent, methodologies created and developed by Mercy, each contributor has clearly been encouraged, inspired, and motivated by her work and witness, thereby answering her famous call (echoing the call of Jesus to the daughter of Jairus) extended to the women of Africa: *Talitha cumi* (Mark 5:41).

Introduction

"Treading Softly but Firmly"

African Women, Religion, and Health

Isabel Apawo Phiri and Sarojini Nadar

WHY "TREADING SOFTLY BUT FIRMLY"?

The cabinet drawer was stuck, and for all her violent shaking, pulling and straining, Mercy could not release the stuck drawer. So in sheer exasperation she did the next best thing and headed for the hammer and axe. Filled with determination, she was ready to shatter the drawer, when her helper intervened with the Ga words, *malaka-le*. The words *malaka-le* can be translated to mean "coaxing" or almost "encouraging through gentle tapping."[1] So Richard, the helper, began to gently tap, first to the right, then to the left and as he began an almost rhythm of tapping, the drawer gave way, and opened much to Mercy's relief.

Mercy Amba Ewudziwa Oduyoye related this personal narrative during her insightful presentation at the consultation "On Being Church, African Women's Voices and Visions" in Kempton Park, Johannesburg, in October 2003. To the delight of her audience, she carefully and colorfully recounted her story with the

1

skill and acumen of the great African storyteller that she is.[2] She captivated her audience, but her point was yet to be made. Once she had garnered their attention, Mercy adeptly revealed the theological rationale that lay behind this personal incident. She related how, through all her years of being a theologian, she had come to realize the often ineffectiveness of confrontation as a means to an end. Linking this to women's struggles for gender-justice in religious and cultural settings, she said that such head-on altercations only resulted in the equivalence of cabinet drawers being shattered. For her listeners that day, Mercy's recounting of the jammed cabinet drawer and its coaxing open through gentle tapping, rather than taking a "hammer and axe" to it and thereby in all likelihood destroying it, confirmed her wisdom that treading softly but firmly is often the more appropriate and effective means.

The thrust of her argument is clear. By analogy, the "hammer and axe" theology is not always the most fitting tool when pursuing the cause of gender-justice and liberation for women. Sometimes a "soft but firm" theology is more appropriate. As Mercy has written, "God may not be 'in the thunder' so listen for the thin calm whispers (cf. 1 Kings 19:12) that are coming from African women theologians of the Circle. We are concerned for the health of the church and for religion as such" (Oduyoye 2001a).

In whatever context the history of the Circle of Concerned African Women Theologians is read, the name of Mercy Oduyoye will be certain to feature prominently. Indeed, as the founder of the movement, Mercy was one of the first African women theologians (indeed, for a long time, the *only* African woman) to write and publish theological reflections of any significance, particularly with respect to African women.[3]

"Treading Softly But Firmly," which clearly describes Mercy's approach, serves as a fitting theme for this book, which we see as a quilt made of many different pieces. It certainly is a method that Mercy has used to pry open theological debate among her colleagues, sisters and filial daughters of the Circle. Through their collective voice in this volume, we wish to explore, interrogate, and appropriate this theme, thereby gauging its meaning and usefulness for the Circle as it moves toward its sixteenth year of existence. On an introductory level, we propose to attempt this project in at least three different ways. First, we will explore the need to name the work of African women theologians belonging to the Circle, undergirded as we are by a hermeneutic and theology of liberation. Second, we wish to interrogate the ways in which the work we do as African women theologians relates to African and womanist theology in particular and its identity as an authentic field of study. Third, we will seek to relate our theological work to the wider discipline of theology (especially to those theological forms conceived in the West). In particular, we will investigate the ways in which it occupies and develops its theoretical space as a theological discipline.

Within the pages of one book, we cannot attempt an exhaustive examination of any of these three areas of enquiry. Rather, as African women theologians we seek to open up meaningful avenues of dialogue and enquiry within the wider theological academy, as well as within the Circle itself. Some of the articles contained in this celebration of Mercy Oduyoye already address some of these areas in detail, while others implicitly focus on specific aspects of the discussion. In total, we invite you, the reader, to join in this examination and elucidation of the work and witness of Mercy Oduyoye and the unique and important contribution she has made to the development of African women's theology and to the liberation project of African women as a whole.

WHAT'S IN A NAME? CIRCLE THEOLOGY

Mercy has simply called the theology being done by the Circle "African women's theologies." Circle theologians, on the other hand, have not always been so explicit in the naming of their work. In the fifteen-year history of the Circle, a diversity of names have been used: Circle theology; communal theology; *bosadi (English meaning?)* hermeneutics; cultural hermeneutics; womanist theologies, and African women's theologies. We want to suggest that a method based on "Treading Softly But Firmly" is a new and innovative model within which we might work.

The need to critically think through the issues surrounding the way in which we name ourselves was highlighted at a Circle consultation in 2004. Called to discuss models of engendering theological education, a robust and spirited debate ensued among Circle theologians as to whether we should name ourselves feminists or not. The discussion, albeit heated at times, highlighted our need as African women theologians to continue the struggle to find a theoretical basis for our work. Although many of us were trained in the tools of Western theologies, we have yet to systematically and theoretically interrogate their meaningfulness within our context as African women. Coupled with this, as African women we saw the need to establish ourselves differently (although with similar agendas) from the feminist cause, which we perceive as being largely Western, white, and middle-class.

Before embarking on the task of naming, we need to establish what characterizes our work as theologians. Within the main contours of African women's theological interests, we can point to three factors that may contribute to the problem of "naming." First is the need to continually interrogate the "triple-bind" of gender, race, and class, each of which is as important to African women as gender is to white feminists. Second, there is a need to find a balance between the activist and the theoretical planes as activism is a defining feature of the African women's liberation project. Third is the necessity of formulating new methods and theories appropriate to African modalities of theologizing that, although distinctive from those of the West, still maintain a critical approach. While this list is by no means exhaustive, it does capture the status of the present debate.

THE TRILOGY OF RACE, CLASS, AND GENDER

African women theologians, like their African-American counterparts, recognize the need for race and class to be an integral part of the discourse surrounding gender, rather than as marginal or adjunct discourses. The key issue, of course, is that, like our feminist and womanist sisters, our work is framed by an ideology and concern for the liberation of women, and yet we struggle to find ways in which to name what we do. We do not want to be called feminist, because of its seeming neglect of race and class; neither do we want to be called womanist because, as some have argued, the experiences of African-American women are different from those of African women (see Phiri 1997, Oduyoye 1990). African women theologians, however, realize the need to be in constant dialogue with all liberative theologies being done by women. Some are still wary of the cultural imperialism that might be present in some of these discourses (see the article by Ogbu Kalu in this book).[4] Nonetheless, there are some Circle theologians who have, despite the controversy, still chosen to bravely name their work feminist or womanist, albeit suffixed or prefixed by the term African. Musimbi Kanyoro (1995), Teresa Okure (1993), Musa Dube (1996), and Sarojini Nadar (2003) are some examples in point.

Others within the Circle struggle profoundly with this issue. Madipoane Masenya embodies this struggle to some extent, and we are not sure that she has resolved it through her use of the *bosadi* hermeneutic. Masenya's work reveals her struggle to situate her arguments within the larger debate in which women practice liberation hermeneutics. This is particularly true in regard to her critique of other African women working within a liberation paradigm (for example, Oduyoye 1992, 1995, 1998; Okure 1992, 1993), whom she accuses of demonizing African culture.

It seems to us that by opting for a specifically cultural hermeneutic, namely the *bosadi* approach, Masenya is reluctant to critique those aspects of culture that oppress women. Even though she claims that she does recognize that culture has both positive and negative elements for women, she chooses to ignore the negative aspects while bringing forth the positive (Masenya 1996, 157). This criticism aside, Masenya's work must be recognized as a bold attempt to name her work in a way that vividly captures the African context. Indeed, Masenya charts a shift in naming her work first as a black feminist construct within feminist theology, and then as African womanist hermeneutics, and most recently as a *bosadi* hermeneutic (Masenya 1997, 15). These shifts clearly reveal the struggle implicit in employing feminist categories of interpretation while remaining true to her commitment to women within African culture and, particularly, Northern-Sotho culture.

Musa Dube has taken the issue of race and class most seriously in her work developing a postcolonial reading of the Bible. Her book, *Postcolonial Feminist Interpretation of the Bible* (2000), based on her doctoral research, clearly testifies to this.

Notwithstanding the attempts by the aforementioned scholars, we would suggest that much more work remains to be done in this area if we are to keep the lines of conversation open, in particular that of scrutinizing the ways in which race and class interconnect with gender.

BETWEEN THEORY AND ACTIVISM

A second feature of African women's theologies is their commitment to "grassroots" women living in faith communities. The Circle Action Plan developed at the 2002 Circle Pan African Conference requires that African women become "bilingual," speaking the language of the academy and that of their communities, not just linguistically, but culturally and socially.

The commitment to "grassroots activism" is often reflected in the style and content of the publications that emerge from the Circle, targeted as they are toward "grassroots" women. However, the need for our voices to be heard in the academy has also been highlighted by the attempts of African women scholars to develop bold and innovative theoretical spaces. Musimbi Kanyoro's "cultural hermeneutics" and Musa Dube's "postcolonial readings" are striking examples of this trend. Inherent in these new theoretical models are deep-seated communal commitments to African women struggling daily with issues such as HIV/AIDS, poverty, and domestic violence.

A note needs to be appended as to how we approach the issue of HIV and AIDS. Within the South African context, many women and others are committed to campaigning for the government to provide post-exposure prophylaxis (PEP) to rape survivors and for an effective and comprehensive anti-retroviral treatment (ART) plan to those infected by the HIV virus, particularly for the prevention of mother-to-child transmission (PMTCT) of the virus by pregnant and nursing women. But this involves some highly contested issues. Exacerbated by President Mbeki's rhetoric of denial, many choose to utilize the term as HIV/AIDS, in order to highlight the causal link between HIV and AIDS. On the other hand, there are those diagnosed as HIV+ who prefer the term to be designated HIV and AIDS, arguing that although HIV can and will eventually lead to AIDS, being diagnosed HIV+ does not mean that one has full-blown AIDS. With proper nutrition, access to medication, and overall well-being, one can live positively with the HIV virus for a number of years, possibly until an effective cure can be found. As editors we have allowed for both uses, recognizing that each side of the argument has merits. What it does highlight, however, is the way in which our work is informed by our activist stance and our commitment to those who suffer the most.

We would submit, therefore, that an important second contributing factor to the reluctance of African women to name our liberation project for women is our struggle to find terminology that adequately captures both sides of our activism—the radical "head-on" approach often appropriated by African women in the face of impervious obstacles, and the more subtle approach of "treading softly but firmly." For African women, partnership, interdependence, and mutuality are as important as freedom in our struggle.

NARRATIVE ACTIVISM

Although we have perhaps suggested that Circle women awkwardly bridge the divide between the activist and the theoretical space at times, this does not mean that we have sacrificed the theoretical upon the altar of activism. In fact, to the contrary, we would submit that Circle women have often charted innovative methodologies that fall outside the ambit of traditional Western methodologies. One such method, garnered from within the enculturation project begun by African male scholars yet distinct from it, is the narrative method. African women theologians have frequently and unabashedly used this method of theologizing as a powerful and potent method to critique oppressive practices in African religio-culture. By using the established and time-honored method of storytelling, we have critiqued traditional practices, answering in the affirmative to Audre Lorde's question as to whether the master's tools can after all be used to break down the master's house. As a result — unlike our male counterparts—we African women theologians have not merely stamped our endorsement on religion and culture, but we have declared our "critical solidarity" with African religio-culture. In other words, while remaining true to our African roots, we have never ceased, through the telling of our stories, to point out those aspects of culture and religion that demonize and oppress women.

The above three factors might constitute a valuable starting point for widening the circle of discussion that Mercy Oduyoye opened over sixteen years ago when her vision was to motivate more African women to write about their experiences of religion and culture. We are now at a critical stage where we can no longer simply be content with writing about those experiences; we need to theorize about them in such a way that we make space for ourselves to be heard in our communities, in our churches, mosques and temples, but also in the local and international academy.

RELIGION AND HEALTH

True to the interreligious vision of the Circle, the articles in this book do not deal solely with one religion, but draw from the Christian beliefs and practices as practiced in Africa and African Indigenous Religion. Africa is home to African Indigenous Religion, the Baha'i Faith, Buddhism, Christianity, Hinduism, Islam, Judaism, and Rastafarianism. Each religion contains its own guidelines on how women should be treated. The Circle has published many books on how religion and culture have been used to enhance and harm women's lives.[5]

This book is an addition to the Circle's growing literature on women and health in the context of African religions and culture. It focuses on how religion influences women's thoughts, emotions, personalities, and social relationships as they seek communion with God. It is also a bold critique of how religion has enhanced or denied women's health. Health is understood in its broad context, encompassing the physical, emotional, psychological and social domains. We are honoring Mercy Oduyoye at a time when Africa is struggling with HIV/AIDS. The Circle started responding formally to HIV/AIDS in 2002 and has already published four books on the subject (see Phiri et al. 2003, Dube and Kanyoro 2004, Hinga et al. 2005, Akintunde et al. 2005). Within this book we have concentrated on specific issues that deny women's health: HIV/AIDS, rape, and gender-based violence that is in the home, religious institutions, sacred writings, and within society. The papers utilize religious modeling to show the importance of women's and children's health. Women are motivated by religion to be in the forefront in seeking health. African Indigenous Religion and Christianity are both replete with resources that bring healing to women and the African community from the multiple sources of oppression that otherwise deny them health. Women draw from their religious heritage and spirituality to become health providers to themselves and their families and communities in times of peace and conflict.

The interdisciplinary nature of the work of the Circle is reflected in the articles that appear in this volume. Through different disciplines and perspectives, the central theme of women, religion, and health is explored, reflecting many theological and religious conversations with Mercy Oduyoye.

ORGANIZATION OF THE BOOK

This book is divided into four parts of a patchwork quilt that tells the story of Mercy Oduyoye and deals with issues that are passionate concerns of hers.

Part I of our quilt is entitled "Celebrating Mercy Amba Ewudziwa Oduyoye." In "Beads and Strands: Threading More Beads in the Story of the Circle," Musimbi Kanyoro celebrates Mercy as the visionary behind the formation of the Circle of Concerned African Women Theologians. She takes the reader behind the scenes to show the important role Mercy played in founding, cultivating, and nurturing the Circle. She highlights the growth of the Circle and the difficulties it has encountered in the process of creating a space for African women theologians to theologize in community. Finally, she reflects upon crucial questions vital to the future of the Circle.

Letty Russell, a long-standing supporter of the Circle and a close friend of Mercy, continues the story of Mercy in the chapter "Mercy Amba Ewudziwa Oduyoye: Wise Woman Bearing Gifts." Letty skillfully weaves the story of the magi bearing gifts for the infant Jesus, as recorded in Matthew 2, with the story of Mercy, as the mother of African women's theologies. Letty goes on to analyze Mercy's publications and experiences in the international ecumenical community in order to show how she has used her pioneering position to bear good gifts to African women despite the severe opposition that she has often faced.

Nyambura Njoroge, in her chapter entitled, "Let's Celebrate the Power of Naming," salutes Mercy Oduyoye for her courage to publish the story of her own pain as a childless African Christian woman. Building on this, Nyambura furthers Mercy's call for a life-giving theology of procreation and eschatology that brings healing, transformation, and hope. Finally, Nyambura uses Mercy's story as a springboard to share her own agony and pain in naming the abuse of power in churches and theological institutions.

Part II of our quilt focuses on African women, the Bible, and health. In "'Texts of Terror,' The Conspiracy of Rape in the Bible, Church, and Society: The Case of Esther 2:1–18," Sarojini Nadar begins her discussion by quoting Mercy Oduyoye's reading of the story of the rape of Dinah. Sarojini pursues the theme of women's health by focusing on sexual violence that has been concealed within the Bible. She has chosen the book of Esther to reveal the structural rape of women present in the biblical text and society. She maintains that "texts of terror," unless read and exposed, will "continue to hurt women in our courts, cities, townships, rural areas, and the church as well."

In her chapter, "Women and Health in Ghana and the *Trokosi* Practice: An Issue of Women's and Children's Rights in 2 Kings 4:1–7," Dorothy Akoto places into parallel the story of 2 Kings 4:1–7 and the *trokosi* practice of slavery of virgin girls. She describes with dexterity the liberation of African women through the work of Mercy and the Circle. Dorothy identifies one thread that runs parallel through both, namely, that "women's rights and health are bound together with children's rights." She thus encourages the Circle to constantly deal with both these issues.

Part III of the quilt deals with "Women as Traditional Healers in Africa." In "Dealing with the Trauma of Sexual Abuse: A Gender-based Analysis of the Testimonies of Female Traditional Healers in KwaZulu-Natal," Isabel Apawo Phiri explores the issue of rape and pregnancy as experienced by female traditional health practitioners who have sought traditional methods of healing and have used traditional healing to help other rape survivors. Isabel goes further by breaking the silence around the issue of same-sex relationships among traditional healers, a claim that seems to contradict the commonly held view that homosexuality is a Western import into African societies.

In "Adinkra! Four Hearts Joined Together: On Becoming Healer-Teachers of African Indigenous Religion/s in HIV & AIDS Prevention," Musa Dube asks "How can African Indigenous Religion/s lecturers become healer-teachers by teaching AIR/s for HIV & AIDS prevention?" She has sought to answer this question by analyzing the holistic approach of African diviners among the Batswana. Musa cogently argues that if this method is used in HIV prevention strategies, the participatory process of the infected/affected community and specialist educators/project managers/activists, social workers, spiritual leaders, health specialists, policy and law makers would lead the community to write its own diagnosis. Such a participatory process would highlight the relationship of HIV/AIDS with that of poverty, sexual violence against women and girls, gender inequality, youth powerlessness, national corruption, international injustice, racism, and ethnic and sexual discrimination.

Dorcas Olubanke Akintunde argues in her chapter entitled "Women as Traditional Healers: The Nigerian (Yoruba) Example" that within African communities women are health providers through the instrument of care-giving for their families and the community at large. She highlights the need for men to share in the care-giving role as co-creators with women of the human race. She goes on to argue that contemporary Christian women in Nigeria draw from biblical traditions in their care-giving role.

Part IV of our quilt deals with "African Women's Experiences of Health and Healing, Endurance, and Peacemaking." In her chapter, "Women, Poverty and HIV in Zimbabwe: An Exploration of Inequalities in Health Care," Sophia Chirongoma explores the inequalities experienced in accessing the scarce health-care resources within Zimbabwe. She calls attention to the political and economic instability that impact the rural poor and women in particular. When this is protracted upon Zimbabwe's high HIV prevalence rate, it becomes a disaster that calls for urgent action by all, especially the faith communities.

In "Women and Peacemaking: The Challenge of a Non-Violent Life," Susan Rakoczy highlights the peacemaking efforts by women as individuals and as groups. She asserts that although Christianity has often been used to justify war, its essential core message is one of peace. Jesus was a peacemaker. So should be his followers. Sue shares the stories of two women of faith who chose to work for peacemaking. The important contribution of South African women to peacemaking under apartheid is also highlighted. Finally, using a focus group of intercontinental women, Sue highlights the traditional efforts of African women to make peace in times of conflict.

In "Stand Up and Walk, Daughter of My People: Consecrated Sisters of the Circle," Sr. Marie-Bernadette Mbuy Beya shares the story of the Circle through the eyes of a Roman Catholic religious woman situated in the war-torn Democratic Republic of Congo. She highlights in particular how, through the inclusive spirit of Mercy Oduyoye, African Roman Catholic religious women have gained their voice to speak out against all forms of oppression in the church and society. Finally, Bernadette describes how her own organization, the Bonne Espérance (Good Hope), has been used to further the aims of the Circle.

In her chapter, "From Mere Existence to Tenacious Endurance: Stigma, HIV/AIDS, and a Feminist Theology of Praxis," Denise Ackermann continues with the theme of women's health and religion by unpacking in a systematic way the gendered nature of stigma and HIV within society and the church. She argues persuasively that "if this debate does not take place in religious institutions, if it is silenced by cultural taboos and centuries of Christian moral teaching that has shown little understanding of embodiment, human sexuality will continue to be seen by many as something shameful, and sexual behavior will automatically be stigmatized."

Fulata Lusungu Moyo draws the attention of the reader to Christian teachings about healing in "Navigating Experiences of Healing: A Narrative Theology of Eschatological Hope as Healing." She draws upon her own experience of nursing a terminally ill husband and her experience as a widow to analyze the content of the messages that she received from well-wishers. She concludes by stating that although she was expected as a woman to remain strong in the face of her personal pain, she too had pastoral needs. She suggests that the terminally ill need to be involved in decision-making and the establishment of an eschatological hope in the present, instead of the imposition of prayers and continuous words of encouragement.

Part V takes the form of dialogue with Ogbu Kalu, a family friend of Mercy Oduyoye. Professor Kalu reflects on possible future areas of conversation between the Circle and African-American women theologians. In "Daughters of Ethiopia: Constructing a Feminist Discourse in Ebony Strokes," Kalu identifies five reasons for a dialogical theological methodology between African-American women and African women.

A CLOSING WORD OF THANKS

Finally, in view of all that Mercy has achieved, it is only proper to recognize with gratitude the profound contribution that she has made to theology and religion in general and to the creation of the Circle in particular. We encourage readers to follow up on these important themes by reading the second volume to this book, which will be published by Cluster Publications at the beginning of 2006. It is our hope that the observations, analysis, and visions set out here to honor Mercy Oduyoye will be carried forward, engaged, embraced and critiqued. Mercy would want no less.

NOTES

[1] Elizabeth Amoah has cautioned us that the Ga word *malaka-le* can also mean "I shall deceive her/him/it." Given this literal translation, the use of this word within this book might be construed to describe "deceptive theologies." Our intention, however, is to use the phrase in the context and spirit in which Mercy originally used it and which bespeaks her character and temperament.

[2] Oduyoye has often made the call for African women to use narrative as a theological method. In her book *Introducing African Women's Theology* (2001a, 16), she describes this method in detail.

[3] See the article by Musimbi Kanyoro in this collection.

[4] *Agenda* (2001 and 2002), a feminist journal published in South Africa and committed to empowering women for gender equity, dedicated two volumes to the theme of "African Feminisms," exploring the way in which African women committed to gender-justice name and articulate their work.

[5] See the books listed on the Circle website: http://www.thecirclecawt-.org/

REFERENCES

Akintunde, Dorcas Olubanke, Elizabeth Amoah, and Dorothy B. E. A. Akoto, eds. 2005. *Cultural Practices and HIV/AIDS: African Women's Voices*. Accra: Sam-Woode Ltd.

Dube, Musa W. 1996. "Readings of Semoya—Batswana Women's Interpretations of Matt. 15:21–28." *Semeia* 73: 111–29.

———. 1997. "Toward a Postcolonial Feminist Interpretation of the Bible." *Semeia* 78: 11–26.

———. 2000. *Postcolonial Feminist Interpretation of the Bible*. St. Louis, Missouri: Chalice Press.

——— and Musimbi R. A. Kanyoro, eds. 2004. *Grant Me Justice! HIV/ AIDS & Gender Readings of the Bible*. Pietermaritzburg: Cluster Publications; Maryknoll, New York: Orbis Books.

Hinga, Teresia, Anne Kubai, Philomena Mwaura, and Hazel Ayanga. 2005. *Women, Religion and HIV /AIDS in Africa: Responding to Ethical and Theological Challenges*. Pietermaritzburg: Cluster Publications.

Kanyoro, Musimbi R. A. 1995. "Cultural Hermeneutics—An African Contribution." In *Women's Visions: Theological Reflection, Celebration, Action*. Edited by Ofelia Ortega. Geneva: World Council of Churches, 18–28.

———. 1999. "Reading the Bible from an African Perspective." *The Ecumenical Review* January, 1–8.

——— and Mercy Amba Oduyoye, eds. 1990. *Thalitha Qumi: The Proceedings of the Convocation of African Women Theologians*. Ibadan, Nigeria: Daystar University Press.

Masenya, Madipoane J. 1996. "Proverbs 31: 10-31 in a South African context—a Bosadi (Womanhood) perspective." Unpublished D.Litt. et Phil. Dissertation. University of South Africa.

———. 1997. "Reading the Bible the Bosadi (Womanhood) way." *Bulletin for contextual theology in Southern Africa and Africa* 4:15-16.

Nadar, Sarojini. 2003. "Power, Ideology and Interpretation/s: Womanist and Literary Perspectives on the book of Esther as Resources for Gender-Social Transformation." Unpublished Ph.D. dissertation. University of Natal.

Oduyoye, Mercy A. 1990. "The Circle." In *Talitha Qumi! Proceedings of the Convocation of African Women Theologians 1989*. Edited by Mercy Oduyoye, M. Kanyoro. Ibadan: Daystar Press, 1-30.

———. 1992. "Women and Ritual in Africa." In *The Will to Arise: Women, Tradition and the Church in Africa*. Edited by Mercy Amba Oduyoye and Musimbi R. A. Kanyoro. Maryknoll, New York: Orbis Books, 9–24.

———. 1995. *Daughters of Anowa: African Women and Patriarchy*. Maryknoll, New York: Orbis Books.

———. 1998. "African Women's Hermeneutics." In *The Power of Naming: A Concilium Reader in Feminist Liberation Theology*. Edited by Elisabeth Schüssler Fiorenza. Maryknoll, New York: Orbis Books, 124–31.

———. 2001a. *Introducing African Women's Theology*. Sheffield: Sheffield Academic Press.

———. 2000b. "The Story of a Circle—Circle of Concerned African Women Theologians." *The Ecumenical Review*, January. http:// www.findarticles.com/p/articles/mi_m2065/is_1_53/ai_71190358/ (accessed 12 June 2005).

Okure, Teresa. 1989. "Women in the Bible." In *With Passion and Compassion: Third World Women Doing Theology*. Edited by Virginia Fabella and Mercy Amba Oduyoye. Maryknoll, New York: Orbis Books, 47–59.

———. 1992. "The Will to Arise: Reflections on Luke 8:40–56." In *The Will to Arise: Women, Tradition and the Church in Africa*. Edited by Mercy Amba Oduyoye and Musimbi R. A. Kanyoro. Maryknoll, New York: Orbis Books, 221–30.

———. 1993. "Feminist Interpretations in Africa." In *Searching the Scriptures: A Feminist Introduction*. Vol. I. Edited by Elisabeth Schüssler Fiorenza. New York: Crossroads, 76–85.

Phiri, Isabel Apawo. 1997. "Doing Theology in Community: The Case of African Women Theologians in the 1990s." *Journal of Theology for Southern Africa* 99, November, 68–76.

———, Beverley Haddad, and Madipoane Masenya, eds. 2003. *African Women, HIV/AIDS and Faith Communities*. Pietermaritzburg: Cluster Publications.

PART I

CELEBRATING
MERCY AMBA
EWUDZIWA ODUYOYE

1

Beads and Strands

Threading More Beads in the Story of the Circle

Musimbi R. A. Kanyoro

RECOGNIZING THE CHALLENGE

In a chapter in Mercy Amba Ewudziwa Oduyoye's 1995 book *Daughters of Anowa* entitled "Beads and Strands," she explains her fondness for the art of beadwork. The artists who sort and thread beads envision creating something beautiful. Many others have sought to tell the story of the Circle of Concerned African Women Theologians, each adding their individual beads to make our strand longer and prettier (see, for example, Njoroge 2001, Ackermann 2000, Phiri 1997, and Kanyoro 1997). I consider it a great privilege to add a Geneva-based color of beads to the already beautiful beadwork that is the Circle. I speak from the point of view of one who has worked very closely with Mercy Oduyoye, who founded the Circle in 1988. This "strand" is in honor of Mercy for her immense contribution to the Circle. In her own words, "the Circle is unique in being the initiative and vision of one woman, which gained enthusiastic welcome, and support of EATWOT women in Africa and subsequently that of many more" (Oduyoye 1997, 1–2).

BACKGROUND

The Circle is the space for women of Africa to do communal theology. Musa Dube, a Circle theologian, asserts, "A circle of women describes those who are seated together, who are connected and who seek to keep the interconnectedness of life" (Dube 2001b, 11). Circle members are women who are rooted in Islam, Christianity and African traditional religions. They are indigenous African women and also African women of Indian and European origins. These concerned women are engaged in theological dialogue with the cultures, religions, sacred writings and oral stories, which shape the African context and define the women of this continent. Circle members attempt to reflect together on issues of justice across boundaries of gender, faith and belief.

The Circle is a movement still in its infancy. It is a privilege for us to have the opportunity to record what we do, see and hear. Faithful history has the potential of sustaining and strengthening the foundation on which the future will be built.[1] It is the role of eyewitnesses to keep track of the facts and provide the context and interpretation for those who will come after us.

A VISION IS BORN

In her article, "Reflections from a Third World Perspective: Women's Experience and Liberation Theology" (Oduyoye 1994), Mercy articulates the ecumenical background that provided the incubatory space for the Circle. For many years, she was almost the only woman from Africa who wrote theology for publication. Her writing, verbal skills and extraordinary visionary mind opened doors for her in the ecumenical and international arena where she is still recognized as a mover and shaker. For many years she was the lone theological voice of African women. Such a role no doubt put her in a dilemma as well as in a position of privilege. But Mercy is not one to brood over these things. She is the emblem of the African woman of whom she writes in her poem "Women with Beads": "Here I sit, not idle, but busy stringing my beads" (Oduyoye 1995, vii).

The Mercy that I have come to know and admire is one who gets up and "is on the go" even when the going is hard. It is my contention that rather than lamenting the dearth of writings from African women, she was motivated to change the situation. Njoroge (2001, 252) suggests that Mercy began gathering women for the Circle in 1978. This gained momentum during the World Council of Churches-initiated study "The Community of Men and Women in the Church."[2] When I first met Mercy in 1988, she had files, lists, and letters from many African women. All we needed do was to "sort, thread and make them into nice strands" for them to become the Circle of Concerned African Women Theologians.

THE HANDMAID'S STORY

The Circle was officially inaugurated in 1989 at Trinity College, Legon, Ghana. The road to Ghana was nurtured by the International Planning Committee. The Committee was composed mainly of women from Africa who were then members of the Ecumenical Association of Third World Theologians (EATWOT). I joined them during a meeting in Geneva in August 1988. During this meeting, they identified religion and culture as the crucial foci for creating a liberative theology that would respond to the needs of women in Africa. These women then mooted the idea of bringing into being the Circle. According to recorded file notes, the proposed Circle was to be made up of women interested in holding a Biennial Institute for Women in Religion and Culture. They defined the main purpose of membership in the Circle as the commitment to be concerned about the lack of theological literature by women of Africa and the willingness to change the situation. The press release of 25 September 1989 captured the mood well when it stated that this group of concerned African women theologians "will concentrate their efforts on producing literature from the base of religion and culture to enrich the critical study and empowering practice of religion in Africa."

The first International Planning Committee consisted of Dr. Mercy Oduyoye, convener (Ghana); Dr. Betty Ekeya (Kenya); Dr. Sr. Rosemary Edet (Nigeria); Dr. Sr. Bernadette Mbuy Beya (Zaire); Dr. Elizabeth Amoah (Ghana); Dr. Brigalia Bam (South Africa); Ms. Rose Zoe Obianga (Cameroon); and Dr. Musimbi Kanyoro (Kenya).

A short word about each one of them, as they were in 1988, will suffice for now until future historians bring them alive in other in-depth studies.

- In 1988 Mercy Oduyoye was Deputy General Secretary of the World Council of Churches. She was the first African woman from south of the Sahara to hold such a high position in the WCC. Mercy had served in years past within the WCC Youth Department and had numerous other connections to the WCC.

- Betty Ekeya was teaching religion at Egerton University in Kenya. Shortly after the inauguration of the Circle, Betty left for the United States and has subsequently not been directly involved.

- Sr. Rosemary Edet was teaching religion at the University of Calabar in Nigeria. Sr. Edet continued actively as the Coordinator for the Nigerian Circle until her death from cancer in 1993.

- Brigalia Bam was the General Secretary of the South African Council of Churches. Brigalia worked in Geneva as the Director for the WCC Sub-unit on Women before her return to South Africa.

- Sr. Bernadette Mbuy Beya was in the Community of Religious Sisters in Lubumbashi, Zaire. She was doing pastoral work. She continues to be active in the Circle at the national and regional level.

- Elizabeth Amoah was teaching religion at the University of Ghana, Legon, where she is at present. She continues to be active in the Circle.

- Rose Zoe Obianga was teaching linguistics at the University in Cameroon. She continues to be associated with the Circle, although not actively.
- Musimbi Kanyoro was the Executive Secretary for Women in Church and Society, with the Lutheran World Federation (LWF) and was living in Geneva. She was Circle coordinator from 1996 until 2002, when Isabel Phiri, a professor of African theology at the then University of KwaZulu-Natal took over the reins.

SHAPING THE VISION

This first International Planning Committee undertook several tasks. One was to define parameters for the Circle. The planning committee built on the foundation clearly thought through by Mercy. It was agreed that the Circle should not become an organization with a structure and headquarters. While it was obvious that the Circle would need some funds for its work, it was resolved that it must be driven by the commitment of African women to write and publish and not by external factors such as money. The Circle was to be a space for women to mentor each other by doing communal theology. Thus the Circle was to remain an open-ended forum, always hospitable to new people. Hierarchical structures of leadership such as president, chairperson, or general secretary were not seen as essential. It was envisaged that members would spontaneously take up any task that needed to be done, and apply themselves appropriately to it.

The meetings of the Planning Committee were chaired on a rotation basis by all present. Each one took part in writing the minutes. It was understood, even without discussion, that the Circle would charge no membership fee, and writing would remain the criteria for membership. Circle members were free to write and publish in fora other than the Circle. The important fact was for African women to nurture and support one another as writers. Circle women would engage in debate and dialogue with all other theologians, women and men, in Africa and beyond.

TESTING THE WATERS

Members of the Committee assigned each other tasks. For example, with the help of their administrative staff, Oduyoye and Kanyoro began to prepare a database of African women who had studied theology. This task was implemented by building on lists already collected over many years by Mercy, Brigalia Bam and other members of the Committee through their work as lecturers. In addition, letters were sent to theological schools asking for lists of their past students. Other ecumenical people also offered names of women whom they knew, and we carried out a search following the clues given. To find such women was difficult, because many had changed their names following marriage, but we did our best.

A questionnaire was designed and circulated widely by ecumenical people traveling to places on the African continent. In addition to the questionnaire eliciting some personal data, it announced a conference and its theme and solicited papers for the conference. Those who responded and wrote a paper earned themselves a paid ticket to Accra, Ghana, to read their paper. In this way, we built up a database with nearly one hundred names of women who had studied Bible texts, Bible translation, religion, theology, ministry, anthropology, sociology, and linguistics. These women were all committed to the concept of forming the Circle. They all identified strongly with religion and culture as the overall theme. Sixty-nine women from all over Africa wrote papers and presented papers during the first Circle meeting.

More than two hundred churchwomen from Ghana attended the inauguration of the Circle. The Ghanaian church women who followed the conference day by day keenly supported what we told them about the Circle. The theme for the convocation was "Daughters of Africa Arise." The Circle meeting took place shortly after the All-Africa Council of Churches had held a well-attended women's meeting in Lomé, Togo, with the theme "Arise and Shine." The similarity of the themes meant that many churchwomen easily identified with the Circle, even though they did not then understand or embrace the idea of writing and publishing.

BREAKING NEW GROUND IN THEOLOGY

From the beginning, the International Planning Committee stated clearly that Circle theology was to address issues important to the women of Africa. The suggested subjects were far from the traditional theology we all knew. Sr. Bernadette Mbuy Beya was requested to research "The African Woman and Sexuality." I remember the horror on her face and her wish to change the allotted subject. The Planning Committee teased her out of this fear by persuading her that being a nun would provide sufficient license to explore the subject with other women in her church. In her recent article, "Violence in the Name of Culture and Religion" (Mbuy Beya 2001), Mbuy Beya reflects back on the early history of the church. She notes the tremendous opportunities that were opened to her and other nuns to work and involve the community around them in discussing a range of issues related to sexuality, including rape, prostitution, and even sexual abuse of women by clergypersons.

The late Sr. Rosemary Edet conducted research on "Christianity and African Rituals." At that time she was clearly opposed to including female genital mutilation (FGM) in her study. She voiced her reservation at that time, warning us not to buy into the Western wholesale condemnation of African culture. The Ghana Convocation of 1989 did not articulate the subject of FGM. This was to be changed in later meetings, and has now become one of the Circle's main concerns. During the early years, although women were willing to break ranks with the theology of inculturation—a theology propagated by African men—they nevertheless hesitated to differ with each other.

EXPANDING THE VISION: CHRISTIAN OR INTERFAITH?

The Circle began through Christian women who were actively involved in their churches and committed to ecumenical cooperation. During the initial meeting of the International Planning Committee, discussion was entertained as to whether we should remain a Christian-based group or develop into an interfaith movement, thereby reflecting the religious diversity of Africa. A number of the members of the committee had studied in secular universities and were familiar with the departments of religious studies in African universities. In African institutions of higher learning, religion and/or religious studies were integrated subjects, and their syllabi often included the study of religious texts and sacred scriptures. We were aware that there were very few women in Africa trained in seminaries because seminary education was linked to ordination and many churches did not ordain women. We also knew that there were less than a handful of faculties of theology on the whole continent. Since our core work was to be research-based, there was a unanimous feeling that it had to be open to religious diversity. The pioneering work of John Mbiti on African religions convinced the group that certain shared cultural norms in Africa transcend faith affiliation.

Rabiatu Ammah, a lecturer in the Department of Religious Studies in Ghana, was the first Muslim woman to participate in the Circle. Since then, others from Ghana, Kenya, and South Africa have participated. Other than in Ghana, the number of Muslim women is still fairly small. At a Circle meeting held in Ghana, August 2001, an oral report by Muslim women indicated that university education is still rare among Muslim women in Africa. In addition, Muslim women usually do not study religion at the universities; they study other subjects. In Ghana, however, there are Muslim women in the Department of Religion as professors and students. One would have expected the same in Nigeria, but the Nigerian Circle has not attracted Muslim women.

A category for those who claimed adherence to African religions was not thought of at the Circle's commencement. This was to change following the 1996 Pan African Conference, where some members of the South African delegation under the leadership of Nokuzola Mndende declared that they belonged neither to Christianity nor to Islam but to indigenous African religion. They were welcomed by the leadership and invited to participate as everyone else. However, on the day they were scheduled to lead the worship, some Christian women refused to listen to the message they had to bring. There are still unresolved questions as to whether indeed Islam and Christianity have completely eroded those African beliefs that lie within each of us. A number of Circle theologians hold the view that since indigenous African religions are an integral part of everyday life, all black Africans share a heritage in them. They argue that it may not be possible to separate religion from culture in this context.

THE SEVEN-YEAR CYCLE OF THE CIRCLE

Another pertinent issue on the agenda of the first International Planning Committee had to do with the design of Circle meetings. As noted above, the Circle inaugurated a Biennial Institute of African Women in Religion and Culture. This concept continues to be confusing both to Circle women and others. The original idea was that the Circle was to work within a seven-year period from 1989 to 1996. The Circle meeting of 1996 would complete the seven-year cycle. Its purpose was to evaluate the work done, stimulate writing projects and publications, and choose a theme for the next seven-year cycle.

Between these seven years, circles would continue to research and meet, present papers, and mentor each other through local or regional institutes. During the institute meetings, women would strategize, formulate and experiment with various methods to enable others to hear African women speak for themselves. These would include holding workshops with communities on the issues of contemporary relevance or visiting and giving lectures in schools and other places of learning. The institutions of theology such as seminaries and universities would be used to create network circles to encourage women to learn from one another about writing for publication. Such small circles would produce books, journals, poems, and letters to newspapers commenting on matters affecting women. Another task in these places of learning would be to build resources on women and culture and on women's theologies for students and researchers. It was anticipated that a plan would be put into place for a strategic study center that would house a library of resources on women's theologies. Within seven years, mobile national, subregional and continental events would take place throughout the whole continent. At the end of seven years, we would come together in a pan-African meeting modeled on the theme of the "Sabbath" year. This cycle of events would then be repeated again, culminating in seven-year continental meetings.

Until 1996, the plan of the International Planning Committee plan was followed, albeit not with as much vigor as anticipated, but with sufficient consistency. I can cite three reasons why I think it worked. First, Mercy Oduyoye was at the steering wheel and she devoted a lot of her time to the Circle, often combining her official duties at the WCC with matters of concern for the Circle as well. She used every opportunity to recruit others and give them specific assignments that were in line with the Circle's goals. Second, Mercy also wrote about the Circle and spoke extensively about it during her global responsibilities and travels. Third, Mercy is very well connected to other networks of churches, women's organizations, academic institutions and theological faculties. She gave the Circle international recognition through theological institutions, ecumenical circles, global networks of women theologians, and funding agencies.

And Mercy knows how to tell a story. She writes and speaks with consummate passion. She believes implicitly in what she does. She is a natural fund-raiser. She obtained financial support from donors and well-wishers for African women to meet in Ghana. She recruited and mentored me, and soon I found myself doing the same. I told the story of the Circle and helped to secure funding from various donors, including my own organization.

THE GENEVA SUPPORT NETWORK

Mercy Oduyoye is a household name at the Ecumenical Center in Geneva. Until 1996, the Circle was basically run from Geneva because Mercy was its driving force. Although the World Council of Churches was her employer, many other organizations in the center claimed a part of her. Her Circle net was cast far and wide, and not only to women but to some men of goodwill, as well. John Pobee, then the Executive Secretary for the

Program for Theological Education (PTE) at the World Council of Churches, was one of those whom Mercy convinced to invest in the Circle. He believed in the concept of the Circle, and supported its efforts on a personal level, and through his unit's work. He attended some of the planning meetings, and shared his ideas freely. He helped raise funding for Circle women to attend international conferences, and he included Circle women in his program as resource persons, or as sponsored participants to ecumenical events. He also encouraged the use of publications written by Circle members.

In his department, other colleagues, especially Ofelia Ortega, were committed to supporting the Circle. Ofelia was also a good conduit for Circle women to engage the WCC with women's theological concerns.

Somewhat providentially, John Pobee was succeeded by Nyambura Njoroge, herself a Circle member who had become part of the Geneva group when she joined the World Alliance of Reformed Churches in 1992. Nyambura Njoroge not only kept the tradition of supporting the Circle, but also took particular interest in helping to strengthen those women who are currently teachers and students within theological institutions.

The Africa Desk of the WCC was another partner recruited by Mercy Oduyoye. The Circle's accounts were managed by the staff of the Africa desk. The two executives, Lal Swai and Richard Murigande, initially gave their support and thereby began an important tradition. Presently it is managed by the newly merged South African institution, the University of KwaZulu-Natal, where the current coordinator, Isabel Phiri, is based.

Another very prominent supporter of the Circle was the WCC Sub-unit on Women. Mercy had established this link way back in the 1980s, when the Circle was but a concept. The Circle was inaugurated during the time of Anna Karin Hammer, the same woman who initiated the Ecumenical Decade of the Churches in Solidarity with Women. Her support for Mercy and the Circle was unwavering. It was, however, her successor, Aruna Gnanadason, who has seen the Circle grow. Aruna is a member of EATWOT and of the Asian Women Theologians. Aruna's support for the Circle has been on many levels: she has supported

Circle events, sponsored Circle women to meetings, and invited and utilized the skills of many Circle women during the Ecumenical Decade, and continues to do so.

Mercy Oduyoye's Geneva network went beyond the people mentioned above. Mercy also worked closely with Evelyn Appia and recruited every other African at the Ecumenical Center in Geneva, whether they were theologians or not. Janet Thompson, a Liberian woman who worked for the Africa Desk, also joined and supported the Circle. The solidarity of women working together went beyond the African staff. The administrative assistants who worked and continue to work with us in Geneva were women ready to be there for us. Annelies Hope and Brigitte Constant worked with Mercy, Diana Chabloz and later Francois Faure worked with John Pobee, and Nyambura Njoroge and Doris Appel work with William Temu. These women are part of the Geneva connection of Circle history, and they form an important part of what we might call "Circle midwives."

I first met Mercy in 1988 when I moved to Geneva. Until that time, I had only read her books. Upon my arrival in Geneva, Mercy took time to share every aspect of the Circle with me. She invited me to join the International Planning Committee and made me a partner. We thought together, designed and carried out things together. Through my involvement I was also able to garner the participation of the Lutheran World Federation (LWF) and recruited as many Lutheran women theologians as I could. I persuaded them to write, facilitating a process whereby they could meet and think together, as well as mentor one another. Countries such as Ethiopia, Madagascar, Tanzania, Namibia, South Africa and Zimbabwe have many Lutheran Circle members because of this partnership. Even in countries where the Lutheran church is very small, such as Nigeria, one still finds Lutheran Circle members. Additionally, like Mercy, I drew others into the Circle, including a number of my male and female colleagues for different types of support. Collette Bouka Coula was among the first we recruited. Recruited originally to voluntarily help us with translations into French, Bouka was from Cameroon and held a doctorate in French and English literature. When Bouka was later transferred by the LWF to Nairobi, not only did we call upon her to be one of the hosts for the 1996 Pan African meetings, but she also traveled with Circle books and gave lectures, introducing the Circle wherever she went in Africa. Collette has subsequently moved to Ethiopia, where she is still intimately involved with Circle matters.

My involvement in the Circle has been possible with the support of Ana Villanueva who has worked with me since 1989 arranging meetings and other support for the Circle. Without her support, coordinating the Circle would have been a difficult, if not an impossible task. This method of using one's own sphere of influence to enhance the Circle continues to be one of the ways of recruiting Circle members. This is a strategy we learned from Mercy.

AFRICAN WOMEN CLAIM OWNERSHIP OF THE CIRCLE

The purpose of the continental meetings was to evaluate the Institute's process and the impact of the publications and to put in place new strategies for influencing institutional and attitudinal changes in Africa. The all-African meeting would then set the priorities for the next seven years and also celebrate the communal journey at whatever point had been reached.

Most women understand the Circle and its emphasis on writing. However, very few of them understand the concept of the Biennial Institutes and the seven-year cycle. During the Pan African Conference in Nairobi in 1996, the participants decided that they wanted to have a say in the leadership of the Circle. They felt a need to formalize the structure in a different way, moving it away from those who had volunteered to work with the founder to a system of elected representatives. Although the Circle had strong roots in Geneva, Mercy had just retired from the WCC and moved back to Ghana. The Conference participants opted for electing an International Coordinating Committee made up of sub-regional representatives (Southern Africa, Eastern Africa, Western Africa, Francophone Africa, and Lusophone, or Portuguese-speaking Africa). They also elected a coordinator for the Committee and two secretaries, one Francophone and the other Anglophone.

The concept of democracy and representation was strong at this meeting. The Pan African meeting felt that the Circle needed to develop its own image and that members should participate in choosing its leadership. They felt that this was an appropriate time to wean the Circle from its mother and founder. I suddenly found myself elected as coordinator. Since I knew that the Circle had succeeded because of Mercy's enormous investment of energy, I was not amused by this election. But there are times when democracy does unexpected things, and this was one of them. Although I had worked with Mercy, she had been the driver. The participants claimed the Circle leadership, but they did not capture the underlying philosophy that had been developed. Reflecting on this event, Mercy told me privately, "I went along with the majority decision, but I still think it lacks dynamism. It was to keep the momentum that I suggested the creation of the study commissions."

The participants present at the Pan African meeting had no idea that everything was done on a voluntary basis. Similarly, it was not clear that Mercy had been using her position at the WCC to travel, recruit and nurture new Circle members. The fact that the Circle had no financial basis to support the new structure was not even debated. The previous meetings had happened in connection with ecumenical meetings enabled by the Geneva-based group, which was largely recruited and nurtured by Mercy Oduyoye. When I was elected to succeed Mercy, I knew that I did not have the kind of wide network that she had, nor the charisma and internal knowledge of the Circle. I knew that we still needed Mercy on the team. I therefore asked immediately for the mandate to co-opt two people whose presence would strengthen the Circle. With that agreement the newly-elected Committee and I decided to invite Mercy back onto the coordination team. We all agreed that she should head the research section since that was our central focus. The big question was whether she would accept our invitation, as she was deeply hurt by the mass decision. She felt misunderstood. She felt that they did not understand what she had done to establish, cultivate, and nurture the Circle. I knew what Mercy had done and I knew that, as I held a full-time job, if I did not have her with me, it was going to be an impossible volunteer task. I decided that I would take the risk personally to invite Mercy back onto the Committee.

Mercy had moved out of Geneva. In her place, Nyambura Njoroge became the partner that I had been for Mercy. I needed her support to sustain the Geneva connection and thus I requested the newly elected committee to co-opt Nyambura to work with us. This was accepted. Nyambura had shown concern for, and leadership among, ordained women. We all saw the need to have her continue with that, but we enlarged her mandate. In this way we gained two new members: the Research Coordinator, Mercy Oduyoye,[3] and the Theological Education and Ministerial Formation Coordinator, Nyambura Njoroge. When Nyambura joined the World Alliance of Reformed Churches in Geneva in 1992, she provided a welcome access to Reformed Churches. This was way beyond our own efforts up to 1988.

A NEW DIRECTION–
THE FORMATION OF STUDY COMMISSIONS

The major changes undertaken by the Coordinating Committee were to inaugurate study commissions on the four priority issues identified at Nairobi in 1996. Again it was Mercy who prepared the proceedings from the 1996 meeting (see Oduyoye 1997). She analyzed the report and brought a strategic approach that began the work in commissions. They were divided into four study commissions, namely Cultural and Biblical Hermeneutics, Women in Culture and Religion, History of Women, and Ministries and Theological Education and Formation.

Each commission included two people trained in the discipline to coordinate the particular study. This involved designing the nature of the study, inviting members from different parts of Africa to carry out relevant field research on the topics identified, and finally to report on the research.

It was also agreed that the two secretaries would be responsible for editing the journal AMKA and that the zonal leaders would convene zonal meetings in their areas between 1996 and 2003, while study commission leaders would work on research and writing. Zonal leaders would also be aware of activities underway in the national Circles in their regions. These changes had some pitfalls. We found that a core group of about fifty women were committed to writing, and each commission leader wanted those writers on their commission. Individual Circle members were expected to choose which commission to align with, but this did not happen.

Zonal leaders found it difficult to function because the Circle had no financial infrastructure to support their travel. Some of the newly elected leaders were not fully aware that all Circle work is voluntary, and when they realized they were expected to volunteer long hours, their commitment decreased.

SETTING A NEW DIRECTION

Although some commissions have continued to produce books, it was clear to me that the 2002 meeting would need to rethink Circle structure. It was important to review the philosophy and history that lay behind the original establishment of the Circle. This required reflecting on our decisions and how we should implement them. One of the recommendations made at the 2002 conference was to look into the possibility of institutionalizing the Circle so that we would become an organization rather than a movement.

The concept of the Circle has attracted many women in Africa, and there is a real desire to be associated with it. However, only a few are willing to sustain and retain the original emphasis on research and writing. Many would like to be associated with the Circle simply to read the writings of African women theologians. They would also like to participate in fora that consider topics of personal interest. The discussion on rites of passage, violence against women, and, more recently, HIV/AIDS has created such interest. For those women, the Circle remains a safe place to analyze and reflect upon these important issues.

Many women in Africa do want to write, but the daily chores and struggles often consume them. Very few have access to a computer or even a typewriter. Because reference books are scarce, one of the biggest problems is often completing bibliographical references. Following a review of the Circle's work, the 2002 Pan African meeting set out a new direction for its future. Although not wanting to be a grassroots-organized institution, we are often pulled in that direction. Concerns were raised that would impact our future in this regard, requiring serious reflection.

CHALLENGES

A second cause for concern is funding. It is time for the Circle to rethink its policy of fund-raising. We need money to enable our meetings to occur, and we need to support research and publication. For fifteen years now, we have proven that we are committed to the Circle. Now we must think of how to sustain the future. We need a promise for tomorrow.

The Circle is also challenged to keep up with technology, which was not so important in the 1980s. Consequently, the Circle has an on-line presence with its own dedicated website, http://www.thecirclecawt.org/. Initially developed by Njoroge Njuguna, the website was recently commercially redesigned, and a contract signed with a web-design company in South Africa to maintain and regularly update the site. It is hoped that Circle members will visit the website and update their bibliographies. Circle publications are also posted on the site. We hope that our books will receive a wider readership now that they can be easily accessed, but this will not happen if we continue to use publishers who are themselves unknown. The first Circle book, *The Will to Arise*, published by Orbis in 1992, is in its fifth printing and easily purchased abroad, but not in Africa. Musa Dube's two books, *Other Ways of Reading* (2001a) and *Postcolonial Feminist Interpretations of the Bible* (2000), are readily available in Africa, as they are in the West. Those published on our continent are not easily available and consequently not widely read. The question of where we publish is urgent and critical.

MOVE TO AFRICA:
RECONNECTING THE CIRCLE
AND THE BIENNIAL INSTITUTE CONCEPT

A bold step was made to transfer Circle operations from Geneva to Ghana when Mercy retired. This enabled her to supervise Circle publications, while building the Institute for African Women in Culture and Religion. The Circle list has grown beyond the abilities of a volunteer coordinator. A total of four hundred women associate themselves with the Circle. More than thirty-four books have been published all over Africa in fifteen years. This is truly a reason to celebrate. Joyce Boham was appointed as liaison officer, and thus became the first Circle member of staff to be remunerated. Her task was to facilitate communication with members, manage Circle meetings, and keep Circle records. Since 2002, this work is being carried out by Lilian Siwila and Bridget Masaiti, who are Isabel Phiri's graduate assistants at the University of KwaZulu-Natal.

Identifying HIV/AIDS as the most pressing concern upon the African continent, the Pan-African meeting was rescheduled from August 2003 to August 2002 to enable the Circle to prioritize its responses and thereby develop appropriate strategies. Women in Africa infected and affected by HIV/AIDS far outnumber men. Stigma stands out as the one single factor that women and others living with HIV/AIDS must fight to overcome. The Circle can initiate straight talk about sex and the stigmas associated with the disease, and thereby assist the process of continuing education. This is imperative if we want to combat this new scourge upon our continent. We are also challenged to discover new ways of speaking theologically about what we have learned and continue to experience in the face of HIV/AIDS.

WHAT IS THE FUTURE OF THE CIRCLE?

Having tasted the waters, we realize that we have a long way to go in order to bring about the change we have long hoped for. According to Tinyiko Sam Maluleke (1996), the men of Africa who lead the church and who have been the pioneers of African theologies are not paying sufficient attention to the voices of African women theologians bearing new witness of God's presence in Africa. Mercy Oduyoye, however, does not agree with this opinion and has written, "It is our focus on Religion and Culture which got EATWOT Africa under Simon Maimela to initiate a monumental study on Religion and Culture." And I believe that it was the growing international recognition of Circle studies on religion and culture that lay behind my invitation to be a keynote speaker at the 1996 World Mission Conference in Salvador, Brazil.

The Circle keeps growing in members and in depth. Today, we are not only larger and more experienced, but we are also more visible, recognized and respected at international ecumenical fora and among other theologians. We are seen as a voice for African women whose voices would not otherwise be heard. As a result, we are beginning to debate with male theologians, whose ignorance of our work sometimes stands out. One of the best examples is Musa Dube's response to Jesse Mugambi (see Dube 2001b).

With our growing influence comes increased responsibility. People look to the Circle for in-depth and practical involvement in the life of communities. Circle women are challenged not only to respond to the dearth of theological literature from African women, but also to play a significant role in helping to create and sustain viable communities of women and men in the church and in society in Africa. Can we initiate a shift so soon in our short history?

CAN WE BORROW A LEAF FROM HISTORY?

Such reflection upon Circle history, will lead to a new call to take on greater responsibilities. We will have to increase our efforts to promote research. We will have to continue to promote cooperation across religious and gender borders. Affirming religious pluralism allows Circle women opportunities to explore questions of the well-being of women writing on our various religions in the context of African cultures. Our hope is that through this process of dialogue we shall come to know one another better; affirm the need for justice and human dignity for all women; and most important, become leading agents in creating a climate in which gender-justice will prevail.

Through participating in face-to-face research and educating each other on the forms of worship and dogmas of our faiths, we have managed to become agents of justice to one another. Here we compare notes and listen to each other's stories of living hopefully within a gender-violent world. We share our pain and tears for the continued oppression that we find inherent in our religions and our cultures. We rejoice that our passion for justice is being awakened despite the prevailing barriers that keep us in "our place." We are learning to value each other's writings and to realize that we owe ourselves the power to change. Our ecumenical encounters prompt us to take our African identity seriously, as it is the basis for our unity. We seek to deepen our commitment to the future of our people, especially girl children and women living in the context of pain and death. Perhaps we can once again reflect on Mercy's vision for the Circle "to hold regular meetings where all concerned African women can come together. It can be biennials or triennials or even annuals, but we must continue to organize, stay visible and available to each other and our communities".[4]

A PROMISE FOR TOMORROW

Our history, short as it may be, holds promise for tomorrow. For many, the promise is for a brighter future for our daughters and us. Our daughters will read books written by us. For women and men alike, the future is a promise of continuity and growth, our covenant with generations yet to come. The Circle's future comes alive through our realization that something exciting has been happening on our continent and to us. We see our names in print and read each other's writings. We see clearly that the stories of women in Africa reflect those of our own lives and those of our foremothers. They speak to our hearts and to our bodies. They give us the impetus to dialogue with one another and with God. Our reflections have created opportunities to pose questions to God about God, our humanity, and the essence of our being. The determination by African women to address the dearth of theological writings by women from the continent has given birth to women's communal theology. It has led to solidarity for us African women and with our global sisters. It has made true the saying of one of our pioneer feminist theologians:

> Women must be able to speak out of their own experience of agony and victimization, survival, empowerment and new life as places of Divine presence and out of these revelatory experiences, write new stories that can tell of God's presence in experiences where God's presence was never allowed or imagined before in a religious culture controlled by men and defined by men's experience. (Ruether 1987, 147)

Critical to our learning has been the realization that African women's commitment to doing theology has come about as a result of the inner conversion by concerned women theologians. It is not motivated by a need to confront, impress, or even win over the church or other religious institutions. If this were the case, we would give up, because many do not read our works. African theology without the faith story of African women is a theology that is incomplete and contextually inept. The distinct gift that we bring to the theology of Africa is to repair this imbalance. Circle theology has posed questions to the content of the theology taught in centers of learning and practiced in religious spaces, as both the theologies of Njoroge and Phiri reveal.

As women of Africa we have come to realize that our liberation partially depends upon us. We have broken the silence to speak for ourselves. In stretching our own theological imagination and our reading of the sacred scriptures, we have become aware of who we are as women of Africa. We have discovered that we are so heavily attached to our traditions and cultures that we must name these as subjects of analysis and critique within the field of theology. This process began early in Circle history, as can be seen in Mercy's 1986 work, *Hearing and Knowing*. It must continue.

And our theology must be communal. In doing communal theology together across gender, culture and religion boundaries we discover and affirm our humanity across borders. Together we have found that there is no option before us but to challenge the culture of patriarchy so dominant on our continent. It affects the way we treat one another as women and the way we handle ordinary situations, including our God-talk. The pioneering work of Mercy Oduyoye and Musimbi Kanyoro has provided a critical framework for doing such cultural hermeneutics.

Finally, after fifteen years of writing, the next phase of our work will inevitably include a review of the impact that our writings have produced. Although it will be the task of other theologians to critique our work, we ourselves will have to begin to critique each other, while formulating alternative and new theories. Thus far, we have enjoyed our journey together and our discovery of basic agreement; but the time has now come to seriously begin an individual analysis of those issues that originally made us one. Our ability to grow further in our interpretation and relationship with each other will be predetermined on our willingness to begin this process. Our future as Circle women and particularly as African women theologians depends on it.

NOTES

[1] At the outset, I want to state that this paper represents my personal views about a small section of the development of the Circle since 1988. Another Circle scholar might provide a different view, but that is the beauty and license of scholarship.

[2] The Fifth Assembly of World Council of Churches (Nairobi, 1975) recommended the study. It was implemented in 1978–1982 under the leadership of Dr. Connie Parvey.

[3] It took courage to request Mercy to come back to the Committee. She did not readily oblige us. It is the special relationship that we had

developed and her commitment to the Circle that really brought her back. I will be forever grateful to her.

[4] Personal communication to the author commenting on an earlier draft of this paper.

REFERENCES

Ackermann, Denise M. 2000. "Claiming Our Footprints, Introductory Reflections." In *Claiming Our Footprints: South African Women Reflect on Context, Identity and Spirituality.* Edited by Denise Ackermann, E. Getmann, H. Kotze, and J. Tobler. Stellenbosch: EFSA Institute of Theological and Interdisciplinary Research, 1–14.

Dube, Musa W. 2000. *Postcolonial Feminist Interpretation of the Bible.* St. Louis: Chalice Press.

———. 2001a. *Other Ways of Reading: African Women and the Bible.* Atlanta/Geneva: Society of Biblical Literature/WCC Publications.

———. 2001b. "Jesse Mugambi Is Calling Us to Move from Liberation to Reconstruction: A Postcolonial Feminist Response." Unpublished paper.

Kanyoro, Musimbi R. A. 1997. "Celebrating God's Transforming Power." In *Transforming Power: Women in the Household of God. Proceedings of the Pan-African Conference of the Circle of Concerned African Women Theologians.* Edited by Mercy A. Oduyoye. Accra-North: Sam-Woode Ltd., 7–27.

———. 2000. "Where Are the African Women in the Theological Debate." *Journal of Constructive Theology* 6: 3–20.

Landman, Christina, ed. 1996. *Digging Up Our Foremothers: Stories of Women in Africa.* Pretoria: UNISA Press.

Maluleke, Tinyiko Ssam. 1996. "Recent Developments in the Christian Theologies of Africa: Towards the Twenty-first Century." *Journal of Constructive Theology* 2 (2): 33–60.

———.1997. "The 'Smoke Screens' Called Black and African Theologies: The Challenge of African Women Theology." *Journal of Constructive Theology* 3 (2): 39–63.

Mbuy Beya, M. Bernadette. 2001. "Violence in the Name of Culture and Religion." Unpublished paper presented at the Pan-African Conference on Religion and Culture, Ghana, 29 July-5 August 2001.

Mombo, E. M. 2000. "Hermeneutics, Gender and Culture: A Circle Perspective." Unpublished paper presented to CATI meeting, August 200.

Nadar, Sarojini. 2000. "Subverting Gender and Ethnic Assumptions in Biblical Narrative: Exploring the Narrative Voice of Ruth." *Journal of Constructive Theology* 6 (2): 67–83.

Njoroge, Nyambura J. 2001. "Talitha Cum! To the New Millennium: A Conclusion." In *Talitha Cum! Theologies of African Women*. Edited by Nyambura Njoroge and Musa W. Dube. Pietermaritzburg: Cluster Publications, 252–53.

Njoroge, Nyambura J. and Musa W. Dube, eds. 2001. *Talitha Cum! Theologies of African Women*. Pietermaritzburg: Cluster Publications.

Oduyoye, Mercy A. 1994. "Reflections from a Third World Woman's Perspective: Women's Experience in Liberation Theologies." In *Feminist Theology from the Third World: A Reader*. Edited by Ursula King. London/Maryknoll, N.Y.: SPCK/Orbis Books, 23–34.

———. 1995. *Daughters of Anowa: African Women and Patriarchy*. Maryknoll, N.Y.: Orbis Books.

———. 1997. *Transforming Power: Women in the Household of God*. Proceedings of the Pan-African Conference of the Circle of Concerned African Women Theologians. Accra-North: Sam-Woode Ltd.

———. 2001. *Introducing African Women's Theology*. Sheffield: Sheffield Academic Press.

Oduyoye, Mercy Amba and Musimbi R. A. Kanyoro, eds. 1992. *The Will to Arise: Women, Tradition, and the Church in Africa*. Maryknoll, N.Y.: Orbis Books.

Parvey, C. F., ed. 1983. *The Community of Women and Men in the Church: The Sheffield Report*. Geneva: WCC Publications.

Phiri, Isabel Apawo. 1997. "Doing Theology in Community: The Case of African Women Theologians in the 1990s." *Journal of Theology for Southern Africa* 99: 68–76.

Ruether, Rosemary R. 1987. "Feminism and Jewish-Christian Dialogue." In *The Myth of Christian Uniqueness: Toward a Pluralistic Theology of Religions*. Edited by John Hick and Paul F. Knitter. Maryknoll, N.Y.: Orbis Books.

Van Shalkwyk, Annalet. 2000. "Writing South African Women's Stories of Transformation: Some Methodological Aspects." *Journal of Constructive Theology* 6 (2): 21–37.

2

Mercy Amba Ewudziwa Oduyoye

Wise Woman Bearing Gifts

Letty M. Russell

INTRODUCTION

There is a cup in my cupboard with "MERCY" glazed on its side. It sits there ready to be used whenever Mercy Amba Ewudziwa Oduyoye arrives in Connecticut, USA, for a visit. She comes as a wise woman from the South, traveling by air rather than camel, but always bearing gifts! When she was working at the World Council of Churches, Mercy was particularly fond of bringing "Swiss chocolates" and pointing out that cocoa was not grown in Switzerland, but rather in places like Ghana on farms such as that of her grandfather's, where she was born (Oduyoye 1988, 38). This woman, who has herself been a gift to so many people on all continents, comes with her box of candy and settles in to share the latest story of her wisdom travels.

That cup sits right next to a camel teapot with three riders glazed on the top. They picture the coming of the wise men from the East to celebrate the birth of Christ. They also represent a story from Matthew 2 that needs to be reclaimed: a story of magi or magicians who have come to be called kings and of the King

43

who had come to die. The many patriarchal overlays of the story and the many colonial interpretations of mission have made it difficult to find the wise women and the good news of Emmanuel, God with us (Dube 2000, 127–56).

Perhaps the story of Mercy, our wise woman from the South, in her long struggles with patriarchy and colonialism on behalf of her beloved Africa and the women of Africa, can help us re-read the story of Matthew 2 "against the grain" and discover more wise women (Wainwright 1994, 641). In this essay I propose to do an exegesis of missing persons that will look again at what is present and missing in the Epiphany story so that we can join with Mercy in the continuing work of God's hospitality and welcome to all people (Bird 1997).

GOD WITH US

Matthew 2:1–6

The birth narratives in Matthew and Luke are each quite different as the authors weave the traditional materials into the themes of their gospel accounts. Focusing on the fulfillment of the tradition of the patriarchs, Matthew begins his story with the faithful Joseph and the story of exile and return, which recapitulates Israel's exile to Egypt and return to Canaan. Using the story in Numbers 22–24 of Balaam, the Magus from the Euphrates who comes with his two servants to Moab and receives an oracle to bless the Israelites, Matthew presents the Gentiles who come to find the Christ child. Like Balaam they prophesy that "a star shall come out of Judah," and the king shall be "exalted" (Num. 24:17, 7; Brown 1992, 412). They symbolize the nations coming to Christ and point toward the end of the gospel when the disciples are to carry the teaching of Jesus to all the nations (Matt. 28:16–20).

One of the most basic themes of the story is that of the mission to the Gentiles. Matthew helps us to see that Christ's continuing presence opens the way for all people to become disciples.

Combined with the Great Commission in Matthew 28:19–20, this theme of the nations coming to believe in Christ and of the church going out to the nations has been used and abused in the Christian churches and in the imperial exploits of countries of the North. Because colonialism, proselytism, and racism are often linked with mission, it has become problematic to many people, especially those in countries of the South (Dube 1998, 224–46).

But this is not the only understanding of mission, for in the story itself is the emphasis on the way that the coming of the Christ Child is part of God coming to be with us as Emmanuel, "God-with-us." This story of God's mission is one of justice and righteousness as God goes about the work of mending the creation through the life and teaching of Jesus that all outsiders are welcome, and through the continuing work of the Holy Spirit.

Another disturbing element in the story is that of the pervasive assumption of *patriarchal order*. The story is *for* everyone, but not *about* everyone. Few women appear in the story, and all the major players in Matthew's scenes are patriarchal figures. The genealogy in Matthew 1 reminds us of Moses' genealogy in Exodus 6:14–27 and situates us in this androcentric framework. We are presented with thirty-nine pairs of male patriarchs in the fifteen verses "genealogy of Jesus the Messiah, the son of David, and the son of Abraham (Matt. 1:2–16)" (Wainwright 1994, 641). Joseph is the center of the story and, like the earlier Joseph (Gen. 37:19), is a dreamer, who receives guidance from God in protecting Mary and the child.

Yet there are cracks in this patriarchal framework. Matthew finally has to mention in 1:16 that Jesus was born to Mary and not to the father in the genealogy. In the story women appear as an anomaly in the patriarchal plans, but God uses women to save the people of Israel. Matthew includes Tamar, Ruth, Rahab, and Bathsheba in the genealogy. They are viewed as dangerous women because they are outside the traditional patriarchal marriage or family structure of Israel. This helps Matthew make clear that God is also able to fulfill the divine promise through the woman Mary (Wainwright 1994, 643).

MERCY AS MOTHER

Mercy can easily join these wise women who lived outside the patriarchal frameworks. In a country where motherhood is as sacred as it was in Israel, she managed to mother many, but bore no children of her own. Married into a patriarchal Yoruba group in western Nigeria, Mercy, nevertheless, has chosen to live in her own matrilineal Akan context in Ghana, and to share an international marriage with Modupe Oduyoye across nations. Into the cracks of colonial theology she has poured creative understandings of the church and mission, and become the mother of African women's theology (Oduyoye 1999, 105–22).

In 1986, while still teaching in Nigeria as senior lecturer in the Department of Religious Studies at the University of Ibadan, Mercy published her first book with Orbis Books, *Hearing and Knowing: Theological Reflections on Christianity in Africa*. Two of her major themes were those we have already encountered in Matthew: the need to rethink mission and the "theology of Soul-Snatching" and to revisit Christian anthropology to include African women's experience (Oduyoye 1986, 19–44; 120–37).

Moving away from the earlier history of missionary efforts of Europeans as an "exercise in cultural occupation," she urged a serious look at ways the gospel could take deep root in Africa only as it became "God-with-us" in African culture (Oduyoye 1986, 32). God's sending action had to do with the way God is present inspiring the gifts of African people, rather than an imposition of white, Western culture. Thus she writes:

> The missionary told the Africans what they needed to be saved from, but when Africans needed power to deal with the spiritual realms that were real to them, the missionary was baffled. The ancestors were to be ignored; infant mortality and premature deaths were purely medical matters. Failure of rains and harvests were acts of God. Childlessness had nothing to do with witchcraft, nor was there any spiritual aspect to any other physical disorder or infirmity.

... The missionaries' superficial assessment of the indigenous culture and its hold on the people who belong to it led to the African's superficial acceptance of Christianity. (Oduyoye 1986, 41)

The Christ story begins with God's sending and with the nations coming to Christ to give thanks for God's love. Focusing here may help us to rethink mission as proselytism by outsiders and to join Mercy in searching out God's presence in the lives, struggles and cultures of African women, men and children.

This wise woman also was full of courage as she moved forward in her developing role as the mother of African women's theology. She actually used the word *feminism* in her book, and talked about the gifts that African women share with men as human beings created in the image of God. In doing so she became one of those dangerous but wise women in Matthew's genealogy. She lifted up the lives and struggles of African women who are always there serving the patriarchal line, and yet usually missing as partners in the leadership and teaching of the churches.

We cannot be happy and unashamed in each other's company if we are hiding behind our gender to shirk responsibility. As baptized people, our suffering is salvific when taken on voluntarily and our sharing of the gifts of others gives us the ability to thank God who made us male and female. Happy and responsible in my being human and female, I shall be able to live a life of doxology in the human community, glorifying God for the gifts I receive in others and for the possibility I have of giving myself freely for the well-being of the community while remaining responsible and responsive to God. (Oduyoye 1986, 137)

BY WHOSE AUTHORITY?

Matthew 2:7–12

As our story of the visit of the magi progresses in Matthew 2:7–12, we discover the tension and conflict highlighted by Matthew between the various male authorities (Wainwright 1994, 636). The magi were a priestly class of Persian or Babylonian experts in the occult, such as astrology and the interpretation of dreams (Matt. 2:1–12; Boring 1995, 141–42). These Gentiles come to Jerusalem, following the light they have seen, in order to pay honor and bring royal gifts to the one whom Matthew names as "King of the Jews." In a scene reminiscent of Pharaoh and the infant Moses, Herod, the other king of the Jews, is set over against the infant Jesus and seeks to slay him. The "chief priests and scribes of the people" speak the authority of scripture as they help to locate the child in Bethlehem. Joseph is guided by dreams in the pilgrimage with Mary and child from Bethlehem, to Egypt, and then back to Nazareth when Herod dies (Matt. 2:19–23; Exod. 4:19).

The patriarchal competition between Herod, the chief priests and scribes representing those Jews who reject the Messiah, and Joseph representing Jews that are faithful to him, and the magi representing Gentiles who welcome him seems to reflect some of the problems in Matthew's church community, which had developed as a Jewish and Gentile congregation and faced many tensions over the interpretation of the law *(Torah)*. At the time of Matthew's gospel, the tensions seem to include conflict with the secular authorities as well as with Jewish groups. In this context, at the end of the first century of the Common Era, Matthew makes use of the prophetic texts and fulfillment narratives to show how Jesus has come to fulfill the law, and points to the continuing presence of the Holy Spirit in the life of the church. The story serves Matthew's purpose of responding to Jewish authorities who question Jesus' messiahship by giving him a Jewish and a divine genealogy with Gentile recognition. Jesus' birth in Bethlehem fulfills the prophecy of the Messiah's birth even though he grew up in Nazareth (Matt. 2:5; Mic. 5:2; Brown 1992, 412).

Matthew's "politics of otherness" in relation to Judaism is problematic in the Christian tradition because it has served to fuel anti-Jewish polemic and negative stereotypes of Judaism (Wainwright 1994, 636). This in turn has helped to legitimatize anti-Semitism and Jewish oppression and persecution (Heschel 1996, 12–13). The mutual hostility in Matthew's account of patriarchal competition has to be resisted as we seek other ways to understand and interpret the story of the birth of this Jewish child to Mary.

Perhaps a crack in this patriarchal competition can be found with Mary and the baby. Yet they hardly play a part in this story and seem more like a frozen Christmas tableaux than real participants. Seen and not heard, supporting cast, not subjects of their history, they are inserted by Matthew into his narrative of patriarchal competition. As Elaine Wainwright points out, "The reproductive power of woman and her role in the birth of the Messiah are affirmed outside of the patriarchal structure. This is further emphasized by linking the woman and the child she conceives to the fulfillment quotation of vv. 22–23" (Wainwright 1994, 643). These almost-missing persons in the story appear as the discordant note to what is going on around them, reminding us of the presence of many wise women in the history of Israel and in Jesus' Jewish ancestry.

In the relationship between mother and child we see not competing kingdoms, but *compassionate kin-dom* (Isasi-Díaz 1993, xi). We are reminded that there is another kind of authority in the gospel story. Matthew also portrays this authority for us as he speaks of Jesus as the embodiment of God's divine wisdom. Jesus is identified with divine Sophia who is Israel's God imaged as sister, wife, mother, beloved, and teacher (Schüssler Fiorenza 1983,133). Sophia-Jesus is a misfit in the midst of patriarchal competition, the one who will care for the people and lead them with the authority of love. This voice of authority invites us to cease our power games and to take up the yoke of discipleship: "Come to me, all you that are weary and are carrying heavy burdens, and I will give you rest. Take my yoke upon you, and learn from me; for I am gentle and humble in heart, and you will find rest for your souls. For my yoke is easy, and my burden is light" (Matt. 11:28–9).

MERCY AS MISFIT

Like Mary and the baby in Matthew's account, Mercy is clearly a misfit in the middle of patriarchal competition and competing kingdoms. Even though she has almost always worked in male-dominated and androcentric organizations, she has used her pioneering presence to open up the possibility of including outsiders into the patriarchal systems of university and church. She has been one to "roll away the stone for others," while still working within the systems to bring about change. Such a position has not always been appreciated in patriarchal systems of male domination. For instance, even now she is labeled as a feminist and troublemaker by many of her colleagues, so that she told me in the summer of 1998 that she could not supervise the thesis of one of the women in our international feminist D. Min. Program because the woman would then be rejected by her university faculty!

In leaving the University of Ibadan and going to the World Council of Churches as Associate General Secretary, Mercy found herself constricted by patriarchal traditions when her church refused to endorse her candidacy unless her husband gave permission for her to go to Geneva. No wonder that she helped to initiate the Ecumenical Decade of the Churches in Solidarity with Women in 1988! As the Decade closed and the results were evaluated by visits to the churches, it was often the case that there was a Decade of women in solidarity with the churches, rather than the other way around. Nevertheless, with the strong support of the World Council of Churches, the Decade has extended the work of Mercy and many other women who are determined that the churches should no longer be a center of patriarchal competition and power, no longer a "men's club" (Oduyoye 1990, 49).

In her book on the Decade, *Who Will Roll the Stone Away? The Ecumenical Decade of the Churches in Solidarity with Women*, Mercy has documented the ways women have come forward to claim their place as partners in the leadership and life of the churches as well as in their societies. She says:

> The church is asked to be in solidarity with women because in the body of Christ the women members are in pain (as are some men) because we seem to be operating as if we are unsure whether women are fully human and therefore to be accounted responsible and accountable. (Oduyoye 1990, 44)

In confronting business-as-usual in the "kingdoms" of our churches and societies, Mercy declared: "In the Decade 1988–98 we seek justice for women, to dream 'bold dreams' for new community" (Oduyoye 1990, 68). In an inescapably clear voice she called for the inclusion of women and their concerns in every story and underlined the importance of *kin-dom thinking* as we seek to stand in solidarity with all those who do not fit in traditional cultures and religious patterns.

Mercy also is aware of Joseph as a representative of the faithful people of God and in her closing appeal for solidarity in community of women and men she recalls the story of Matthew 1 and 2. Mary says, "yes" to God's plan, all "conventional wisdom" to the contrary, and Joseph also hears God's voice and is willing to stand against custom and tradition when he takes a pregnant woman as his wife. "Here is a man who stood in solidarity with a woman he loved and trusted. A man who had an ear tuned to what God is saying to him and to the world" (Oduyoye 1990, 69).

In her search for solidarity, Mercy was very sure that the story of Joseph could have a message for us all. It certainly has had an enduring message for her as she summoned courage to develop African women's theology, combining culture and tradition in weaving them into new and beautiful fabrics and strands of beads. In 1994 she moved beyond the church and university bureaucracies into free-lance teaching and writing, journeying across Africa and around the world to share the riches of what she was learning about the contribution of women to theology. The publication of her second book by Orbis Books in 1995, *Daughters of Anowa: African Women and Patriarchy*, marked this new phase in her creative work as a misfit (Oduyoye 1995a).

In her ground breaking book, Mercy not only confronts the myth that African women are not oppressed, but details the ways African culture is a two-edged sword that provides deep religious and cultural roots for community life, while at the same time it also binds women.

At the core of the culture is an ideology that has absolute priority: corporate personality of the family, clan, or nation is always chosen over the personhood of the individual, especially when that individual is a woman. (Oduyoye 1995a, 15)

Through careful research into the language of myths, folktales and proverbs, Mercy establishes women's place in their communities, and then moves on to how women live their lives in the culture and where women hope to go.

Moving into the area of religion and culture enables Mercy to fashion an African women's theology that is at once responsive to their daily reality, yet full of the riches of their traditions. Mercy came to the United States in 1995 to give the Ensign Lecture at Yale Divinity School. Again she drew on the resources of African women's culture and art to lift up a communal and relational theology, as she spoke on, "Spirituality of African Women: The Sacred from the Writings of Buchi Emecheta" (Oduyoye 1995c). Confronting the authority of the patriarchs, she created her own space for theology and invited those who gathered to enter into a new kinship with the wisdom of African women.

RACHEL WEEPING

Matthew 2:13–23

At the end of Matthew 2 the earlier patriarchal power competition gives way to patriarchal violence and destruction with the slaughter of innocent children in Bethlehem. In a story that parallels Exodus 1:8–2:10, Matthew describes the way this new pharaoh deals with the upstart "King of the Jews." Herod is a cruel ruler and, when he realizes that he had been tricked by the magi, he does not hesitate to make the families of Bethlehem pay the price of his power game: "and [Herod] sent and killed all the children in and around Bethlehem who were two years old or under, according to the time he had learned from the wise men" (Exod. 2:16).

In Matthew's story we see the results of patriarchal logic in which the winners wield power at the expense of the powerless. When power is exercised as a *zero sum game*, those in authority build their power by taking it from those who have less possibility to resist. Sharing of power and inclusion of the many in a *multiplication game* is not even considered.

Matthew, however, does take the multiplication game seriously and lifts it up very clearly as he presents the story of the women and their families crying out in *resistance to this violence*. In Matthew's quotation from Jeremiah 31:15 the suffering multiplies, but so does the compassion. Rachel weeping for her children refuses to be consoled, "because they are no more" (Matt. 2:18). In the midst of this senseless slaughter, the wise women reach out to a God of compassion, knowing that God weeps for them in the midst of injustice and pain.

Here we have echoes of Jesus' own compassion and weeping over Jerusalem as it continues to be caught in the patriarchal competition (Wainwright 1994, 644). In Matthew 23:37 Jesus lifts up one of the Sophia sayings and continues the women's lament: "Jerusalem, Jerusalem, the city that kills the prophets and stones those who are sent to it! How often have I desired to gather your children together as a hen gathers her brood under her wings, and you were not willing!"

And the story of resistance to violence goes on as the one child who is saved from the slaughter continues to confront the power of Pilate, the chief priests and elders. It is his resistance to the *zero sum game* that leads him to the cross where God not only weeps with him, but also calls him to new life through the multiplying power of love.

MERCY AS MS.

Speaking out clearly against patriarchal violence and finding ways to assist women and men to resist this violence has been at the heart of Mercy's organizing task both with the Ecumenical Association of Third World Theologians and with the Circle of

Concerned African Women Theologians. When Mercy began attending EATWOT shortly after it was created in 1976 she was one of a handful of women theologians invited to take part. She was the leading voice at the New Delhi conference on the "Irruption of the Third World," in calling for an "irruption within the irruption" in which women's participation and theological work on behalf of justice be taken seriously (Oduyoye 1983, 246–55). In 1995 she was still calling EATWOT to account at a meeting in New York City, asking the question, "To what extent does patriarchy continue to reign in EATWOT?" in a paper she presented on "The Impact of Women's Theology on the Development of Dialogue in EATWOT" (Oduyoye 1995b).

Her work in cooperation with other women led to the establishment of the Commission on Theology from Third World Women's Perspective in 1983. This Commission carried out an ambitious program of regional and international conferences between the women, and culminated its first phase with a dialogue between First and Third World women theologians in Costa Rica, December 1994. By then the dialogue had been expanded to include women theologians from Eastern Europe, Japan, South Africa, the Pacific and Palestine (Mananzan 1996, 2; Fabella 1993). This dialogue continued and developed with Mercy Oduyoye serving as the first woman president of EATWOT, and Mary John Mananzan from the Philippines serving as the general secretary.

At the conference in Costa Rica on "Women Resisting Violence: Spirituality for Life," Mercy presented a powerful paper entitled, "Spirituality of Resistance and Reconstruction" (Mananzan 1996, 161–72). Drawing on her intensive involvement with ecumenical youth work in Africa and in the WCC, from 1967 to 1974, she underlined the senseless slaughter of the children and families of the African continent through structural adjustment policies, war, drought, and international power plays. She spoke of the refusal of young people and women to stay on the margins of power as they confront a hostile world and resist those who would deny them room to breathe and live. She declared:

> My thesis is that in the struggle to build and maintain a life-giving and life-enhancing community, African women live by a spirituality of resistance, which enables them to transform death into life and to open the way to the reconstruction of a compassionate world. (Mananzan 1996, 162)

Through Mercy's voice these women are joining the women of Ramah, "Rachel weeping for her children" (Mt. 2:18). They reach out to a compassionate God and work to transform Africa "from a hostile space into a nurturing womb and cradle provided by God" (Mananzan 1996, 165).

And this is what Mercy is about in inviting a group of African women to join her in creating the Circle of Concerned African Women Theologians so that women from all over Africa can begin to create their own theology. As Mercy and Musimbi Kanyoro put it: "African women theologians have come to realize that as long as men and foreign researchers remain the authorities on culture, rituals, and religion, African women will continue to be spoken of as if they were dead" (Oduyoye and Kanyoro 1992, 1).

The book on the first meeting of the Circle, which she edited with Musimbi R. A. Kanyoro, shows that the women not only have *The Will to Arise*, but also the insight and gifts that can help to transform theology. Women are writing about their own experiences of tradition and the church in Africa, which are grounded in Scripture and rooted in their own contexts. These women have begun to *let Pharaoh go*, and to write their own lives into theology.

In the work to make sure women's voices continue to be lifted up, Mercy located herself in Ghana at Trinity Theological College in 1998 to create and direct the Institute of Women in Religion and Culture. This Institute of Women provides an ongoing educational base for conferences and workshops. It not only serves the need for leadership development and continuing theological education for women in Ghana, but also furthers the work of women in the Circle from all parts of Africa. Part of her outreach through the program is represented by Mercy's latest book, entitled, *Introducing African Women's Theology* (Oduyoye 2001). Her gifts and those of many African women theologians have continued to multiply so rapidly that such an introduction was needed to the growing literature in this field.

In order to make the Institute a permanent part of the educational ministry of Trinity Theological College, Mercy and the women of the Institute are raising funds to build the *Talitha Cumi Center* on the Trinity campus. Mercy continues to travel and to spread the word about African women's *will to arise*, but she has found a home where she can continue to develop the studies of religion and culture as part of the continuing program of the Circle. Like the family at Bethlehem, she has journeyed far, yet has now circled back, not to Nazareth, but to Legon, where she can continue to teach what it means to be a wise woman and disciple of Jesus.

In our journey with the magi and with the wise woman bearing gifts we have discovered a lot of missing persons who bring many gifts to the Christ Child. Remembering the missing women in Matthew's story, we are reminded that he does not name *three* wise men, but magi from the East who bring three gifts. We also know that we could name the visitors in many ways. From a feminist perspective these magi certainly could be as easily named *Ms, Mother, and Misfit* as Caspar, Balthasar, and Melchior! Matthew 28 tells us that the story continues with all the nations included, so we have also included Mercy because she represents for so many of us what it means to be a wise woman who comes bearing gifts as she continues on her wisdom journey!

REFERENCES

Bird, Phyllis A. 1997. *Missing Persons and Mistaken Identities: Women and Gender in Ancient Israel.* Minneapolis: Fortress Press.

Boring, M. E. 1995. "The Gospel of Matthew: Introduction, Commentary and Reflections." In *The New Interpreter's Bible.* Vol. VIII. Edited by L. E. Keck. Nashville: Abingdon Press, 89–505.

Brown, Raymond E. 1992. "Infancy Narratives in the NT Gospels." In *The Anchor Bible Dictionary.* Vol. III. Edited by D. N. Freedman. New York: Doubleday, 410–15.

Dube, Musa W. 1998. "Go Therefore and Make Disciples of All Nations." In *Teaching the Bible: Discourses and Politics of Biblical Pedagogy.* Edited by F. F. Segovia and M. A. Tolbert. Maryknoll, New York: Orbis Books, 224–46.

———. 2000. *Postcolonial Feminist Interpretation of the Bible*. St. Louis, Missouri: Chalice Press.

Fabella, Virginia. 1993. *Beyond Bonding: A Third World Women's Theological Journey*. Manila: Ecumenical Association of Third World Theologians and the Institute of Women's Studies.

Heschel, Susannah. 1996. "Anti-Judaism/Anti-Semitism." In *Dictionary of Feminist Theologies*. Edited by L. M. Russell and J. S. Clarkson. Louisville, Kentucky: Westminster John Knox Press, 12–13.

Isasi-Díaz, Ada María. 1993. *En la Lucha: (In the Struggle): A Hispanic Women's Liberation Theology*. Minneapolis, Minnesota: Fortress Press.

Mananzan, Mary John, Mercy Amba Oduyoye, Elsa Tamez, J. Shannon Clarkson, Mary C. Grey, Letty M. Russell, eds. 1996. *Women Resisting Violence: Spirituality for Life*. Maryknoll, New York: Orbis Books.

Oduyoye, Mercy Amba.1983. "Reflections from a Third World Woman's Perspective: Women's Experience and Liberation Theologies." In *Irruption of the Third World: The Challenge to Theology*. Edited by Virginia Fabella and Sergio Torres. Maryknoll, New York: Orbis Books, 246–55.

———. 1986. *Hearing and Knowing: Theological Reflections on Christianity in Africa*. Maryknoll, New York: Orbis Books.

———. 1988. "Be a Woman, and Africa Will Be Strong." In *Inheriting Our Mother's Gardens: Feminist Theology in Third World Perspective*. Edited by Letty M. Russell, Kwok Pui-lan, Ada María Isasi-Díaz, and Katie G. Cannon. Philadelphia: Westminster Press, 35–53.

———. 1990. *Who Will Roll Away the Stone? The Ecumenical Decade of the Churches in Solidarity with Women*. Geneva: WCC Publications.

———. 1995a. *Daughters of Anowa: African Women and Patriarchy*. Maryknoll, New York: Orbis Books.

———. 1995b. "The Impact of Women's Theology on the Development of Dialogue in EATWOT." New York: Union Theological Seminary. Unpublished paper.

———. 1995c. "Spirituality of African Women: The Sacred from the Writings of Buchi Emecheta." New Haven, Connecticut: Yale Divinity School. Unpublished paper.

———. 1999. "A Coming Home to Myself: The Childless Woman in the West African Space." In *Liberating Eschatology: Essays in Honor of Letty M. Russell*. Edited by Margaret A. Farley and Serene Jones. Louisville, Kentucky: Westminster John and Knox Press, 105–20.

———. 2001. *Introducing African Women's Theology*. Sheffield, England: Sheffield Academic Press.

Oduyoye, Mercy Amba and Musimbi R. A. Kanyoro, eds. 1992. *The Will to Arise: Women, Tradition, and the Church in Africa*. Maryknoll, New York: Orbis Books.

Schüssler Fiorenza, Elisabeth. 1983. *In Memory of Her: A Feminist Theological Reconstruction of Christian Origins*. New York: Crossroad.

Wainwright, Elaine. 1994. "The Gospel of Matthew." In *Searching the Scriptures: A Feminist Commentary*. Vol. II. Edited by E. Schüssler Fiorenza. New York: Crossroad, 635–77.

3

Let's Celebrate the Power of Naming

Nyambura J. Njoroge

The goal of this essay is to celebrate the enriching power that radiates from the ability to name what is happening in one's life and in the community in the context of injustice, indignity and suffering. This leads to courage that brings hope for healing, transformation and new life. I invite all of us to celebrate this power by exploring "A Coming Home to Myself: The Childless Woman in the West African Space" (Oduyoye 1999), one article by Mercy Amba Ewudziwa Oduyoye—affectionately known as Auntie Mercy by some of us within the Circle. This is my way of celebrating Mercy's life and her many contributions to the shaping of African women's theological voices and to the way African women theologians continue to transform the theological profile of Africa. I also celebrate how Mercy's life and contributions have influenced my own theological journey, especially in discovering the power of naming my pain and loss in the context of death-dealing activities as personally experienced in Kenya and Africa in general.

CELEBRATING THE COURAGE TO ARISE FROM PAIN AND INDIGNITY

In life, especially within Africa, there are many challenges that produce enormous pain, suffering and indignity. During the past twenty years, African women theologians have attempted to name these challenges and to gather courage to address them in ways that are healing, transforming and life-giving. As one of these African women theologians, Mercy Oduyoye has powerfully demonstrated this courage in sharing her own agony as a childless African Christian woman. I believe it is appropriate to celebrate this courage in this volume that honors Mercy because, in her own words:

> Just as Hannah rose, so that day, on the island of Crete, Amba rose to the realization that children are God's gift to creatures who need to survive by procreation. I had prayed to join in obeying the command to increase and multiply, and God was saying a clear no to my offer. I felt free; I felt open and fertile, a new person for whom God has a purpose. It was like putting my life on the altar for God to consume what is not necessary for my journey. Rather than being consumed by childlessness, I rose, like Hannah, as one who had experienced a secret conversation and a secret pact with God. I was convinced that something would be born of this experience. I was pregnant with expectation of great things to come to me from God. I have not been disappointed. What do we expect from the hand of God? For me, it is life lived fully as God would have it, life as a doxology to God, who first loved us. (Oduyoye 1999, 118)

For those who have known Mercy and followed her writings and professional career, these words ring true, leading us to join her in doxology to God.

I want to briefly reflect on my own encounter with this topic. Growing up in the church manse only a few yards from the village maternity clinic where my mother practiced midwifery for seventeen years, I knew many cases of childless women who consulted with my mother, as well as marital problems caused by childlessness that my pastor father had to deal with. My personal encounter with the topic was during my parish ministry in Nairobi in the 1980s. There were many taboo issues that caused women and girl-children great pain, suffering and indignity; but one that left me with very fresh memories was that of childlessness.

The tears of Wanjiru[1] speak for many childless women I knew in the parish. By the time I got to know Wanjiru, she had tried unsuccessfully for sixteen years to conceive a child of her own. Her husband had married another woman and she had decided to adopt a child. That particular day, Wanjiru was in tears because she had received a letter informing her that a child had been found for adoption, but unfortunately she didn't receive the letter until six months after its posting. Wanjiru did not have her own postal address but had used the school address and when the letter arrived it was hard to trace its owner. When Wanjiru went to the adoption office, the adoption order had been closed. Soon afterward, Wanjiru visited my office. I have never forgotten her despair, pain and sense of indignity at being childless. I recalled the advice of the senior minister when I first began parish ministry, warning me never to discuss the topic of children or their fathers unless I knew the women very well, as there were many childless women and single parents in the parish. As a result, the general code of conduct in the parish on issues of childlessness was deafening silence. As I became acquainted with my parishioners, I came to know some of the adopted children, but there were always painful stories behind their adoption, as well as problems associated with the loss of identity and sense of belonging.

Because of this experience and my own inadequacy in pastoral care, counseling and theology, I was one of those Circle members who always wished Mercy would share her personal story as a woman theologian (Oduyoye 1999, 107), a request she graciously acceded to within the article under review. Not only has she provided us with a very personal account of her own childlessness, but

Mercy has instinctively challenged us to create a life-giving theology that directly addresses those taboo topics that bring great pain, suffering and indignity to women's lives. Mercy's article has helped us to know why she does what she does. As Mercy writes, "I would like to claim who I am as a 'woman alone' who inspires community; a woman who prays that the men and women she touches and who touch her will grow and prosper as God would have all humans do; a woman whose life helps effect an earth that is prosperous and at peace" (Oduyoye 1999, 107).

I am one of those African women theologians who have been inspired and empowered by Mercy's boldness, honesty, determination, creativity and fruitfulness. As I have written elsewhere,[2] Mercy has given us a legacy of collaborative leadership worth emulating. This includes the power of naming women's pain and agony due to the lack of biological progeny.

> There is a part of this experience that has not received adequate theological reflection, a story of women's experience that has yet to be told. What I do in this essay is reflect on the experience of women who belong to traditions where naming is according to fruitfulness in childbearing, but who for whatever reason do not join in "increasing and multiplying" the human race. This is an area of silencing crying out for insight and for words. (Oduyoye 1999, 105)

In conclusion, she writes:

> The issue I have been addressing may have only marginal relevance for feminists, womanists, and mujerista theologians, the theological sisterhood in the Western world; but in a community of women-centered theologians, where one hurts, all should hurt. In the context of liberating eschatology, therefore, I make bold to raise a question so personal and so "old-fashioned" that it may embarrass even my African sisters. The "child factor" in Africa (and perhaps elsewhere) is complex, and its public faces are daunting; but nothing is more oppressive than the ordinary meanings imposed on the absence of children in a marriage. The

silence that shrouds the issue compounds its potential for the disempowering of women. Shall we continue to be silent, or shall we help shape a theology that is life-giving in a situation that is otherwise a context of death? The one who sits on the throne says, "See, I am making all things new" (Rev. 21:5). Shall we not seek life for the childless? (Oduyoye 1999, 119)

By writing from her own experience, Mercy has broken one chain of conspiracy that patriarchy and its collaborator, sexism, use to debase women's identity and dignity. This is something truly worth celebrating. In her article, Mercy has taught us the value of being vulnerable, honest and true to ourselves. But this lesson comes with great responsibility.

A CALL FOR A LIFE-GIVING THEOLOGY

As African women theologians, our celebration is complete only when we hear and respond to Mercy's central cry for creating a life-giving theology of procreation and eschatology. In her article, we hear an unambiguous, yet intense voice, calling us as African women theologians to create a life-giving theology, a theology that addresses the trauma women undergo in the quest for a child of their own (Oduyoye 1999, 112). Put simply, Mercy passionately calls us to assist churches to formulate teachings, counseling methodologies, and materials that help women, men and their families to realize that there is more than one way of being fruitful in the eyes of God: "There is no aid for the judgments of inferiority and shame, no clarity for the childless couple from an alternative theological view of their forms of fruitfulness, their participation in the glory of God. Only passive resignation is offered in an inadequate eschatological perspective" (Oduyoye 1999, 116).

Silence and passivity are not options. As women, we are called to be fruitful and creative. We can discover how by re-imagining the Bible and raising new questions that lead to renewed vision and faith. For instance, the songs of Hannah (1 Sam. 2:1–10) and

Mary (Luke 2:46–55) can empower women even when our many prayers for a child appear to go unanswered. Consequently, the answer to Mercy's many prayers was:

> Increase in humanity.
> Multiply the likeness to God for which you have the
>   potential.
> Multiply the fullness of humanity that is found in
>   Christ.
> *Fill the earth with the glory of God.*
> Increase in creativity.
> Bring into being that which God can look upon and
>   pronounce
> "good," even "very good." (Oduyoye 1999, 118;
>   emphasis added)

Filling Africa with the glory of God is a challenge to each one of us as African women. This is particularly daunting in the context of extreme poverty, chronic hunger, systemic violence, the HIV/AIDS pandemic, malaria, and the social injustices of globalization, each of which conspires against Africa's natural and human resources. As a result, the whole of Africa cries out for a life-giving theology that can bring healing, transformation and hope. And yet we must provide a balm in Gilead. In addition, we are called to address issues related to our Christian understanding of immortality. In this area, Mercy has posed many pertinent and important questions:

> If the Bible does not finally anchor people's worth solely in their power of procreation, then why is there not a stronger eschatology that would counter the craving to continue particular genetic lines, to reproduce ourselves as concrete evidence of our immortality? What constitutes immortality? The immortal ones whose "photocopies" we see around us are themselves no longer here; only their spirits and what they stood for abide. *To be remembered by children is not the only way to desirable immortality.* The "immortal" ones who people our archives and history books were not all persons

of honor and great love. What kind of immortality are we craving? (Oduyoye 1999, 116; emphasis added)

As African women theologians we have the potential to give birth to a life-giving theology that will multiply the fullness of humanity as well as bring life after death through Christ. Mercy's personal search for a life-giving theology and eschatology shows powerfully that childless women can actively embrace this state of life and work toward enhancing and enriching humanity, suffering with those who suffer as did Jesus Christ (Oduyoye 1999, 118–19). This is precisely what Mercy attempted to achieve in creating the Circle of Concerned African Women Theologians and the *Talitha Cum* Center in Accra, Ghana. The best way to celebrate these astonishing achievements is, in Mercy's words, to assist "the church to acknowledge and raise up the diversity of God's gifts and to celebrate all the ways of bringing forth life" (Oduyoye 1999, 119). She gives us a role model worthy of emulation: "The bruises and the sounds of the stone throwing, intentional and unintentional, are still fresh in my mind. Only my soul remains undaunted and un-embittered" (Oduyoye 1999, 112). She also wrote, "To participate in the ever-widening stream of resurrection people is to know fruitfulness, to be transformed (Oduyoye 1999, 119).

Mercy has been our role model in a number of ways. Her article cited here demonstrates a model of ethics and a spirituality of resistance and transformation that grew out of her pain and agony of being childless. Powerfully, she has named the different ways the African community and Christian churches have perpetuated stigmas and feelings of inferiority and shame upon childless women. Through seeking God's will for her life, Mercy not only found the strength to resist, but also the means toward her own transformation. By refusing to accept that biological progeny is the only way to participate in increasing and multiplying humanity, Mercy set in place a model for other women to emulate. Furthermore, Mercy's life and ministry have demonstrated that there is diversity in God's giftedness that results in many forms of fruitfulness, biological and beyond, and transforms the way we think about the theology of procreation and eschatology.

In this process, Mercy's ethics and spirituality of resistance and transformation have challenged one of the fundamental beliefs in African religion and culture, a belief that has caused great misery to countless childless women and men.

> In Africa, it is at one's death that children count most, for reproducing the human race is seen as a religious duty. One is never really a full and faithful person until one has a child. Among the Asante, burial rituals for childless persons are enacted in a way that is supposed to ensure that they are not reincarnated. Some would not call on childless ancestors in libation or name children after them. In is an inauspicious state, not to be encouraged and not to be celebrated. (Oduyoye 1999, 113)

As I have written elsewhere, the pioneering Gikuyu Christian women resisted the ritual of female circumcision for their daughters (otherwise known as female genital mutilation or FGM) by adopting an ethic of resistance and transformation. Likewise, Mercy has spoken a resolute NO to a practice that can hold deadly consequences for African women in their pursuit of bearing a child (Oduyoye 1999, 118).

On the other hand, by passionately and powerfully naming her pain and agony of childlessness and by resisting stigmatization by crying out for a life-giving theology of procreation and eschatology, Mercy has modeled for us a theology of lament.[3] In my view, Mercy's narrative has given African women who find themselves languishing in pain and indignity "permission" to name their own pain and to cry out for help, something which until very recently was considered a sign of weakness and lack of faith. By addressing the global HIV/AIDS pandemic in Africa and gender-based violence, now endemic on the continent, African women theologians are creating a theology of lament (see Dube and Kanyoro 2004). Slowly we are breaking the chain of omission and silence by giving voice to our lament in theology, sermons, and prayers in our churches. This is something worth celebrating.

Although I have tried within my own writings to give insight and language to those areas of women's lives (including childlessness) that are silenced and ignored, encountering afresh the words of Mercy as she names her own traumas and pain has renewed my courage to name my own pain, loss and sense of indignity and to continue developing a theology of lament. As I write, I recognize how desperately I am in need of a life-giving theology that will help me arise from the trauma and numbness that have encompassed me following a death in my family, a great loss that demanded that I return to childrearing soon after my last-born celebrated her twenty-first birthday. In addition, I am dealing with the trauma and pain of a relative who, after being raped, fell into a deep depression and attempted suicide. My heart is so grieved that the only theological language I know is that of lament. I echo the words of the psalmist:

> Give ear to my prayer, O God;
>   do not hide yourself from my supplication.
> Attend to me, and answer me;
>   I am troubled in my complaint.
> I am distraught by the noise of the enemy,
>   because of the clamor of the wicked.
>
> My heart is in anguish within me,
>   the terrors of death have fallen upon me.
> Fear and trembling come upon me,
>   and horror overwhelms me.
> And I say, "O that I had wings like a dove![4]
>   I would fly away and be at rest;
> truly, I would flee far away;
>   I would lodge in the wilderness;
> I would hurry to find a shelter for myself
>   from the raging wind and tempest."
>   (Psalm 55:1–3a, 4–8)

As I share my own experience of pain and great loss, I know that many African women have walked the self-same pathway.

They too yearn for a life-giving theology that will bring a balm in Gilead.[5] Among Mercy's writings (and I cannot claim to have read them all) this particular article helps me to celebrate the courage to arise from my own pain, loss and sense of indignity and, with others, seek healing, transformation and the newness of life. Mercy remains an important role model as we continue to create an African feminist theological ethics that reaffirms women as moral agents and as agents of transformation.

THE POWER OF NAMING: A PROPHETIC VOICE

In addition to providing us with a legacy worth emulating, Mercy has been a prophetic voice in a continent that is languishing in a litany of woes that devalue and diminish women's fruitfulness and creativity. Fortunately, we find through the Circle and other emerging prophetic voices courageous attempts at naming these woes. Some male theologians have added their prophetic voices (*JTSA* 2002, West and Zondi-Mabizela 2004). Taking our cue from Mercy, with courage, we should name and expose those things that diminish life in the body of Christ, especially on issues to which the leadership of the church responds with a deafening silence.[6] In particular, I have in mind the urgent need to name and expose the abuse of power and trust, widespread corruption, institutional mismanagement and poor governance that exists within the churches and other ecumenical and theological institutions.[7] Back in the late 1970s when Mercy started to gather names of theologically trained women in religious departments of universities and theological institutions, few of us existed. Today, we not only have hundreds of ordained pastors and priests, but also a growing number of holders of masters and Ph.D. degrees in various theological disciplines. Some have chosen to be theological educators and administrators.

We can no longer look at the church and its institutions only from the pews or the periphery. Although we are members of the highest church synods and sit on the councils of its constituent institutions, we are still small in number. We cannot wait for our numbers to swell before we name the abuse of power and trust (including sexual abuse), corruption, institutional mismanagement and poor governance within its patriarchal and hierarchical institutions. Mercy did not wait for others to name her experience, but rather courageously exercised the power of naming and exposing degrading practices and attitudes throughout her life. In the process, she exercised her God-given gifts of bringing forth life and raising a prophetic voice.

> I therefore had to work things out for myself, believing that I am no less in the image of God because I have not biologically increased and multiplied. I reflected on the taunts, the condolences, the blaming, and I concluded that these efforts to explain "why" one is childless are futile and false. . . . I found models of faith who had not biologically increased and multiplied but who participated in glorifying God. I prayed for strength to move beyond the theological impasse and to be at home with my *kra Amba*. I believed that what my soul desires is in what I am and what I live. (Oduyoye 1999, 116–17)

Working globally and ecumenically with theological institutions and theological education by extension programs, I regularly confront situations of grave abuse of power and trust and other injustices that have at times rendered some institutions and churches almost unmanageable and unproductive. Whereas women are not always innocent subjects when abuse of power and trust occur, I still believe the Circle stands on a strong platform from which it can effectively tackle this scourge. As Mercy has demonstrated, it is possible to be a prophetic voice under challenging and difficult circumstances.

African women theologians can learn from the prophetic voice of the first African (Kenyan) woman Noble Laureate, Wangari Maathai. Around the same time Mercy was busy reaching out and gathering us together as Circle women, Wangari was tackling the issue of the environment, creating in 1977 the Green Belt Movement (GBM). Eventually as rural women and others became aware that environmental rights are tied to issues of human rights, democracy, governance and peace, the GBM participated in challenging abuses of power and trust, corruption and bad governance in the Kenyan government, to the extent that Maathai and others were silenced, insulted and tortured, although they never gave up.[8] As we challenge those in power, we must exercise leadership values that uphold the standards of honesty, integrity, dignity, justice, peace and wholeness of life. We must work to develop a responsible and effective leadership that brings forth creativity and fruitfulness. As Maathai pointed out in her Noble Peace Prize acceptance speech in December 2004, those of us privileged with [theological] education have an immense responsibility placed upon our shoulders: "I call on leaders, especially from Africa, to expand democratic space and build fair and just societies that allow the creativity and energy of their citizens to flourish. Those of us who have been privileged to receive education, skills and experiences and even power must be models for the next generation of leadership" (Maathai 2004, 4).

We should not be afraid to share our own stories of abuse of power and trust (even in our own homes), corruption, institutional mismanagement and poor governance. It is sometimes weak and poor leadership that drives many women to an early grave or to live in endless suffering.

A PRAYERFUL WOMAN

Finally, for those who may not know Mercy personally, her articles reveal a woman of prayer and spirituality. As we struggle with naming life-diminishing and death-dealing issues, it seems only appropriate to conclude this essay with one of her published prayers, written while spending time with the Holy Spirit, awaiting her connecting flight at Heathrow Airport:

> Holy Spirit,
> Advocate and Comforter
> In you we celebrate
> The liberating presence of the living Christ.

You blow where you will,
Refreshing, renewing and inspiring
Like fire you purify.
Purify us.

Holy Spirit,
Advocate and Comforter
You expose what is evil in the world
You convict the world of sin
Like fire, you purify.
Purify us.

Holy Spirit,
Carry from us
Our narrow personal concerns to
Uphold, preserve and care for creation.
Nourish, sustain and direct us
Holy Spirit, Advocate and Comforter
Like fire, you purify
Purify us, we pray.

Holy Spirit,
You are the power at work in us
Source of faith, joy and hope.
When you give us breath we live;
Breathe on all creation.
Give new life to the earth,
We pray you.
    (Amoah & Martin 2001, 52–53)

NOTES

[1] Not her real name.

[2] In Njoroge 2005, I discuss at length how I met Mercy and the legacy she has established in reaching out and gathering African women theologians and the creation in 1989 of the Circle of Concerned African Women Theologians.

[3] Lament has been largely omitted in prayers in worship as well as in sermons and theology in western Christendom, which is largely responsible for the spread of Christianity in Africa. For further discussion see Billman and Daniel 1999.

[4] The words "On the Wings of a Dove" became the theme of the worldwide campaign on overcoming violence against children and women launched on 25 November-10 December 2004 by the World Council of Churches in Geneva as part of the Decade to Overcome Violence: Churches Seeking Reconciliation and Peace, 2001–2010.

[5] As I share the story of rape of my relative with friends and some Circle members, I am appalled to learn how prevalent rape and incest is among us, especially with our children and siblings in schools and in the streets.

[6] For instance, on issues related to violence against children and women and especially sexual violence against female bodies of all ages, despite the fact that some non-governmental organizations (NGOs) have attempted to create awareness and seek for solutions. For further discussion and updates on the plight of women and girl-children with respect to sexual violence, including when it is used as a means of torture and weapon of war, see the Amnesty International website http://www.amnesty.org/

[7] I have attempted to address the issue of leadership in a number of articles. See References for further details.

[8] Maathai has shared about her ordeal with the Kenyan regime of former President Daniel Arap Moi. See Motavalli 2004.

REFERENCES

Amoah, Elizabeth and P. Martin, P., eds. 2001. *Heart, Mind and Tongue: A Heritage of Woven Words*. Accra: Sam-Woode Ltd.

Billman, Kathleen D. and Daniel L. Migliore. 1999. *Rachel's Cry: Prayer of Lament and Rebirth of Hope*. Cleveland, Ohio: United Church Press.

Dube, Musa W., ed. 2003. *HIV/AIDS and the Curriculum: Methods of Mainstreaming HIV/AIDS in Theological Programs*. Geneva: WCC Publications.

——— and Musimbi R. A. Kanyoro, eds. 2004. *Grant Me Justice! HIV/AIDS & Gender Readings of the Bible*. Pietermaritzburg/Maryknoll, N.Y.: Cluster Publications/Orbis Books.

JTSA. 2002. *Special Issue: Overcoming Violence against Women and Children. Journal of Theology for Southern Africa*, 114.

Maathai, Wangari. 2004. "Nobel Prize Acceptance Speech." City Hall, Oslo, Norway, http://nobelprize.org/peace/laureates/2004/presentation-speech.html (accessed on 27 January 2006).

Motavalli, J. 2004. "Africa's Green Belt Movement: Wangari Maathai's Movement Is Built on the Power of Trees." *E Magazine*, 7 July 2004. http://nobelprize.org/peace/laureates/2004/presentation-speech.html (accessed on 27 January 2006).

Njoroge, Nyambura J. 1995. "Fountain of Life." In *Theology, Ministry and Renewal of God's People: Sixteen Bible* Studies. Edited by John Pobee. Geneva: WCC Publications, 78–86.

———. 1996a. "Groaning and Languishing in Labour Pains." In *Groaning in Faith: African Women in the Household of God*. Edited by Musimbi R. A. Kanyoro, A. and Nyambura J. Njoroge. Nairobi: Acton Publishers, 3–15.

———. 1996b. "Hannah, Why Do You Weep?" In *Violence Against Women: Reflections by Kenyan Women Theologians*. Edited by Grace Wamue and Mary Getui. Nairobi: Acton Publishers, 21–26.

———. 1997. "'Woman, Why Are You Weeping?'" *The Ecumenical Review* 49 (4): 427–38.

———. 1999. "Honoring Courageous Women: Troublemakers in the Face of Injustice." In *Networking for Reconciliation*. Edited by E. C. Miescher and M. J. Arana. Basel: Basileia Verlag, 191–201.

———. 2000a. *Kiama Kia Ngo: An African Feminist Ethic of Resistance of Transformation*. Accra: Legon Theological Studies Series Project in collaboration with Asempa Publishers.

———. 2000b. "A Tribute to Rizpah: A Spirituality of Resistance and Transformation." In *Of Rolling Waters and Roaring Wind: A Celebration of the Woman Song*. Edited by Linda Katsuno-Ishii and Edna J. Orteza. Geneva: WCC Publications, 66–68.

———. 2001a. "The Bible and African Christianity: A Curse or Blessings?" In *Other Ways of Reading: African Women and the Bible*. Edited by Musa W. Dube. Atlanta/Geneva: Society of Biblical Literature/ WCC Publications, 207–36.

———. 2001b. "A Spirituality of Resistance and Transformation." In *Talitha Cum! Theologies of African Women*. Edited by Nyambura J. Njoroge and Musa W. Dube. Pietermaritzburg: Cluster Publications, 66–82.

———. 2001c. "Talitha Cum! To the New Millennium: A Conclusion." In *Talitha Cum! Theologies of African Women*. Edited by Nyambura J. Njoroge and Musa W. Dube. Pietermaritzburg: Cluster Publications, 245–59.

———. 2001d. "Come Now, Let Us Reason Together." *Missionalia* 29 (2): 232–57.

———. 2001e. "Transforming Ministerial Ecumenical Formation." *The Ecumenical Review* 53 (3): 306–18.

———. 2002. "Reclaiming Our Heritage of Power: Discovering Our Theological Voices." In *Her-Stories: Hidden Histories of Women of Faith in*

Africa. Edited by Isabel A. Phiri, Deverakshanam Betty B. Govinden, and Sarojini Nadar. Pietermaritzburg: Cluster Publications, 39–57.

———. 2005. "A New Way of Facilitating Leadership: Lessons from African Women Theologians." *Missiology: An International Review* 33 (1): 29–46.

Oduyoye, Mercy Amba and Musimbi R. A. Kanyoro, eds. 1990. *Thalitha Qumi*. Ibadan: Daystar Press.

Oduyoye, Mercy Amba, ed. 1997. *Transforming Power: Women in the Household of God*. Accra: Sam-Woode Ltd.

———. 1999. "A Coming Home to Myself: The Childless Woman in the West African Space." In *Liberating Eschatology: Essays in Honor of Letty M. Russell*. Edited by Margaret A. Farley and Serene Jones. Louisville, Kentucky: Westminster John Knox Press, 105–22.

Rakoczy, Susan. 2004. *In Her Name: Women Doing Theology*. Pietermaritzburg: Cluster Publications.

Umlilo, Thandeki. 2002. *Little Girl, Arise: New Life after Incest and Abuse*. Pietermaritzburg: Cluster Publications.

West, Gerald O. and Phumzele Zondi-Mabizela. 2004. "The Bible Story That Became a Campaign: Tamar Campaign in South Africa (and Beyond)." *Ministerial Formation* 113. Geneva: WCC Publications, 4–12.

Women's Shelter Project 2000. 2001. *Stories of Courage Told by Women*. Gaborone: Lightbooks.

World Council of Churches. 2004. *Ministerial Formation* 113. Geneva: WCC Publications.

PART II

AFRICAN WOMEN, THE BIBLE, AND HEALTH

4

"Texts of Terror"

The Conspiracy of Rape in the Bible, Church, and Society: The Case of Esther 2:1–18

Sarojini Nadar

The brute force that pounced on me and carried me away, kicking and screaming, later took flesh and blood in the person of Shechem, said to be a prince. This royal rapist could not have known who I was, let alone my name. I was but clay in his hands as he pounded and squeezed vigorously until I would yield what would please him. I was just a part of silent nature to be worked until I produced or became what would please men. That I screamed and scratched meant nothing. I was female and should expect to be raped. Not a word from me is recorded anywhere. That for me is the saddest part. Do I have a say in how my life is managed? Am I and the women I went out to seek just chips on a patriarchal bargaining table? (Quoted in Gnanadason 1993, 48–49)

This is a re-telling of the rape of Dinah (Gen. 34), in the context of a Bible study by Mercy Amba Ewudziwa Oduyoye.[1] In her creative re-telling of the story, Oduyoye reveals at least three key features of her theology, and Circle theology in general, the last of which is the most significant here. The first is that experience is a legitimate source of theology. As Teresa Okure points out, African women's "primary consciousness in doing theology is not method, but life and life concerns—their own and those of their own peoples" (Okure 1995, 77). In contexts where patriarchy still dominates, where women are beaten and raped each and every day, the choice to read these texts in the light of our experiences as women is vital.

The second feature can be found in the very act of re-telling the story from Dinah's perspective. Feminists and womanists have argued for the power of story-telling for a long time (see Phiri, Govinden and Nadar 2002). The patriarchal Bible silences the voices of women, whether as victims of rape or as agents in their own right. We do not hear their voices. Everything about women is filtered through the voice of the narrator, who is male. Oduyoye, in re-telling the story from the perspective of Dinah, "takes back" some of this lost power. This re-telling evokes Elizabeth Schüssler Fiorenza's call for "creative actualization" in her book *In Memory of Her: A Feminist Theological Reconstruction of Christian Origins* (Schüssler Fiorenza 1983). She goes against the "master narrative" of the patriarchal Bible, and tells the story from the point of the victim, the underdog.[2]

Finally, and of most significance for this paper, in creating space to re-read this "text of terror" (see Trible 1984) from the perspective of a woman, Oduyoye makes the implicit point that the Bible cannot be dismissed—even those texts that are difficult to read have to be exposed, interrogated, deconstructed and re-interpreted until a liberating message or at least a voice that women can identify with can be found. It is on this foundation that the present essay is written.

The rape of women[3] especially within biblical literature and its subsequent covert endorsement by biblical writers and interpreters alike is a cause for great concern.[4] The issue of rape is intricately related to issues of gender, power, ideology, sexuality, and interpretation. In this paper, I will first examine how these issues operate in the text of Esther. Second, by deconstructing these notions in a literary-womanist reading of chapter 2 of Esther, I will seek to show how the text colludes in the approval of the rape of women, and how such readings, designated as "Word of God" are construed as "natural." Finally, I will argue that since the Bible plays such a pivotal role in the lives of women in Africa, it is imperative that we break with these traditional modes of oppressive reading by engaging critical ways of reading the biblical text, such as the ones I will propose in this reading.

A study cited in *The Cape Times* conducted by Lloyd Vogelman of the University of the Witwatersrand from the Centre for the Study of Violence and Reconciliation was able to conclude that "South Africa has the highest rape statistics in the world for a country that is not at war. It is estimated that 1 in 2 women will be raped in her lifetime in South Africa" (24 October 1991). Responding to this situation, Karen Buckenham has made the important observation:

> To prevent rape, we need to challenge societal beliefs and cultural values that promote and condone sexual violence. The silence surrounding rape by society at large, including the church, denotes its acceptance, and allows it to continue. (Buckenham n.d.: 29; see also Maluleke and Nadar 2002, 5–17; Dube 2001)

These two quotations reveal important concerns for interpreters/readers of the Bible. The first quotation exposes the scourge of sexual violence against women in South Africa, while the second discloses an implicit damning accusation against the complicity of both church and society in the crime of sexual violence against women. As I have asked in a previous paper, "How is it that we find suffering bodies of used and abused women right from biblical times into our very own century in the midst of people that claim to be religious, in the midst of people who engage in religious discourse?" (Nadar 2002, 113). I have argued that the answer to this lays, to a considerable degree, in the text that feeds the religious discourse, in this case, the Bible. I further argue that unless we transform the ways in which we read the Bible, not only within the academy but also in our communities of faith, we will perpetuate the justification of the rape and abuse of women. To achieve such transformative readings, I submit that liberative academic interpretive resources need to be shared with faith communities so that gender-social transformation can begin (see West 1999, Cochrane 1999, Philpott 1993, Haddad 2000).[5]

TAKING THE BIBLE SERIOUSLY

For African biblical scholars to simply theorize about oppression in the biblical text or the biblical text's history seems self-indulgent, especially since the majority of Africans (again particularly women) who read or listen to the Bible view it as a source of inspiration in their daily lives and not as a document under scientific scrutiny (Oduyoye 1998, 124–31). I submit, therefore, that it is irresponsible for the biblical scholar to ignore such readers since there is overwhelming evidence for the pivotal role that the Bible plays in most communities of faith, particularly amongst the poor and working class.[6] In other words, I am arguing that the biblical scholar who claims to be committed to liberation has to take into account the communities of faith who interpret the Bible and the way in which their interpretations either liberate or oppress. In this respect, Itumeleng Mosala has acknowledged that Black theology as a theology of liberation in South Africa has failed to "become a useful weapon in the hands of the oppressed and exploited Black people themselves. It has remained the monopoly of educated Black Christians and has often been unable to interest the white theologians against whose theology it was supposedly developed. Further it has been unable to develop organic links with the popular struggles of especially the black working-class people, the most exploited segment of the community" (Mosala 1989, 2).

These arguments were penned at a crucial time in apartheid South African history, some years before the release of Nelson Mandela. Whether his argument still holds true for Black theology currently remains to be seen, as the relevancy of Black theology as a liberation discourse within post-apartheid South Africa is a topic of hot debate. My use of Mosala's concern over the class positions and class commitments of Black theology is to apply it to the current period of academic biblical criticism. While it remains true that biblical scholars have discovered new reading methodologies that have promoted readings of the Bible that liberate rather than oppress,[7] the problem remains that most of these methods, although claiming to read the Bible for liberation, actually liberate very few people—indeed mostly those within the academy who have been looking for alternative methodologies! Apart from a few academics (namely, African, Asian and Latin American), most biblical scholars who are supposedly practitioners of liberation hermeneutics have been unable to develop organic links with such poor and oppressed faith communities in whose name liberation hermeneutics is practiced. Yet, the Bible remains, in these communities of faith, both central and normative for the way people live their lives.

The fundamental difference between the interpretive strategies of the academy and the interpretive strategies of the faith communities lies in the latter's belief in the authority of scripture.[8] Black liberation scholars in South Africa have attempted to take seriously the way in which faith communities view the Bible as the "Word of God," by making this their exegetical starting point (see Boesak 1984, Tutu 1984). Itumeleng Mosala has been more than candid in his critique of this exegetical starting point of liberation hermeneutics. He argues that "The insistence on the Bible as the Word of God must be seen for what it is: an ideological maneuver whereby ruling-class interests evident in the Bible are converted into a faith that transcends social, political, racial, sexual, and economic divisions" (Mosala 1989, 18).

I agree with Mosala when he states that the Bible "is the product, the record, the site, and the weapon of class, culture, gender, and racial struggles" (Mosala 1989, 193). Feminist and womanist scholars have held this for a long time with respect to the patriarchal character of the biblical text. However, even though some scholars have totally abandoned the Bible, claiming it has nothing positive to say about women (see Daly 1978, 1996), there are still those who, committed to the emancipation of women, continue to struggle with the text in order to find liberating messages for women. More important, women within faith communities also struggle with the biblical text to find a God who liberates rather than oppresses. In defense of Mosala, he does not argue that we abandon the biblical text altogether, rather he calls for "a 'projective' appropriation of biblical texts in such a way that the absences and silences in these texts may serve as spaces from which the thrust of alternative significations and discourses may be launched" (Mosala 1989, 189). What Mosala is adverse to are interpretations that collude with the ideology behind the final form of the biblical text, by appealing to the text in its final canonical form.

Contrary to Mosala's plea for a return to a historical materialist reading of the text, I would suggest that given that our goal is liberation—not just in the academy but within our communities—postmodernist-literary methodologies are more helpful than historical-critical ones. I would maintain that postmodernist-literary methods open up the text to new and multiple interpretations in a way that historical-materialist methodologies do not allow. As asserted above, faith communities begin with the assumption that the Bible is the Word of God. For scholars wanting to enable liberation within our communities, refutation of this understanding would be totally irresponsible. In saying this, I do not suggest that scholars must themselves believe that the Bible is the Word of God. Rather, they must take seriously the ways in which the Bible operates within the community as the inspired and authoritative Word of God. Mosala seems to think that this is a difficult, if not impossible task:

> What, then, do we mean by the Bible as the "Word of God?" The ideological import of such a theological question is immense, because presumably the Word of God cannot (by definition) be the object of criticism. Furthermore, the Word of God cannot be critiqued in the light of black experience or any other experience. The only appropriate response is obedience. (Mosala 1989, 16–17)

Mosala's argument seems to suggest that if scholars buy into the notion of the Bible as the inspired "Word of God," a meaningful critique is not possible, due to the divine authority that becomes attached to the biblical text. His argument only holds true however if a single methodology is applied to the text: namely the historical materialist. In other words, by constantly trying to read behind the text in order to expose the hegemonic motives that lie behind the text, the scholar might alienate the community that reads the "text as text." In contradistinction, I suggest that literary methods, particularly those that belong to the postmodernist paradigm, could help bridge the gap between how academic scholarship and faith communities read the Bible, in a way that historical materialist exegesis can not.[9]

Finally, reading the biblical text for transformation is not a self-evident methodology. There are currently several debates surrounding the value of reading the biblical text in such a way. Notably, one such scholar who has developed her thinking in this regard is Elisabeth Schüssler Fiorenza. Since her earlier work, *In Memory of Her*, Schüssler Fiorenza has moved substantially from an academic and what she has called a "gender studies" approach to that of a "critical feminist interpretation for liberation approach" (Schüssler Fiorenza 1983, 79). I situate myself as a womanist scholar in this paradigm of scholarship, treading carefully amongst the shaky spaces that lie between the theoretical and activist planes of reality. As such, this paper does not aim at developing a merely theoretical and academic hermeneutic, but more important, an activist approach that will produce an emancipatory reading for women who are victims of rape and abuse. This is clearly reflected in the reading I will now attempt.

LITERARY-WOMANIST ANALYSIS OF ESTHER 2:1–18: PLOT AND TIME

Esther 2:1–18 seems—at least on the surface—to be concerned with a beauty contest. Virgins are gathered in the king's harem, from which he will choose a new wife. It certainly does seem innocent enough. What we are not told is what happens to the bodies of all the virgin women who, we are told, go into the king's palace at night and return in the morning, and do not return to the palace again until the king decides that he has "delighted" in them and wants to see them again. If we read the text carefully we will see that the king is spending a night with each of the virgins. They are not simply paraded before him in beautiful gowns. Yet what happens to these virgins when they go into the king's room at night? I suggest that their bodies are violated and raped, being treated as mere objects of desire. The virgins are as violated as the Levite's concubine in Judges 19.

In this section I therefore want to demonstrate why chapter 2:1–18 should be read as a text of terror. Utilizing the literary devices of plot and time, I will first present a brief analysis of the way in which the plot works within this text, and then I will provide an analysis of the way in which time operates within this text.

Chapter 2 of the Book of Esther opens with Queen Vashti having been deposed for not appearing when the king summoned her to show off her beauty to all his male friends who were "merry with wine" (1:10). Chapter 2 documents the search for one who is "better than Vashti." Although Vashti is immediately deposed, the king takes a long time to decide who will be his new bride. His power as king allows him to sanction a nation-wide search. The reader expects that this greater choice will allow the king to choose much more carefully than he did previously. This time he should not end up with another wife like Vashti, who publicly disobeyed and humiliated him. His careful choice of a new bride should help in solving the complication of the old wife's disobedience. For this, the reader expects that the king would have carefully chosen criteria for the potential candidates for queen. However, it seems that the only criteria they had to fulfill was that they had to look beautiful (hence the twelve months of cosmetic treatment that the young virgins had to undergo at the house of Hegai the eunuch) and be good in bed. (After spending a night with all the girls, the king would only call back a girl that "delighted" him [2:14]). Eventually, the king finds a girl who fulfils these criteria in the person of Esther and with her introduction as the king's new wife a state of equilibrium is once more reached in the palace.

Analyzing the Use of Plot

Plots are usually structured along a pattern of "equilibrium-complication-equilibrium." Vashti's "disobedience" introduces a state of complication, but Esther's ascension to the throne, re-introduces equilibrium. This is the way in which this plot seems to work—through establishing and re-establishing the power of the male over the female. As Pam Morris has argued, "Plot structure represents a perception of reality. Traditional structures show female destiny to be the passive acceptance of restricted choice, stoicism in suffering and punishment for transgression" (Morris 1993, 34).

The Book of Esther appears to contain the traditional plot structure that Morris is speaking about. This is indicated by Vashti's deposal and Esther's apparent submissive acceptance of her appointment as the new queen. In this, it once again becomes apparent that the king's arbitrary power (in that he chooses a wife in a way that clearly violates not only her, but all the women in the harem) is the vehicle that drives the plot forward. This arbitrary power embodied through the character of the king re-appears in all the following scenes of the narrative as well.

The plot becomes one of the vehicles through which the narrative's ideologies are transported. Within the narrative, this is carried within the framework of three distinct trajectories. The first suggests that plots contain inherent mechanisms that guide the reader from one event to the next until a "satisfactory" ending is reached. If we agree that this is the only way a plot functions, then we accept, with regard to the patriarchal ideology in the text, that the plot of Esther wants to entice us into the "logic" of the story—that men are initiators of action and only men are the custodians of power. As Morris further asserts, "To be heroic, plots tell us, men must embrace action, seeking to shape circumstances to their will, whereas for women heroism consists of accepting restrictions and disappointments with stoicism" (Morris 1993, 32).

The second trajectory suggests that even though the narrative seems to chart out a plot that seeks to direct us in a certain way, the text actually contains elements that, if followed carefully, might lead us in a different direction. For example as Clines has shown through his exploration of the (non)exposition in the narrative, the text wants to give more significance to the story of Vashti than mere expositional significance (Clines 1998, 9–11). By choosing to read the text in this way, we "oppose the ideological implications of classic plot structures, prizing open alternative spaces of freedom for women within the text against the often relentless logic of the story" (Morris 1993, 33).

The apparent logic of the plot structure of the Esther narrative seems to imply that power lies with the males and the Persians only. Perhaps later in the text this may be proven otherwise. However, within this chapter it certainly seems to be the case.

The final trajectory is the role of the reader in the understanding of the plot. When reading the narrative through womanist lenses, Esther's ascension to the throne may be interpreted as her buying into the patriarchal game. It may alternatively be interpreted as a victory. A womanist reader knows how to follow the plot of how she gets there, since womanist readers know how to survive without deliberately being excluded from the system. A womanist reader will be in tune with the plot developments that culminate in Esther's gain of power in the end, even though this might seem to be at the expense of her gender power. Ironically, it is the ambiguity of the power relations in the narrative that floats the plot. Hence, even though it might seem that Jews and women are powerless in the narrative of Esther, it is only through their acquisition of covert power that the denouement of the plot is reached. As Lilian Klein has argued, "powerless women and Jews can invoke power as long as they maintain required appearances" (Klein 1995, 175). Nevertheless, even though Esther did what she had to do in order to survive, I would argue that this chapter constitutes a "text of terror."

Analyzing the Use of Time

Analyzing the use of time in this narrative will also show why this text should be read as a "text of terror." The Book of Esther opens with a phrase that seeks to set the narrative in a concrete historical moment in time, namely the reign of the Persian king Ahaseurus (Xerxes I). At the same time, however, it suggests that the narrative was written much later: "This happened in the days of Ahaseurus" (1:1).[10] As Yairah Amit has shown, "chronological markers not only tell the reader how much time has elapsed, they may also serve more complex requirements" (Amit 2001, 107). By analyzing the significance of a few of these chronological markers, I will now seek to demonstrate how these time markers highlight the issues of power and gender oppression with particular reference to rape.

The text continues, "In the third year of his reign, he gave a banquet for all his ministers and officials" (1:3). We are told that it is in this period of banqueting (that is, in the third year of his reign) that Vashti is deposed. The time marker "after these things" (2:1) that begins the search for a new bride, indicates that little time has passed between the deposal of Vashti and the nationwide pursuit for a new queen.[11] The next time marker is found within Chapter 2: "When Esther was taken to King Ahaseurus in his royal palace in the tenth month, which is the month of Tebeth, in the seventh year of his reign, the king loved Esther more than all the other women; of all the virgins she won his favor and devotion, so that he set the royal crown on her head and made her queen instead of Vashti" (2:16–17).

It is clear from this text that four years have now passed since the king began his search for a new queen and before Esther "wins his favor." One of these years was spent preparing the virgins with cosmetic treatments. After their cosmetic makeovers the time came for each girl to enter the king's palace. Another time marker indicates the amount of time that the girl spent with the king: "In the evening she went in; then in the morning she came back to the second harem in custody of Shaasgaz, the king's eunuch, who was in charge of the concubines" (2:14).

This process goes on for three years before Esther is chosen as queen. The time markers contained in these chapters suggest at least two things: first, the king takes four years to choose a new queen, and second, apart from the one year that the women spent receiving cosmetic treatments, he had sexual intercourse with each of the virgins, which is indicated by the fact that each of them went into the palace from the virgins' harem, spent a night with the king, and then returned not to the harem of the virgins, but to the harem of the concubines.[12]

These time markers hold great significance with respect to the king's character as an all-powerful monarch, whose every need, including sexual, had to be taken care of, irrespective of the women he violated in the process. The scope of this paper does not allow an in-depth character analysis of the king. My point here is to show that time markers can point to a number of important traits, such as characterization, that lie within a narrative. In this case, the long period of time that the king takes to choose his new bride reflects his power. Even though the narrative is comprised of short sentences to quicken the pace of the narrative, this device seems to suggest that the text does not want to dwell on this issue. It is a womanist reading that picks up such issues as the abuse of power that is summarily "brushed off" in the context of short sentences, thus highlighting how biblical narrators conspire in the rape of women. Undoubtedly, interpreters of the Bible also appear to be co-conspirators in this "cover up" by "brushing off" the rape of the virgins in order to reach the conclusion of the plot. I argue, therefore, that biblical scholars and interpreters in faith communities (who usually rely on the Bible as the word of God, as described in detail at the outset of this essay) need to take careful notice of these reference points within the corpus of the biblical text so that the bias against women and the horror of rape is not perpetuated.

The pericope that describes the king's "liaisons" with the women seems to inscribe rape into the text (albeit through staccato sentences). At the same time it construes to erase it by focusing the reader's attention on the "glorious" occasion of Esther being chosen as queen. As Higgins and Silver point out:

> Analyses of specific texts, when read through and against each other, illustrate a number of profoundly disturbing patterns. Not the least of these is an obsessive inscription— and an obsessive erasure—of sexual violence against women (and against those placed by society in the position of

'woman'). The striking repetition of inscription and erasure raises the question not only of why this trope recurs,
but even more, of what it means and who benefits. How is
it that in spite of (or perhaps because of) their erasure, rape
and sexual violence have been so ingrained and rational-
ized through their representations as to appear 'natural' and
inevitable to women as to men? Feminist modes of 'reading' rape and its cultural inscriptions help identify and
demystify the multiple manifestations, displacements, and
transformations of what amounts to an insidious cultural
myth. In the process, they show how feminist critique can
challenge the representations that continue to hurt women
both in the courts and on the streets. (Higgins and Silver
1991, 2)

CONCLUSION

Higgins and Silver succinctly capture the main points that I
wish to make in this paper. First, they show how flippantly and
dismissively rape is presented in literature (as well as in society),
thus making it appear a natural occurrence. This is clearly seen
in the Book of Esther: The virgins with whom the king forcibly
had sexual intercourse are categorized according to the euphe-
mistic adjective "delight"; hence, the girl that "delighted" the
king the most was asked to return. Second, they point to the short
way in which rape and sexual violence are represented within a
text so as to make their occurrence appear natural—before they
are "erased" from further discussion. As a result, only two verses
are spent on the choosing process before the text moves on to
the main event, the crowning of Esther as queen. And, of course,
Esther needs to be crowned queen in order for the plot to progress
and the "more important" aspect of the plot to be fulfilled, namely
the salvation of the Jews. Third, unless one reads the text from a
feminist perspective it is difficult to uncover the masked references to sexual violence, which are covered up ingeniously by the
literary devices of time and plot structure as was shown throughout this paper. Failure in this regard will thus help to perpetuate

the violence implicit in our interpretations. Finally, unless these texts are read and exposed, they will continue to hurt women in our courts, cities, townships, rural areas, and, I would argue, the church as well.

As Renita Weems has so astutely asserted:

> All of this underscores the fact that reading is not the passive, private, neutral experience that we have previously believed. To read is to be prepared in many respects to fight defensively. It is to be prepared to resist, to avoid, to maneuver around some of the counterproductive impulses within the text. In short, reading does not mean simply surrendering oneself totally to the literary strategies [such as plot and time structures] and imaginative worlds of narrators. It also means at the very least that one must be conscious of the ways in which symbolic speech, for example, draws us into its designs and attempts to mould our beliefs and identity. (Weems 1995, 101)

Within this paper I have aimed to show that the literary devices of plot and time used ingeniously by the narrator serve to point us in a certain direction leading to meaning. This is not always a one-way road, as literary devices meet and interact with readers, who have particular concerns and who are already "ideologically positioned" (Beal 1997, 85). Hence, even though the narrative of Esther might seem to be already plotted, feminist, womanist and African women biblical scholars cannot and should not be satisfied with this state of affairs. Instead, we need to constantly interrogate, appropriate and transform these texts so that irresponsible interpretation is not constantly perpetuated, putting women's lives at further risk.

NOTES

[1] As presented at a preparatory meeting for the July 1993 Ecumenical Global Gathering of Youth and Students (EGGYS), Geneva, February 1993.

[2] Monica Melanchthon explains that "master narratives are stories that are so familiar that they seem inevitable and obvious in their meaning, even when they happen to us. Master narratives are the stories we were taught and they teach us about who does what and why. Perhaps the best way to counteract master narratives is to offer new, compelling, and even more interesting stories—stories that sustain us, inspire others, and aim to subvert. Sometimes these stories are crowded out of public awareness by the dominance of the master narrative. These are counter narratives which arise both in autobiographical and in fictional accounts and in stories of women. . . . Indeed it is proved to be an effective method for conscious raising" (Melanchthon 2000, 78).

[3] The legal definition of rape in South Africa has been criticized for being defined in extremely narrow ways. With a view to promulgating new legislation, the South African Law Commission was asked to review the Sexual Offences Bill and make recommendations for a more suitable definition. I quote parts of their recommendation: "In terms of our common law, rape is committed by a man having intentional unlawful sexual intercourse with a woman without her consent. Non-consensual anal or oral penetration does not constitute rape in common law, although it can constitute indecent assault. Sexual intercourse is restricted to the penetration of the vagina by the penis. The Commission proposes the repeal of the common law offence of rape and its replacement with a new gender-neutral statutory offence. The essence of the Commission's proposal on rape centers on 'unlawful sexual penetration.' The Commission says sexual penetration is unlawful *per se* when it occurs under coercive circumstances. Coercive circumstances include the application of force, threats, the abuse of power or authority, the use of drugs, and so on. Sexual penetration is defined very broadly by the Commission to include the penetration 'to any extent whatsoever' by a penis, any object or part of the body of one person, or any part of the body of an animal into the vagina, anus, or mouth of another person. Simulated sexual intercourse is also included under the Commission's definition of 'sexual penetration'" (South African Law Commission 1999). For the purposes of this paper, I am particularly interested in the recommendation of the South African Law Commission to include "coercive circumstances" in the definition of rape, particularly with regard to the abuse of power or authority. In my view this broader definition resonates well with the text of Esther 2:1–18, which I will analyze further within this paper. When conducting a Bible study on this text with participants at a workshop organized by the Centre for Constructive Theology (CCT), women pointed out that even if what is reported to have occurred in this text is not rape, it certainly constitutes an abuse of power: women in such vulnerable power-situations are reported to have "consensual sex" with powerful men who do not give them any choice in the matter.

[4] Renita J. Weems asserts that "violence against women is virtually always cast in sexual terms. Women are punished with rape, beatings, exposure of their private parts, and mutilation of their bodies. . ." (Weems 1995, 3).

[5] It must be noted that the length and the scope of this paper does not allow a detailed description of what "shared interpretive resources" involve, or the findings of such a venture. For a more detailed analysis, see Nadar 2003, 232–317.

[6] In saying this, I am not suggesting that the Bible does not play important roles in other class/social sectors of the church.

[7] The advent of feminist, womanist, African women's theologies, *mujerista* and a host of other women liberation methodologies, ideological criticism, post-colonial criticism and such significant discourses testify to this shift.

[8] The issue of authority may be directly linked with the reality that people of faith read with other people of faith, not simply as an individual or scholarly activity. For example, Stephen Fowl argues, "The authority of Scripture, then, is not so much an invariant property of the biblical texts, as a way of ordering textual relationships. To call Scripture authoritative also establishes a particular relationship between that text and those people and communities who treat it as authoritative. In the absence of a community or communities of people who are struggling to order their lives in accord with that Scripture, claims about the authority of Scripture begin to look rather abstract and vague" (Fowl 1998, 6).

[9] This is especially true of those who belong to the positivist-scientist paradigm that endorses the belief that there is only one "correct" interpretation.

[10] Although there are a number of serious questions concerning the historicity of the narrative, it is not relevant for the purposes of this paper to dwell on this issue. For the latest discussion in this regard, see Bush 1996.

[11] See Bechtel, who suggests that although the meaning of "after these things" is imprecise, "the scene has all the symptoms of the 'morning after'" (Bechtel 2002, 28). Michael Fox also notes that the "after these things" does not imply a long lapse in time as "Xerxes does not seem like the sort of person to persist in his anger for very long" (Fox 1991, 172).

[12] *Contra* Karen Jobes, who argues that "During the intervening years Xerxes was off fighting a disastrous war with Greece. . . . Shortly after his return from Greece, Esther was chosen as his new consort" (Jobes 1999, 94). Jobes makes these statements as if they are self-evident and that this is what actually took place; indeed, she seems quite oblivious to the number of issues of historicity that surround the book of Esther. Further, she insists that feminist critics should not perceive this as an act of sexism, since

Herodotus also reports that five hundred young boys were gathered each year and castrated to serve as eunuchs in the Persian court. Hence Jobes can starkly conclude, "One might argue that the young women actually got the better deal. The gathering of the virgins, whether consensual or not, is not sexism. It is a brutal act typical of how power was used in the Persian court. Everyone, whether male or female, was at the disposal of the king's personal whims" (Jobes 1999, 94).

REFERENCES

Amit, Yairah. 2001. *Reading Biblical Narratives, Literary Criticism and the Hebrew Bible*. Minneapolis, Minnesota: Fortress Press.

Beal, Timothy K. 1997. *The Book of Hiding—Gender, Ethnicity, Annihilation, and Esther*. New York: Routledge.

Bechtel, Carol M. 2002. *Esther: Interpretation—A Biblical Commentary for Teaching and Preaching*. Louisville, Kentucky: John Knox Press.

Berlin, Adele. 2001. *The JPS Commentary—Esther*. Philadelphia: The Jewish Publication Society.

Boesak, Allan. 1984. *Black and Reformed: Apartheid, Liberation and the Calvinist Tradition*. Johannesburg: Skotaville.

Buckenham, Karen. n.d. "Rape." In *Violence Against Women Resource Pack*. PACSA Manual for Churches. Pietermaritzburg.

Bush, Frederick W. 1996. *Word Biblical Commentary—Ruth, Esther*. Dallas, Texas: Word.

Clines, David J. A. 1998. "Reading Esther from Left to Right—Contemporary Strategies for Reading the Biblical Text." In On *the Way to the Postmodern*. Edited by D. J. A. Clines. Sheffield: Sheffield Academic Press.

Cochrane, James. 1999. *Circles of Dignity—Community Wisdom and Theological Reflection*. Minneapolis, Minnesota: Fortress Press.

Daly, Mary. 1978. *Gynecology: The Metaethics of Radical Feminism*. Boston: Beacon Press.

———. 1996. *Beyond God the Father: Toward a Philosophy of Women's Liberation*. London: The Women's Press.

Dube, Musa W., ed. 2001. "Other Ways of Reading—African Women and the Bible." Atlanta: Society of Biblical Literature; Geneva: World Council of Churches Publications.

Fowl, Stephen E. 1998. *Engaging Scripture—A Model for Theological Interpretation*. Oxford: Blackwell Publishers.

Fox, Michael. 1991. *Character and Ideology in the Book of Esther*. Columbia: University of South Carolina Press.

Gnanadason, Aruna. 1993. *No Longer Silent: The Church and Violence Against Women*. Geneva: World Council of Churches Publications.

Haddad, Beverley. 2000. "African Women's Theologies of Survival—Intersecting Faith, Feminisms, and Development." Unpublished Ph.D. diss., University of Natal.

Higgins, Lynn A. and Brenda R. Silver. 1991. *Rape and Representation*. New York: Columbia University Press.

Jobes, Karen H. 1999. *Esther: The NIV Application Commentary*. Grand Rapids, Michigan: Zondervan.

Klein, Lilian R. 1995. "Honor and Shame in Esther." In *A Feminist Companion to Esther, Judith and Susanna*. Edited by A. Brenner. Sheffield: Sheffield Academic Press.

Maluleke, Tinyiko Sam and Sarojini Nadar. 2002. "Breaking the Covenant of Violence against Women." *Journal of Theology for Southern Africa* 114: 5–17.

Masenya, Madipoane J. 1999. "Biblical Authority and the Authority of Women's Experiences: Wither Way?" *Scriptura* 70: 229–40.

Melanchthon, Monica. 2000. "Hidden Histories, Open Opportunities: Women in Theological Education." Report of the International Network in Advanced Theological Education (INATE) Workshop (Budapest, Hungary, 2–7 September).

Morris, Pam. 1993. *Literature and Feminism*. Oxford: Blackwell Publishers.

Mosala, Itumeleng J. 1989. *Biblical Hermeneutics and Black Theology in South Africa*. Grand Rapids, Michigan: Eerdmans.

Nadar, Sarojini. 2002. "Gender, Power, Sexuality and Suffering Bodies: Re-reading the Characters of Esther and Vashti for Social Transformation." *Old Testament Essays* 15 (1): 113–30.

———. 2003. "Power, Ideology and Interpretation/s: Womanist and Literary Perspectives on the Book of Esther as Resources for Gender-Social Transformation." Unpublished Ph.D. diss., University of Natal.

Oduyoye, Mercy Amba. 1998. "African Women's Hermeneutics." In *The Power of Naming: A Concilium Reader in Feminist Liberation Theology*. Edited by E. Schüssler Fiorenza. Maryknoll, New York: Orbis Books.

Okure, Teresa. 1989. "Women in the Bible." In *With Passion and Compassion: Third World Women Doing Theology*. Edited by Virginia M. Fabella and Mercy Amba Oduyoye. Maryknoll, New York: Orbis Books.

———. 1995. "Feminist Interpretations in Africa." In *Searching the Scriptures: A Feminist Introduction*. Edited by Elisabeth Schüssler Fiorenza. New York: Crossroads.

Philpot, Graham. 1993. *Jesus Is Tricky and God Is Undemocratic—The Kin-Dom of God in Amawoti*. Pietermaritzburg: Cluster Publications.

Phiri, Isabel Apawo, Better Deverskshanam Govinden; and Sarojini Nadar, eds. 2002. *Her-Stories: Hidden Histories of Women of Faith in Africa*. Pietermaritzburg: Cluster Publications.

Plaatjie, G. K. 1997. "Mary Magdalene in the Gospel of John in the Context of Readings by Southern African Christian Township Women." Unpublished M.Th. Thesis. University of Natal.

Schüssler Fiorenza, Elisabeth. 1983. *In Memory of Her: A Feminist Theological Reconstruction of Christian Origins*. New York: Crossroads.

———. 1998. *Sharing Her Word: Feminist Biblical Interpretation in Context*. Boston: Beacon Press.

South African Law Commission, 1999. "Sexual Offences: The Substantive Law." Executive Summary, Discussion Paper 85, Project 107. http://www.law.wits.ac.za/salc/discussn/sexsum.html/ (accessed 8 June 2005).

Trible, Phyllis. 1984. *Texts of Terror: Literary Feminist Readings of Biblical Narratives*. Philadelphia: Fortress Press.

Tutu, Desmond Mpilo. 1984. *Hope and Suffering: Sermons and Speeches*. Grand Rapids, Michigan: Eerdmans.

Weems, Renita J. 1995. *Battered Love: Marriage, Sex, and Violence in the Hebrew Prophets*. Minneapolis, Minnesota: Fortress Press.

West, Gerald O. 1999. *The Academy of the Poor—Towards a Dialogical Reading of the Bible*, Sheffield: Sheffield Academic Press.

5

Women and Health in Ghana and the *Trokosi* Practice

An Issue of Women's and Children's Rights in 2 Kings 4:1–7

Dorothy B. E. A. Akoto

Our Mother, Our Shepherd—Mercy Amba
    Ewudziwa Oduyoye

[1] Our Mother, Our Shepherd—Auntie Mercy,
For your industry as a theologian, and educationist,
Your training and teaching tirelessly,
    we never know want.
Your dependants and more are provided for.

[2] You jealously guard the legacy and
    values you uphold.
As theologian and educationist, academician,
You ensure the welfare of all and sundry.

[3] When sickness and waywardness beset,
    Your instructions and guidance

96

direct toward right paths of order.
   Health is restored.

[4] Even when life becomes tempestuous,
   The future seems unknown and scary,
when situations are threatening and trying,
   there is no cause for alarm,
for your teachings, your instructions,
   are always there to show the way.
Your words of chastening are a source
   of purification and encouragement.

[5] Jealously, you guard the good because
   you are *obaa simaa* (*lit:* ideal woman).
You are *nyornu* (*lit:* maker of things good).
Your eyes are always fixed on the prize.
   Your words of praise, comfort and
encouragement, make you an educator "laureate"
for they nullify feelings of bitterness and
   hatred, restoring peace and calm.

[6] Our Mother, Our Shepherd—Auntie Mercy,
the good and "right-full" paths, in which you
offer training, your tender love and care will always
   abide.
As long as life lasts and the Circle lives,
we will continue to bask in your amazing
   motherliness.
Surely, your guidance, your counsel, your industry,
   will be appropriated forever.[1]

This poem is dedicated to Mercy Amba Ewudziwa Oduyoye
in recognition of her pioneering work in founding the Circle of
Concerned African Women Theologians. Since 1989, the Circle
has ably served our African sisters (and brothers) on the continent of Africa, as well as those within the diaspora. Many other
women have also benefited. Conscious awareness has been raised
of issues surrounding gender, and the violence meted out toward
women and children has been laid bare. The Circle has been

instrumental in addressing women's issues not only through engagement and activism, but also through the publication of articles and books; thereby providing an enabling environment in which health and healing can flow into situations of physical, emotional, and sociological ill-health, leading African women back to health. As Katie Cannon has correctly pointed out, the work of the Circle is two-dimensional, "giving literary expression to religious aspirations and reformulating African women's intimate life with God in the context of African culture" (Cannon 1992, vii–viii).

The aim of this chapter is to argue that the issue of women's health in Africa should be synonymous with the rights of children and women. It will deal with matters of Bible and interpretation, as befits Mercy, a devoted Christian and theologian. In particular, I will engage 2 Kings 4:1–7 as a women's health issue, and as an issue of women's and children's rights in Ghana today. In particular, I will parallel the biblical passage to that of *trokosi*,[2] which is practiced in some Ghanaian societies, and to the work of Mercy and the Circle.

WOMEN AND HEALTH

Women's health is more at risk than the health of others. Indeed, the issue of women's health is multi-faceted and includes not only the physiological, but also the psychological, social and economic domains, among others. Before I attempt to delve further into this topic, I need to ask "What is health?" *Webster's Ninth New Collegiate Dictionary* defines "health" as "the condition of being sound in body, mind or spirit, especially, freedom from physical disease or pain or the general condition of well-being." Additionally, R. K. Harrison in his entry within *The Interpreter's Dictionary of the Bible* depicts health and healing as "curing or restoring to health a sick person, whether by closing wounds, repairing results of accidents or surgical disease or treating effectively specific pathological conditions of the body or mind. It is the absence of disease. . . . A healthy person exhibits the state of body and mind in which all functions are being discharged harmoniously" (Harrison 1962, 541–42). Physical strength and well-being constitute health. The description of David in 1 Samuel 16:18 as "skillful in playing, a man of valor, a warrior, prudent in speech, and a man of good presence; and the Lord is with him," projects him as an all-encompassing healthy personality. The apocryphal Book of Sirach includes a poem on health:

> Better off poor, healthy, and fit
>   than rich and afflicted in body.
> Health and fitness are better than any gold,
>   and a robust body than countless riches.
> There is no wealth better than health of body,
>   and no gladness above joy of heart.
>   (Sir. 30:14–16)

Health can be deduced from the Hebrew word *shalem*, which literally means "healthy" or "whole," from which derives the word *shalom*. *Shalom* encompasses a complete state of soundness of the entire human condition, both physical and spiritual.

These various definitions of health seem to suggest that "health" involves completeness in all aspects of life. Cheris Kramarae and Paula Treichler, in their work *A Feminist Dictionary*, define "health" as "a state of well-being and freedom from disease and pain, which should be considered a "basic right and a high social priority" (1985, 187). The emphasis on the value of health suggests that it is an indispensable and basic right that must be prioritized.

In *Healing the Child Within: Discovery and Recovery for Children of Dysfunctional Families* (1989), Charles Whitfield makes the powerful assertion that there is a child within each person who is vital, active, creative and fulfilled, thereby reflecting the true self. He further elaborates on this child within by asserting that when s/he is not nurtured or allowed freedom of expression the individual begins to live as a victim and experiences difficulties in resolving emotional trauma. This gradually becomes an accumulation of unfinished psychological and emotional business and leads to chronic anxiety, fear, confusion, emptiness and unhappiness. Some causes of ill-health—emotional or mental—among African women can be explained by the foregoing assertion. African women have, for the most part, been denied the freedom to be themselves, resulting in their ill-health. I believe that this is an issue of human rights.

Nyambura Njoroge, in *Kiama Kia Ngo: An African Feminist Ethic of Resistance and Transformation*, invites women to renounce patriarchy with all its accompanying oppressive dehumanization and unite toward transformation. She sees the Gikuyu Women's Guild of the Presbyterian Church of East Africa as a group that expresses faith in both word and action toward healing. Teresia Hinga, in her article "Jesus Christ and the Liberation of Women in Africa," advocates that "for women to achieve their freedom, they will have to cultivate confidence in themselves, such that their actions spring from themselves rather than being motivated by imitation of any role models" (Oduyoye and Kanyoro 1992, 185). For a long time African women have lacked faith and confidence in themselves. As a result they have imitated those they considered role models and have thereby inhibited their own freedom to be transformed into "healthy" women.

CHILDREN'S AND WOMEN'S RIGHTS

Rights, as defined by *Webster's Ninth Collegiate Dictionary*, is "something to which one has a just claim," "power or privilege to which one is justly entitled," and as "the cause of truth and justice." As Mercy Oduyoye asserts:

Men and women are sexually distinct beings who do not necessarily have to be identified with the opposite sex in marriage or other forms of complementarity. We [women] may have to reorient our thinking so that we see communion as a relationship devoid of hierarchical relations and power-seeking. When we have learned more about our humanity perhaps we will also be able to understand what God is telling us about divinity. (Oduyoye and Kanyoro 1992, 23–24)

Mercy's argument that through the knowledge of ourselves we can probably understand God is to the point.

During the International Year of the Child (1977) the United Nations Children Educational Fund (UNICEF) issued a statement on the Rights of the Child. This included the right to:

- Affection, love and understanding.
- Adequate nutrition and medical care.
- Free education.
- Full opportunity for play and recreation.
- A name and nationality.
- Special care if handicapped.
- Be among the first to receive relief in times of disaster.
- Be a useful member of society and develop individual abilities.
- Be brought up in a spirit of peace and universal brotherhood [sisterhood].
- Enjoy these rights, regardless of race, color, sex, religion, national or social origin. (Wehrheim 1979, 30)

These constitute genuine rights of the child. The question is, however, whether these ideals have been adhered to. UNICEF, together with its global partners, has worked hard to implement this declaration, although it must be admitted that there is still much to be done, particularly on the African continent. The inhumanity perpetuated by civil and ethnic wars and other forms of conflict persists. Sudan, Rwanda, Zaire, Sierra Leone, and, not too long ago, Liberia are cases in point. In Zimbabwe, innocent children have been raped and tortured by Security Police and Youth Brigade members. In northern Uganda, the Lord's Resistance Army utilizes child soldiers in their insurgency campaigns. Severe famine, caused by drought, has claimed the lives of countless children and adults. Communities are fraught with disease and poverty, such as HIV/AIDS, tuberculosis, malaria and chicken pox. Dehumanizing practices are carried out in the name of tradition. In her article "The Christian Widow in African Culture," Daisy Nwachuku captures well the situation, using the words of a female health researcher, C. O. Adebajo, "[I]t is an established fact that the more severe the effects of any harmful practices are, the more likely it is that the victims will be either women or children. Men have been, generally, involved in the less severe forms of traditional practices" (Nwachuku 1992, 57). Children and women are the victims.

THE CONTEXT– 2 KINGS 4:1–7

The story of 2 Kings 4:1–7 belongs to the Deuteronomic tradition of the former prophets, which includes the books of Deuteronomy through 2 Kings, with the exception of Ruth. Its genre is that of a miracle story, and it is the first in a chain of seven stories of similar genre. It, and the six others following, are attributed to an Elisha-cycle of sagas, which scholars attribute to folklore. They are probably intended to glorify the prophet but are intertwined with some form of moral code in order to give them theological value.

In this story, a poor widow pleads with a man of God, Elisha, to save her two orphaned sons from the creditor of her dead husband. The man of God, moved with compassion, encourages the poor widow to put her faith to work by using what she possesses— an otherwise insignificant jar of oil—to grant justice to her and her children. This woman does not have what would be considered a bodily ailment, but rather she appears to be emotionally ill. Through a humanitarian act, the man of God produces a miracle of multiplication of the widow's oil, to heal or liberate her and her family from the claws of slavery.

The poor widow's two sons are about to be taken into slavery to pay the debt her husband had owed before his death. Completely confused, she rushes to Elisha, the leader of the prophetic guild to which her husband had belonged, with a report and a desperate plea that he should tell her what to do (v. 2). This story is set just before that of another desperate woman's plea to Elisha. In contradistinction, the second woman is a wealthy Shunamite (2 Kings 4:8–37). Both are facing situations of health and their rights, and those of their children. The Shunamite has lost her only son and goes to seek out the prophet for his help. This arrangement

emphasizes the gravity of the situation of the first woman, as highlighted in 2 Kings 4:1–7. When she is questioned by the prophet
about what she possesses, she declares, "Your servant has nothing in the house, except a jar of oil" (v. 2). For an African woman,
this story is a projection of a real existential situation. It exempli-
fies the harshness of a traditional cultural practice. Widowhood,
with its accompanying hardships, can be an ordeal and threatens
the emotional health of both women and children. The woman
in this story is a widow whose husband was a member of a prophetic guild, which, although not celibate, was coenobitic. She
faces several issues. Apart from losing her husband, the cultural
prospect of losing her two children to slavery for the debt of her
dead husband also confronts her.

Mosaic law, or Israelite cultural practice, allowed a creditor to
take a debtor and his children into slavery. If the debtor was dead,
his children could be taken into slavery until the debt was repaid.
This is evident in passages such as Exodus 21:2, Leviticus 25:39–
41, Nehemiah 5:4, 5, and Matthew 18:25. This practice seems to
parallel the *trokosi* practice in some Ghanaian societies. The *trokosi*
is a young virgin given up by her family in propitiation for the
sins committed against the gods by her ancestors. The young,
innocent virgin becomes a slave-wife of a fetish priest, who is
usually old enough to be her grandparent. He has children with
her in a loveless relationship. While in the former case, the slaves
could be freed in the year of Jubilee (see accounts in Exodus and
Leviticus), the *trokosi* could not be freed. This woman could not
stand the thought of her sons being enslaved, hence her intentional step to avoid it. When asked what she has at home, she
responds "nothing but a jar of oil" (v. 2). Insignificant though
this might be, the prophet instructs her to "borrow vessels from
all your neighbors, empty vessels and not just a few" (v. 3) and,
behind closed doors, to fill them with her oil. This was a real test
of her faith. Her unquestioning obedience results in the miracle
of multiplication of the oil. As long as there were sufficient vessels, the oil flowed. The faith of her children was also tested.
They cooperated to receive the miracle of their own salvation.
The unquestioning obedience shown by both mother and children serves to miraculously multiply what they had. Even after

filling the vessels, she still had to ask the prophet what to do with the oil that had been multiplied. "Go, sell the oil and pay your debts, and you and your sons can live on the rest" (v. 8), instructs the prophet.

This story can be structured as a drama, with four distinct scenes:

1. The woman desperately pleading for her children (vv. 1–2);

2. The dialogue between the woman and the prophet, culminating in her borrowing "empty vessels and not just a few" (v. 3) from her neighbors;

3. The woman filling the borrowed vessels with the oil with the active help of her sons (5–6); and

4. The woman returning to give the prophet feedback on the miracle, and the prophet's final instruction to go pay her debts and live off the remaining with her sons (v. 7).

This story can be compared with our relationship with Mercy. With our active cooperation, Mercy initiated the formation of the Circle and it has continued to live up to its aim. When African women were on the verge of enslavement to dehumanizing cultural practices, Mercy could not stand by while such enslavement ensued. In her own words, the initiation of the Circle had "its genesis in the need to probe the effects of religion and culture on African women's lives" (Oduyoye 1996, 31). She holds the opinion that "no amount of men's words can substitute for women's own articulation of the vision of this community which both men and women theologians should help to build" (Oduyoye 1996, 32). I submit that certain oppressive cultural and religious practices bring about most of what can be termed "ill-health" issues of women. As such, women must be in a position to unite in fighting for their health as a God-given right.

The son of the prophet Elisha has been identified by Josephus (*Antiquities of the Jews* IX. 4, 2), a Targumic source, as Obadiah, the chief steward of King Ahab, who supposedly hid one hundred prophets in a cave. It is claimed that the money owed must have been for the upkeep of the hidden prophets and that Obadiah must have died before he could repay the debt. The foregoing is a text-critical issue but looking at us as individuals before the Circle was formed, we could say we too were in a similar dialectical situation. We hid others and were hidden. We fed others and were, in exchange, fed traditional religious and socio-cultural modalities in a system dominated by patriarchy. Our death, and the death of those things that caused our pain and dehumanization, culminated in our appeal as African women for deliverance.

Like the widow and her progeny, we too suffered because of the death of others. Our suffering was the result of our husbands' indebtedness to African cultural practices, such as *trokosi* and associated widowhood rites. We and our children suffered all kinds of dehumanization. Yet, we did not have the courage to ask, "Why should the living be made to bear the punishment of the dead?" Even though the claim of the creditor in this story, to take the debtor's children into slavery, is culturally inclined, we must ask if it is just. In our African society where the Bible is taken literally and adhered to as the word of God, we should ask whether many cultural or religious customs practiced under the guise of scriptural authority should continue to be propagated. Female ordination continues to be debated in many Christian circles without any concrete resolution. The erroneous hermeneutics with which certain concepts of the scriptures are treated continue to be used to prevent the ordination of women and keep them from attaining leadership positions. We should ask if such scriptural authority used to keep women and their children in bondage should continue to be propagated even in this present age and context.

MEDIATION OF HEALING

How can health be mediated to women in order to grant them and their children the rights they deserve? I believe Mercy was right when she stated:

We seek to discard these fetters of culture. We seek full humanity and some principles to guide our lives in community. The meaning of full humanity cannot be defined by only one sector of humanity without listening to the voices, the hurts, and the delights of all the Fatimas. Even more important, what constitutes the fetters of oppression should be defined by those who experience it and not those who simply observe it. (1995, 82)

As African women we must take up the challenge and intentionally free ourselves from the chains of culture and religion, like the widow of 2 Kings 4:1–7. Like the widow's sons, we must participate actively in the healing process by being inclusive in solidarity and by sharing power. Our pace has been set by Mercy and we must rise to the task. The Circle has become our prophet and, with compassion, continues to multiply the little we possess. As Justin Ukpong has argued, contextualization is a means of creating links between African culture and Christian values. This must be our watchword. The foundation laid for us by Mercy is that of a liberation theology and we are called upon to be transformed and develop our talents.

Gwinyai Muzorewa has called us to produce fruits that "will be faithful to the African [I add, feminist] way of thinking," an "epistemology that will yield a distinct African theology" (1985, 84). As African women, we need to take ourselves to God just as we are in order to experience God's power of healing. We also need to love not only ourselves but all our significant others (such as our husbands and children) and try to maintain our safety in the face of the violence of the world. As Musimbi Kanyoro counsels, "unless women also get into the area of Bible translation, the thought system of women will remain unreflected in the texts which are received. The language of the Bible will also remain masculine until the women take up the will to arise and influence this aspect of the Christian base" (Kanyoro 1992, 99).

This counsel, I think, must be taken seriously to enable us African women to challenge theological rhetoric and break down the sexual barriers set by culture. This will enable us to promote socio-economic equality by making friendships that are free of dualistic and hierarchical tendencies set between the sexes and ages. This will promote the biblical concept of wholeness. Our talents must be used fully in building just communities in which we can give ear to those hurting among us. Through education, training and awareness-building programs, we can embrace everyone in reconciliation as God accomplished through Jesus Christ. Women's voices must be heard on those legal issues affecting women, children, and men, ensuring that appropriate structures are put in place so that the patriarchal project of dehumanization is effectively dissembled.

CONCLUSION

This article has attempted to address some of the issues that affect the health of women. It has been noted that women's health issues and those of human rights cannot be divorced from each other. Although the issues I have tackled in this chapter relate specifically to African women and children, they are nevertheless universal in scope. Additionally, health issues are not solely physical ailments. They also involve emotional and psychological issues and include anything that militates against the completeness of a person's being. Health, understood in this way, forms a basic and intrinsic right. The case of 2 Kings 4:1–7 ably illustrates how cultural practices affect women's health. Further, I have underlined the importance of Mercy's call for the re-interpretation of religion and culture in the light of the hurtful experiences of women at this point in time. I have sought to demonstrate what Mercy achieved and helped us as African women theologians to achieve through her formation of the Circle. We have received a call to healing. Such healing, in my opinion, can only come about when women and men are in that true partnership that depicts community.

Finally, in her beautiful poem on beads, which opens *Daughters of Anowa: African Women and Patriarchy*, Mercy alludes to that sense of *shalom*, that total feeling of health and wholeness that can be ours in God:

> I am in the process of giving birth
> To myself—recreating Me
> Of being, the Me that God sees.
> I am Woman

I am African
My beads mark my presence
And when I am gone
My beads
will remain.
(Oduyoye 1995, iv)

True to your words, Mercy, you have re-created yourself, and have called us to re-create ourselves into that which God desires us to be. We are women and African. Our beads (our achievements) mark who we are meant to be. When we are called home, our beads will remain.

NOTES

[1] Adapted from my recasting of Psalm 23 originally as a dedication to my mother, published in West and Dube 2000, 266–67.

[2] Literally, a young virgin given up by her family in propitiation for the sins committed by her ancestors against the gods.

REFERENCES

Akoto, Dorothy B. E. A. 2000. "'The Mother of the Ewe and Firstborn Daughter as the 'Good Shepherd' in the Cultural Context of the Ewe Peoples: A Liberating Approach." In *The Bible in Africa: Transactions, Trajectories and Trends*. Edited by Gerald O. West and Musa W. Dube. Leiden: Brill.

Boston Women's Health Collective. 1997. *Our Bodies, Ourselves: A Book by Four Women*. New York: Simon & Schuster.

Cannon, Katie G. 1992. "Foreword." In *The Will to Arise: Women, Tradition and the Church in Africa*. Edited by Mercy Oduyoye and M. Kanyoro. Maryknoll, New York: Orbis Books, vii-viii.

Cheatham, Aanne, Mary C. Powell, and Gloria Anzaldua. 1996. *This Way Day Break Comes: Women's Values and the Future*. Philadelphia: New Society Publishers.

Cunningham, Sarah. 1992. *We Belong Together: Churches in Solidarity with Women*. New York: Friendship Press.

Fabella, Virginia and Mercy Amba Oduyoye, eds. 1988. *With Passion and Compassion: Third World Women Doing Theology*. Maryknoll, New York: Orbis Books.

Gilkes, Cheryl Townsend. 2001. *If It Wasn't for the Women.* Maryknoll, New York: Orbis Books.

Harrison, R. K. 1962. s.v. "Healing, Health." *The Interpreter's Dictionary of the Bible.* Edited by G. A. Buttrick et al. Vol. II. Nashville, Tennessee: Abingdon Press, 541–48.

Hinga, Teresia. 1992. "Jesus Christ and the Liberation of Women in Africa." In *The Will to Arise: Women, Tradition, and the Church in Africa.* Edited by Mercy Amba Oduyoye and Musimbi R. A. Kanyoro. Maryknoll, New York: Orbis Books.

Kanyoro, Musimbi R. A. 1992. "Interpreting Old Testament Polygamy through African Eyes." In *The Will To Arise: Women: Tradition and the Church in Africa.* Edited by Mercy Amba Oduyoye and Musimbi R. A. Kanyoro. Maryknoll, New York: Orbis Books, 87–100

Kanyoro, Musimbi R. A. 1997. *In Search of a Round Table: Gender, Theology and Church Leadership.* Geneva: World Council of Churches Publications.

Kemdirim, Protus O. and Mercy Amba Oduyoye. 1998. *Women, Culture and Theological Education.* Enugu, Nigeria: SNAAP Press Ltd.

Kramarae, Cheris and Paula A Treicher. 1985. *A Feminist Dictionary.* Boston: Pandora Press.

Mananzan, Mary John, Mercy Amba Oduyoye, Elsa Tamez, J. Shannon Clarkson, Mary C. Grey, Letty M. Russell, eds. 1996. *Women Resisting Violence: Spirituality for Life.* Maryknoll, New York: Orbis Books.

Martey, Emmanuel. 1993. *African Theology: Inculturation and Liberation.* Maryknoll, New York: Orbis Books.

Muzorewa, Gwinyai H. 1985. *The Origins and Development of African Theology.* Maryknoll, New York: Orbis Books.

Nebenzahl, Donna. 2003. *Faces of Change: Around the World Womankind.* New York: The Feminist Press.

Newsom, Carol A. and Sharon H. Ringe. 1992. *The Women's Bible Commentary.* Louisville, Kentucky: Westminster/John Knox Press.

Njoroge, Nyambura J. 2000. *Kiama Kia Ngo: An African Christian Feminist Ethic of Resistance and Transformation.* Legon: Legon Theological Studies.

Nwachuku, Daisy N.1992. "The Christian Widow in African Culture." In *The Will to Arise: Women, Tradition, and the Church in Africa.* Edited by Mercy Amba Oduyoye and Musibmi R. A. Kanyoro. Maryknoll, New York: Orbis Books, 54–73.

Oduyoye, Mercy Amba. 1986. *Hearing and Knowing: Theological Reflections on Christianity in Africa.* Maryknoll, New York: Orbis Books.

_____. 1995. *Daughters of Anowa: African Women and Patriarchy.* Maryknoll, New York: Orbis Books.

_____. 1996. "Spirituality of Resistance and Reconstruction." In *Women Resisting Violence: Spirituality for Life.* Edited by Mary John Mananzan,

Mercy Amba Oduyoye, Elsa Tamez, J. Shannon Clarkson, Mary C. Grey, and Letty M. Russell. Maryknoll, New York: Orbis Books, 161–71.

Oduyoye, Mercy Amba, and Musimbi R. A. Kanyoro, eds. 1992. *The Will to Arise: Women, Tradition, and the Church in Africa*. Maryknoll, New York: Orbis Books.

Townes, Emilie M. 1997. *Embracing the Spirit: Womanist Perspectives on Hope, Salvation and Transformation*. Maryknoll, New York: Orbis Books.

Ukpong, Justin S. 1984. *African Theologies Now: A Profile*. Eldoret, Kenya: Gaba Publications.

Vennard, Jane E. 1998. *A Way to Intimacy: Praying with Body and Soul with God*. Minneapolis, Minnesota: Augsburg Press.

Villarosa, Linda, ed. 1994. *Body and Soul: A Black Women's Guide to Health and Emotional Well-Being*. With Angela Davis and June Jordan. New York: Harper.

Wehrheim, Carol A. 1979. *Children's Needs and Rights: A Doing the Word Issue Guide*. New York: United Church Press.

Whitfield, Charles L. 1989. *Healing the Child Within: Discovery for Adult Children of Dysfunctional Families*. Deerfield Beach, Florida: Health Communications Inc.

PART III

WOMEN AS TRADITIONAL
HEALERS IN AFRICA

6

Dealing with the Trauma
of Sexual Abuse

A Gender-based Analysis of the Testimonies
of Female Traditional Healers in KwaZulu-Natal

Isabel Apawo Phiri

I first met Mercy Amba Ewudziwa Oduyoye in 1989 at the launch of the Circle of Concerned African Women Theologians in Legon, Ghana. I was filled with unspeakable joy to hear an African woman speak so frankly about the pains of African women in the church and society. I identified with every word she spoke; it was as medicine to my troubled soul. It was during this first Circle conference and my contact with Mercy Oduyoye that my Ph.D. research topic was conceived. Thereafter, I read every article and book authored by Mercy Oduyoye. In 1991, I was greatly honored to visit her home in Geneva, where she shared with me her collection of articles. I felt further honored when a year later she accepted my invitation to be accommodated at my student cottage at the University of Cape Town, South Africa. Thus, I was able to reciprocate that embodiment of African hospitality that Mercy has written so extensively about in her publication *Introducing African Women's Theologies*. Since completion of my

113

Ph.D. studies, I have used Mercy Oduyoye's books and articles in my own teaching. I hold her in high esteem as both a scholar in African theology and as the founder of the Circle of Concerned African Women Theologians. It is because of Mercy Oduyoye that African women theologians have come together to seek healing through theologizing together. I therefore count it a great privilege to contribute an article in a publication that is to her honor.

From 1948 to 1994, apartheid was the official government policy of racial segregation and political and economic discrimination against non-European groups in South Africa. But racial discrimination existed long before the beginning of formal apartheid. The enforcement of the apartheid policy over a period of nearly five decades led to the systematic domination and oppression of black people that caused physical "pain and psychological trauma on millions of black South Africans" (Human Rights and Health 1998, 1). When South Africa changed from apartheid to a democratic form of government and the majority black people came to power in April 1994, the new government chose the route of unity between the majority black people and the minority white. For this to happen, the government realized that the whole nation had to go through a process of truth-telling concerning what took place during the apartheid regime so that people would know what it is that they were forgiving before reconciliation of the different racial groups could take place. This route was chosen because, as observed by Eric Brahm, "Human rights violations create massive trauma, which can in turn fuel additional human rights violations and so on. Feelings of trauma can generate feelings of frustration and revenge that can produce a cycle of violence and perpetuate feelings of victim-hood on all sides of the conflict" (Brahm 2003, 2).

To break this cycle of violence it became necessary for the new government to set up a Truth and Reconciliation Committee (TRC), under the leadership of Archbishop Desmond Tutu; it sat for two and a half years to hear people's stories of human rights abuses from victims and perpetrators alike. "The task of the TRC was defined as 'coming to terms with the past' and 'reaching out to the future'" (Zeichner 1998, 1). The TRC submitted its report to the government on 19 October 1998. Whether the TRC fulfilled its mandate is a subject of socio-political and theological debate (see Maluleke 1997, Villa-Vicencio 1997). Some felt betrayed by the new democratically elected government of South Africa for its unwillingness to adequately compensate for hurt and suffering. Others felt betrayed by the TRC when those perpetrators who did not tell the whole truth were given blanket amnesty from further prosecution. This said, what is generally accepted is that the TRC provided an important space for survivors of oppression from apartheid to begin the process of healing from trauma to wholeness. The report made it clear that the effects of apartheid have continued to haunt the people of South Africa and will continue to do so for a very long time. What was important, however, was that by telling their stories of pain, survivors of violence could take control of their own lives and thus contribute toward their own inner healing.

The process of telling stories to initiate healing from the trauma caused by violence clearly showed that there was an invasive element of gendered violence operating under apartheid. Women not only suffered from institutionalized racism and classism, but also from an endemic patriarchy commensurate with the previous white oligarchic apartheid state. This resonates well with the argument of Eric Brahm who has pointed out that women have unique trauma-healing needs:

> Women are often in particular need of trauma healing. They may themselves be victims of traumatic experiences such as rape or incest. However, they are also more likely to be left behind after husbands and children are killed in conflict. Women are often humiliated, feeling that they could do nothing to stop the violence. What is more, the loss of a husband or children can make it difficult for women to provide for their families, thereby adding further humiliation. (Brahm 2003, 5)

A number of articles have subsequently been published reflecting on the women's TRC hearings in Johannesburg, Durban and Cape Town (Goldblatt 1996, Goldblatt and Meintjies 1997,

Madladla-Routledge 1997, Olckers 1996, van Schalkwyk 1999, Ackermann 1998). All these publications show that there was a gendered dimension to apartheid.

One also notices that there was a critical gap in acknowledging women traditional healers as victims of apartheid as well as survivors who have continued to contribute toward the healing of their communities from trauma. This paper chooses to concentrate on this group of women because they include, in great measure, those 70 percent of South Africans that utilize traditional modalities of healing (United Nations Integrated Regional Information Network, 10 September 2004). This significant number warrants further attention. The testimonies that this paper tries to analyze have nothing to do with apartheid *per se*. The healing process to which they refer only has an indirect link with the TRC.

METHODOLOGY

This is the third paper (see also Phiri 2003a, 63–78; Phiri 2003b) in an ongoing research project about African women religious leaders that utilizes the methodology of oral history and African women's theology to tell the stories of suffering and trauma. The research is part of the Sinomlando Center, whose aim is to retrieve the silenced memories of religious people who suffered such trauma under apartheid. It gives visibility to the voiceless so that their experiences can contribute to the telling of the history of faith communities in South Africa. Its period does not end with the dawn of the democratic state of South Africa in 1994, but goes forward to examine the current high rate of crime in South Africa, which, in our view, is a direct reflection upon the continuing effect of the previous apartheid system. As stories of trauma are told, the interface between Christianity and African religion as practiced in South Africa becomes clearly visible. This study therefore readily acknowledges the fact that the majority of African Christians are still influenced by the beliefs and practices of African religion, especially in times of crisis, even though they may not acknowledge it publicly (Setiloane 1986, i; Fiedler

1997, 190). African theology acknowledges that African religions and culture are some of its sources (Pobee 1997, 45–56). In addition, African women theologians have also declared that African theology needs to be critical of its sources so that it should not be seen as promoting the oppression of women (Kanyoro 1996; Oduyoye 1998, 359–373; Oduyoye 2001).

This paper is based on a series of interviews conducted with twelve African women healers, commonly known as *sangomas*, who are based in the eThekwini and Umsunduzi municipal areas and the town of Newcastle, all within the Province of KwaZulu-Natal, South Africa. While the research on this topic began in 2002, the information that has been used in this paper is mainly based on follow-up interviews that I and my research assistant Lindiwe Mkasi conducted between June 2003 and September 2004. Almost all the interviews were conducted in Zulu. Together, we attended one cleansing ritual and a virginity-testing celebration. We also conducted a group interview with five traditional healers in Newcastle, in northern KwaZulu Natal. We have interacted with some women traditional healers through the various programs of the Center for Constructive Theology,[1] which gave us the opportunity to ask follow-up questions when I felt we needed further clarification. The study required a series of interviews that involved meeting each interviewee more than twice. The first visits were to build trust and then more information was gathered with each visit. We found the *sangomas* very willing to share their stories because they felt they had been marginalized for a very long time. This project is a retrieval of their silenced voices.

Most of the *sangomas* gave permission to have their conversations tape-recorded and transcribed in Zulu and later translated into English.[2] Each interviewee was given a copy of the interview on an audio tape and a manuscript in Zulu as a way of giving back to the community after taking something from them. Following the write-up of each academic paper, a workshop was conducted with the women to give them as a group feedback on the research. Such workshops have proved to be very valuable in gaining new insights on the issues being researched.

Oral history methodology was favored in this case because, while a lot has been written on women in African religions (Anti

1996; Mbiti 1988, 69–82; Phiri 1996, 161–71), there is a general silence in the literature about traditional healers as religious leaders who contributed to the healing of trauma as a result of suffering under the system of apartheid. The original choice of whom to interview was based on a "snowball-rolling" methodology. The interviews also followed in-depth interviews using the methodology of story telling. Important for us were the personal stories, which gave depth to the issues that each woman raised.

A *SANGOMA'S* STORIES OF CRIME

Nompilo Mangondo[3] is a *sangoma* currently based in Durban. Her story is an example of an experience of trauma that took place during the time of political violence in Lindelani. Nompilo left school in grade eight because she was constantly sick. Her mother, who was also a *sangoma*, recognized her sickness as a calling to become a *sangoma*. In 1989, at the age of twelve, she was already in training to become a *sangoma*. She did not respond to the the first trainer and had to change to one who mixed Christianity with traditional healing. She remembers that it was a time of political violence among the different political organizations of Lindelani. While she was in training, at the age of fourteen, the "comrades" came to the house where she was being trained, armed with weapons and looking for their *thwasa* mother.[4] They surrounded her house because they said her brother was a security police informer. The *thwasa* mother was badly beaten in full view of her trainees. The "comrades" said they were waiting for the *thwasa* mother's brother to appear or they would kill all of them. Knowing that they meant what they said, the *thwasa* mother made herself disappear[5] in the presence of the "comrades" and the trainees. All the trainees were kidnapped and were taken to another house where they were to be killed. Nompilo escaped from that house, changing her *sangoma* attire to ordinary clothes in order not to attract attention. All the gun shots fired at her missed.

After six months Nompilo became sick again. It was obvious to the whole family that she needed to go back to Lindelani to her *thwasa* mother in order to complete her *sangoma* training. Her biological mother helped to trace her *thwasa* mother who had moved to another place. Nompilo resumed her training.

When Nompilo was about to graduate from the *sangoma* training at the age of fifteen, her *thwasa* mother sent her to run an errand. As she was walking from Lindelani to Matikwe, dressed in her *sangoma* trainee attire, a vehicle stopped for her. There were two men in the vehicle, one white and the other black. Before she knew what was happening, she was grabbed, forced into the vehicle and sped off to the sugar plantations in Verulam where at gunpoint she was gang-raped. Nompilo emphasized that until then she had been a virgin. At the place where she was gang-raped, she saw a number of corpses of girl children, which made her realize that this was not just rape, but that there was a distinct possibility of her being killed as well. She attempted to escape but could not run very far as she was bleeding badly. The two men took her in the vehicle and dropped her near a bus stop. Nompilo could not walk. A woman she did not know picked her up and took her to her biological parent's home. She was taken to St. Joseph's Hospital, where she received treatment. She was also tested for HIV and pregnancy. Both were negative. She was told to come back a month later for another pregnancy test and after a further six months for another HIV test. The second pregnancy test was positive while the second HIV test remained negative.

No charges were filed with the police because her mother feared that the police would give her the option to abort the baby. As religious people, they did not believe in abortion. Nompilo went through a traditional healing ritual to remove the evil spirits of the rape experience. A cow was slaughtered for her cleansing ceremony at home. On the day that she was raped, the cow that was to be used for her coming-out ceremony died mysteriously. This was interpreted as the cow having died in her place. She later graduated as a *sangoma*, gave birth to a "mixed parentage" baby boy, whom she has continued to nurture though he remains a constant reminder of her ordeal. Through another traditional ritual, the child was incorporated into Nompilo's father's family (Mangondo 2004a, 2004b, 2004c).

INTERPRETATION OF NOMPILO'S EXPERIENCE
FROM A GENDERED PERSPECTIVE

The story of Nompilo was chosen because it highlights a number of themes that are relevant to our present topic and were also found in the stories of other *sangomas* that we interviewed. It will be used as a discussion point as we draw on the other stories of *sangomas*.

Interaction between African Religion and Christianity

The story of Nompilo highlights the fact that *sangomas* as a group experienced violence that was specifically aimed at them because of their profession. The *thwasa* mother was attacked because of the crime of her brother. Nompilo escaped gun shots aimed at her because of the association she had with her *thwasa* mother. It is not clear why her parents' home was burned. What is clear, however, is that the violence she was subjected to led to even more violence, including being forced to relocate, thus being taken away from the sacred burial place of her ancestors. Land has great religious significance for African people, something the apartheid regime did not understand, as was particularly demonstrated in their policy of forced removals. These removals traumatized people at different social and psychological levels, including the religious level.

Nompilo was raped while wearing her *sangoma* attire. In the Black community, a religious uniform is treated with utmost respect. Therefore to be raped while wearing a religious uniform, as in the case of Nompilo, is an extreme sign of disrespect for one's profession and an insult to her belief in God. Yet, it was her faith in God that helped her to cope with the abuse and to go on with life.

In Nompilo's family, Christianity and African indigenous religious beliefs co-existed peacefully. As already mentioned, her father was a practicing Christian. Nompilo and her mother and sister are all *sangomas* who at times attend an African Initiated Church (AIC). The children are raised within the two traditions. This was the experience of most of the *sangomas*. Mrs. Zuma, who conducted a cleansing ritual for Lindo Gumede's family, is a founder of her church and also a practicing *sangoma*. Jane Myembe, a student of the Theological Education by Extension Award program, is also a practicing *sangoma*. Her husband is a leader of an AIC (Zuma 2004, Gumede 2004, Myembe 2004).[6]

From the *sangoma's* interview, we can see clearly that there exists a free flow of beliefs and practices between the two religions. However, when the research project was being designed, it was incorrectly assumed that African religious women leaders had nothing to do with Christianity.[7] Through the interviews and participation in the rituals, we learned that women healers can be divided into two categories. The first category includes women traditional healers who continue in their church membership. The second category consists of women traditional healers who have totally disassociated themselves from Christianity and practice only African traditional religion.

Our research has established that the *sangomas* in the second category were at one time members of churches and yet later made conscious decisions to leave in favor of maintaining African culture and religion. They belonged mainly to the Roman Catholic, Presbyterian, and Durban Christian Center (charismatic) churches. The *sangomas* in this category see Christianity as a Western religion associated with Western civilization, which came to destroy traditional African culture. They stated that their ancestors told them to leave the church and practice healing without mixing it with Christianity. However, they still claimed to be in touch with *Mveliqangi* (the Creator)[8] as the source of their healing ministry through the ancestors.

The first category of *sangomas*, those who have remained in the church, belonged to the United Congregational Church of Southern Africa (UCCSA), Zion Christian Church (ZCC), and Nazarite Church (Shembe). Some of the *sangomas* claimed to have leadership positions within the church, including that of a church elder, a minister with theological training, and a Theological

Education by Extension Award student. Of particular interest to this paper was the apparent hypocrisy that existed among some of the church leaders. While the churches did not allow *sangomas* to be members, and even threw scorn and condemnation at them, some of these church leaders were their clients at night! One *sangoma* argued that Jesus had a healing ministry and they too are called by *Mveliqangi* through the ancestors to the healing ministry. They did not see any difference between the God of the Old Testament, who accepted sacrifice, and *Mveliqangi*, who is the spiritual source of their ministry.

Women's Experiences of the Crime of Rape

Rape is a traumatic experience. Women all over the world live in constant fear of being raped by both strangers and people they know (Phiri 2000, 85–110). While there are different reasons given as to why men rape women and children, ultimately rape is about power. It is used as a weapon of domination. Thus, women and children are raped during war as a sign of conquest by one group of soldiers against another.

During the apartheid regime, rape was also used by men as a weapon to dominate women. As Annalet van Schalkwyk has shown, "There was a keen awareness by the police of the nature of gender power relations, and how these power relations could be used to threaten and abuse their victims. This determined how women in the struggle against apartheid experienced torture, which often took the form of sexual violence" (van Schalkwyk 1999, 13).

Nompilo is not the only *sangoma* who shared her story of rape and pregnancy. While Nompilo belongs to a few women of faith who have broken the silence over rape to seek healing and take control of their lives, there remain many other women of faith who have not yet found the words to describe what happened to them and who still live with the fear and trauma. Sometimes women choose silence out of embarrassment or humiliation. In relation to issues of childlessness, Mercy Oduyoye describes a question that she was asked by a traditional healer in the presence of her parents as unspeakable and unprintable because it was so embarrassing. While she lied in her response, she knew that everyone who heard the answer knew that she had lied (Oduyoye 1999, 111). This is an example of an experience that many women who have gone through gender-based trauma can identify with. This could be one reason why most rape cases are never reported to the police.

Thandi Mthethwa,[9] a prominent *sangoma* with a high-profile husband, told us she had never before shared her experience of being gang-raped as a teenager and bearing a child from that experience (Mthethwa 2004). Thandi's consolation was in the fact that the man she subsequently married knew about her experience, but decided to marry her anyway and adopt the child that was conceived out of the rape.

The issue of whether to keep a child from a rape is indeed an ethical one that divides many people of faith. Nompilo's mother was very clear from the outset that the ancestors would not advise her daughter to undergo an abortion. In the case of all the women traditional healers we interviewed, abortion was not an option—even in the case of rape, despite the fact that the child was a constant reminder of the trauma that they endured. They argued that as people of faith their healing does not include terminating life, despite the way that life came into being. The five Newcastle-based *sangomas*, interviewed at Madadeni, Newcastle (22 July 2004), emphasized the importance of performing rituals to cleanse the mother and to incorporate the child into the mother's ancestral family. This ritual is intended to promote forgiveness, healing, and reconciliation with one's self, one's family and the ancestors in order to build a better future. It is not a requirement that the perpetrator be present.

Nompilo was willing to share her experience of rape with anyone who was willing to listen. She claimed to have come to terms with her experience and to have moved on with her life. The experience draws to Nompilo rape survivors who seek her out to share their stories. For those who are willing, she performs a healing ritual. Nompilo and other *sangomas* are creating a safe space for survivors of gender-based violence to share their experiences without fear of being judged. The rituals are holistic. They reach into every aspect of the life of the person who has been violated and thus prepare them for easy integration back into their community. For example, in a culture where the virginity of a girl child is valued, Nomagugu Ngobese, a female traditional healer and co-founder of the *Nomkhumbulwana* festival in Scottsville, Pietermaritzburg argues that virginity testing has become vital. She is of the opinion that revival of the virginity-testing ritual has helped to reduce cases of incest. It has also restored the dignity of girl children (Ngobese 2004). As described elsewhere (Phiri 2003a), during a virginity-testing ritual that we attended, the girl children who were found to have lost their virginity were interviewed and divided into two groups. Those who lost their virginity through rape underwent a cleansing ritual and thereafter were treated as virgins. Interestingly, while the cleansing ritual is supposed to restore their virginity, they are not allowed to participate in planting seeds at the *Nomkhumbulwana* festival.[10]

While it is not the aim of this paper to debate the merits and demerits of this practice, these rituals provide a religious practice that aims at the restoration of traumatized girl children and women. The healing technique is designed to resonate with the religious worldview of the people, thereby increasing its effectiveness. As a result, it becomes an effective means of therapy.[11]

Same-Sex Relationships and Cleansing

In our interviews, we noted that issues of ritual cleansing were linked to uncleanliness as a result of having sexual relations. It was said that ancestors, who control the *sangomas*, are very clean. Female *sangomas* testified that they operate well when they have not had sexual relations. Their medicines work well and they get many clients.

They argued that ideally *sangomas* should be single, because each area of their life is controlled by the ancestors. Therefore, in a marriage relationship the husband of a *sangoma* is under the authority of the ancestors. This explains why some scholars have argued that women become mediums as a protest to patriarchy and as a way of gaining power (Berger 1976, 157–83). Traditionally the problem of the *sangomas* preferring a life of celibacy was solved by the practice of polygamy. But when the husband of a *sangoma* is a Christian, polygamy becomes unacceptable (unless they belong to an AIC that accepts polygamy). Otherwise the husband must accept a life with long periods of sexual abstinence. When the husband does not respect the ancestors, the ancestors can go against the tradition of the permanency of marriage and ask a *sangoma* to divorce her husband (Ngobese 2004).

One *sangoma* went so far as to suggest that one option that female *sangomas* have is that of same-sex relationships. The ancestors do not oppose such relationships and there is no accompanying ritual of uncleanness that would require constant cleansing practices. We observed that where same-sex relationships were mentioned, the people involved had also been traumatized by rape. Is it possible, therefore, that some female *sangomas* engage in same-sex relationships, not only as a means of keeping their rituals effective, but also as a reaction against the trauma of such abuse and, by extension, heterosexual relationships in particular? Same-sex relationships may thus operate as an effective mechanism in regaining control over their sexuality. The discovery of the practice of same-sex relationships among some *sangomas* goes against the argument that same-sex relationships came to Africa through Western influence. There were, however, some *sangomas* interviewed at Newcastle (21 July 2004) who argued strongly against this practice as a practice that is deviant in African culture.

CONCLUSION

This essay has sought to show that female *sangomas* continue to play a prominent role in bringing spiritual, social, and psychological healing, especially to women, in South Africa. Their stories combine their African traditional religious and Christian heritages, which they draw from with ease. While we may not know the criteria they use, it is clear that whether they mix religious traditions or use one only, they still bring healing to their clients.

This essay has used the story of Nompilo to show that during apartheid *sangomas* experienced political violence that threatened their lives. While gender violence, in the form of rape, was used as a weapon of both the security forces and "comrades" in their attempt to humiliate their ministry, the resulting trauma of women and girls can be healed through traditional cleansing rituals.

Whether one agrees with the practice of virginity testing or not, this paper has sought to show that while female *sangomas* promote its use, it is seen as another way to bring healing to abused girls and women. The *sangomas'* concept of healing is holistic in that it includes every aspect of life. This is in contrast with Western healing systems that appear to compartmentalize the patient. This paper has also sought to touch the sensitive issue of the existence of same-sex relationships among the *sangomas*, under the approval of the ancestors, as a way of keeping their practice effective. This may confirm the existence of this practice in Africa, independent of the incursion of Western civilization. As *sangomas* are considered custodians of African culture, to find same-sex practices among the *sangomas* raises a number of questions around the secrecy given to such practices in African culture. As some s*angomas* argued strongly against this practice as a deviation from African culture, more research is required to establish how widespread it is before any serious conclusions can be drawn.

NOTES

[1] The Center for Constructive Theology was established in 1996 at the Faculty of Theology at the then University of Durban-Westville, KwaZulu-Natal, South Africa, as a positive response to the challenges of transformation and reconstruction in the new South Africa. It now functions independently and is currently housed at the Diakonia Center in the city of Durban. Its objective is to bridge the gap between formal theological education and the practical concerns and the needs of the people of South Africa through research, advocacy and outreach.

[2] Although permission was given to record and store the material, not all of the respondents gave permission for their personal stories to be shared in this publication.

[3] Nompilo Mangondo is a pseudonym.

[4] The woman who was training them to become *sangomas* is called *thwasa* Mother. She is also commonly known as their ancestral mother.

[5] She made herself disappear using her spiritual powers. Nompilo says she could have made all of them disappear if she had an occasion to touch them or explain to them what to do. Unfortunately there was no such opportunity.

[6] All members of the research sample were *sangomas*.

[7] This section represents an adaptation of my work in Phiri 2003b.

[8] *Mveliqangi* is a name for the Creator used by the Xhosas before the coming of Christianity. It has now also become commonly used by the Zulus.

[9] Thandi Mthethwa is a pseudonym. Permission was not granted to give her real name or place of interview.

[10] *Nomkhubulwana* is a Zulu female deity who is responsible for the fertility of land, animals and people. Virginity testing is part of the annual *Nomkhubulwana* festival because only virgins are allowed to take part in the whole festival. This festival existed in pre-colonial Zulu religiosity and was abandoned as more and more Zulus became converts to Christianity. It has now been revived by female traditional healers as a means to fight HIV/AIDS.

[11] I have described elsewhere that "the girls who were found to have lost their virginity for reasons other than rape were counseled about the dangers of sexually transmitted diseases, including HIV; teenage pregnancy and its consequences; and losing opportunities for further studies. Initially, this group of girls was discouraged from further participation in the ceremony. It was argued that the testers did not want a 'bad' influence from this group to be exercised on the 'good' girls. In the current practice, all girls who go for testing are given dots on their forehead. Virginity certificates are given to all girls who are tested. However, the instructors record in their books who is a virgin and who is not. This might be a response to the critique that the procedure of separating virgins from those who are not destroys the self-esteem of the girls who are found not be virgins" (Phiri 2003a, 67).

REFERENCES

Ackermann, Denise M. 1998. "'A Voice Was Heard in Rama': A Feminist Theology of Praxis for Healing in South Africa." In *Liberating Faith Practices: Feminist Practical Theologies in Context*. Edited by Denise M. Ackermann and R. Bons-Storm. Leuven: Uitgeverij Peeters.

Anti, K. K. 1996. "Women in African Traditional Religions." Paper presented at the Women's Center, Eastern Washington University, Cheney, Washington, May.

Berger, I. 1976. "Rebels or Status Seekers? Women as Spirit Mediums in East Africa." In *Women in Africa: Studies in Social and Economic Change*. Edited by Nancy J. Hafkin and Edna G. Bay. Stanford: Stanford University Press, 157–83.

Brahm, E. 2003. *Trauma Healing*. Boulder, Colorado: University of Colorado.

Denis, Philippe and Isabel Apawo Phiri. 2002. "'There Is Also Apartheid in Our Homes': Interviewing Leaders of Black Women's Christian Organizations in KwaZulu-Natal." Paper presented at the School of Theology, University of Natal.

Fiedler, K. 1997. "Even in Church the Exercise of Power Is Accountable to God." In *God, People and Power in Malawi: Democratization in Theological Perspective*. Edited by K. R. Ross. Blantyre: CLAIM.

Goldblatt, B. 1996. "Violence, Gender and Human Rights—An Examination of South Africa's Truth and Reconciliation Commission." Paper presented to the Law and Society Association Annual Meeting, St. Louis, Missouri, United States of America.

————, and S. Meintjies. 1997. "Dealing with the Aftermath—Sexual Violence and the Truth and Reconciliation Commission." *Agenda* 36.

Gumede, L. 2004. Interview by Lindiwe Nkasi and the author, 7 April, Inanda, Durban. Tape Recording.

Human Rights and Health. 1998. The Legacy of Apartheid: A Report by the American Association for the Advancement of Science and Physicians for Human Rights in Conjunction with the Committee for Health in Southern Africa. http://www.phrusa.org/research/methics/safrica.html/ (accessed 17 August 2004).

Idowu, E. Bolaji. 1962. *Olodumare: God in Yoruba Belief*. London: Longmans.

Kanyoro, Musimbi R. 1996. "Feminist Theology and African Culture." In *Violence Against Women*. Edited by Grace Wamue and Mary Getui. Nairobi: Acton Publishers.

Kojo, Anti Kenneth 1996. "Women in African Traditional Religions." Paper presented at the Women's Center, Eastern Washington University, Cheney, Washington, May.

Madladla-Routledge, N. 1997. "What Price Freedom? Women's Testimony and the Natal Organization of Women." *Agenda* 34.

Maluleke, Tinyiko Sam. 1997. "'Dealing Lightly with the Wounds of My People?' The TRC Process in Theological Perspectives." *Missionalia* 25 (3): 324–43.

Mangondo, N. 2004a. Interview by Lindiwe Nkasi, 21 March, Inanda, Durban. Tape Recording.

————. 2004b. Interview by Lindiwe Nkasi, 6 April, Inanda, Durban. Tape Recording.

————. 2004c. Interview by author, 28 July, Inanda, Durban. Tape Recording.

Mbiti, John S. 1988. "The Role of Women in African Traditional Religion." *Cahiers des Religions Africaines* 22: 69–82.

Mthwethwa, T. 2004. Interview by Lindiwe Nkasi and the author, 19 March 2004. Tape Recording.

Myembe, J. 2004. Interview by Lindiwe Nkasi, 15 March. Inanda, Durban. Tape Recording.

Ngobese, N. P. 2004. Interview by Lindiwe Nkasi and the author, Pietermaritzburg. 19 March 2004. Tape Recording.

Oduyoye, Mercy Amba. 1998. "African Women's Hermeneutics." In *Initiation into Theology: The Varieties of Theology and Hermeneutics*. Edited by Simon Maimela and Adrio König. Pretoria: J. L. van Schaik Publishers, 359–73.

————. 1999. "'Coming Home to Myself': The Childless Woman in the West African Space." In *Liberating Eschatology: Essays in Honor of Letty M. Russell*. Edited by Margaret A. Farley and Serene Jones. Louisville, Kentucky: Westminster/John Knox Press.

————. 2001. *Introducing African Women's Theology*. Cleveland, Ohio: Pilgrim Press.

Olckers, I. 1996. "Gendered-Neutral Truth—A Reality Shamefully Distorted." *Agenda* 31.

Phiri, Isabel Apawo. 1996. "African Traditional Religion and Eco-feminism: The Role of Women at Chisumphi Shrine in Preserving Ecology." In *Women Healing Earth: Third World Women on Ecology, Feminism, and Religion*. Edited by Rosemary Radford Ruether. Maryknoll, New York: Orbis Books, 161–71.

————. 2000. "Domestic Violence in Christian Homes: A Durban Case Study." *Journal of Constructive Theology* 6 (2): 85–110.

————. 2003a. "Virginity Testing? African Women Seeking Resources to Combat HIV/AIDS." *Journal of Constructive Theology* 9 (1): 63–78.

————. 2003b. "The Contribution of African Religious Women to National Development." A paper presented at a colloquium: Theological Fragments and Connections, in Honor of Professor John W. De Gruchy. University of Cape Town, 3–5 June.

Pobee, John. 1997. "Sources of African Theology." In *A Reader in African Christian Theology*. Edited by John Parratt. London: SPCK, 45–56.

Setiloane, Gabriel M. 1986. *African Theology: An Introduction*. Johannesburg: Skotaville Publishers.

van Schalkwyk, Annalet. 1999. "Gendered Truth: Women's Testimonies, the TRC and Reconciliation." *Journal of Constructive Theology* 5 (1): 3–48.

Villa-Vicencio, Charles. 1997. "Telling One Another Stories: Towards a Theology of Reconciliation." In *The Reconciliation of Peoples: Challenge to the Churches*. Edited by G. Baum and H. Wells. Maryknoll, New York: Orbis Books.

Zeichner, W. I. 1998. *Thoughts on the South African Truth and Reconciliation Commission Final Report*. http://www.waterzeichner.com/articles/Southaf.html (accessed 17 August 2004).

Zuma A. S. 2004. Interview by Lindiwe Nkasi, 25 March, Inanda, Durban. Tape Recording.

7

Adinkra! Four Hearts Joined Together

On Becoming Healing-Teachers of African Indigenous Religion/s in HIV & AIDS Prevention

Musa W. Dube

"The adinkra[1] *symbol of four hearts joined together teaches togetherness in thought and deed."*

(ODUYOYE 2004, 48)

"A dream becomes a vision when that dream is shared and passed on to others."

(KANYORO 1997, 9)

"Without others, one cannot be."

(MMUALEFE 2004, 17)

THE HIV & AIDS CHALLENGE

To date, the world is host to forty million people living with HIV & AIDS.[2] At least twenty-one million people have died in relation to the diseases. Additionally, the world is also raising about fourteen million orphans and taking care of many critically ill individuals. The pandemic is noted for its social face—it is a pandemic within other social epidemics of poverty, gender inequalities, violence, and the abuse of children's rights, racism, and ethnic and sexual discrimination. Subjugated and marginalized individuals, groups, communities or nations living under conditions that deny their human dignity are more vulnerable to HIV & AIDS. Further, HIV & AIDS attack not only those who are already on the margins of social structures—they further marginalize the marginalized. The poor become poorer, as HIV & AIDS cripple their physical capacity to work and raise funds to pay their medical bills. They lower economic performances of nations by reducing productivity in the market due to HIV deaths, funeral attendance, absenteeism from work due to ill health, and the absence of others who, although well, stay away from work to nurse the sick and feed the orphans. Other vulnerable groups include women, children, grandparents, survivors of war, displaced and disabled populations, and groups discriminated against racially, ethnically, or sexually. HIV & AIDS are accompanied by stigma and discrimination—those who are HIV+ are isolated, rejected, judged, condemned, and feared. In fact, they are often sentenced to social death long before the physical death comes. Given its link with social injustice and its wide impact, "*a broad social movement needs to be mobilized* to tackle the links between inequality, poverty, gender discrimination, and the AIDS epidemic" (UNDP and Botswana Government, 2000, 26; emphasis in original).

Many governments, NGOs, faith-based organizations, private companies, and families are now actively engaged in HIV & AIDS prevention. This engagement came with the realization that HIV & AIDS is not just a medical issue, but a social-justice issue that affects all aspects of life. To be effective, an HIV & AIDS prevention strategy has to promote both short- and long-term goals. The short-term strategy tends to promote abstinence, condoms, faithfulness (the so-called "ABC"), and care-giving, despite its limitedness. On the other hand, the long-term strategic focus on addressing poverty, gender inequality, civil and spousal violence, child abuse, racism, ethnic and sexual discrimination, national corruption, and international injustice more often than not makes the ABC strategy ineffective. The realization that HIV & AIDS are social justice issues that pervade all aspects of life has prompted a multi-sectoral strategy—an approach that challenges all departments, disciplines, and sectors to struggle with how they can become part of promoting prevention of HIV & AIDS and give quality care to the infected and affected, to be part of breaking the silence and stigma, and to address the social injustice that drives the epidemic. African indigenous religion/s (AIR/s)[3] are confronted by the same challenges, particularly because the African worldview remains the framework that informs the response toward the pandemic in many parts of sub-Saharan Africa.

In this paper, I wish to explore how AIR/s can respond to the HIV & AIDS challenge and become part of the healing process (Dube 2003a, 2003b). My main question is: *How can AIR/s lecturers become healer-teachers by teaching AIR/s for HIV & AIDS prevention?* To address this question, I will begin by examining the problem of addressing HIV & AIDS without taking into consideration the AIR/s worldview, which informs people's response in most African contexts. Here I will focus on imposed naming and testing policies and how they violate the community-based African cosmology. Second, I will explore some AIR/s concepts on divination and healing as philosophical frameworks that can enhance the struggle against the spread of HIV & AIDS among individuals and communities. I will conclude by exploring the pedagogical implications of being HIV & AIDS activists and AIR/s lecturers.

Given the diversity within African cultures, my examples will be drawn primarily from Southern Africa, particularly Botswana, which is my cultural setting. However, I will also draw from scholars from other African regions, particularly from the work of Mercy Amba Ewudziwa Oduyoye, the woman who has taught us to live out the message of the *adinkra* symbol of four hearts joined together. Through her vision of beginning the Circle of Concerned African Women Theologians, Mercy Amba Oduyoye brought African women from all over Africa and, indeed, the world to a fellowship of laboring for salvation, justice, and liberation with joined hearts.

A MAJOR PROBLEM: TACKLING HIV & AIDS
WITHOUT THE AIR/S COSMOLOGY

Colonized Knowledge and Structures

The structural epistemology that assumes that the West/North holds the best answer for the whole world—civilization, progress, language, science, faith, its brand of democracy, medicine, law, education, environmental care, development, and freedom—was established in colonial times and continues today, informing the economic, political, and reproductive policies that are often recommended to all world wide. The global approach to HIV & AIDS has been no different. Western categories of understanding and preventing HIV & AIDS became the standard approach in extremely different contexts around the world. Twenty-four years after the first scientific discovery of HIV & AIDS, it is important to ask: What is lost when HIV & AIDS prevention proceeds without fully factoring in the AIR/s worldview in African contexts? What lessons have been learned? I will use two examples to illustrate the tragedy of operating within the "colonial framework" and then I will focus on the naming of HIV & AIDS and strategies of prevention that disregard the worldview of AIR/s.

The Naming of AIDS:
American Ideas of Discouraging Sex

During the early 1980s, when HIV & AIDS were medically discovered outside the African continent, it was named as HIV (Human Immunodeficiency Virus) and its effects were named AIDS (Acquired Immunodeficiency Syndrome). Since then, it is not an exaggeration that HIV & AIDS remain largely and officially named in the colonial languages of English and French—even when the African continent is among those most affected. In the early days of the pandemic, some Batswana attempted to name the disease according to symptoms of culturally known diseases, but this was discouraged.

I am sure that many advantages in using one universal name can be outlined, but the disadvantages of imposing one universal name are equally serious. In Botswana, HIV & AIDS remained a distant myth that had nothing to do with the people. The long gestation period of HIV before it becomes AIDS did not help this situation. The fact that HIV & AIDS were scientifically discovered from outside was also a factor, for it could remain a foreign disease or, as teenage school-going students point out, AIDS stands for "American Ideas of Discouraging Sex." The process of national self-distancing has been deadly, since it gave HIV & AIDS sufficient time to spread before the community mobilized to be active in their prevention. The point here is that most African nations have not allowed themselves to officially name HIV & AIDS in African languages that would speak to African people, who are among the hardest hit by this pandemic. This in itself reflects a colonial mentality; rather than assisting in HIV & AIDS prevention, it has helped doom millions.

Testing Policy:
"One's Trouble Is Bound to Affect One's Neighbor"

The second example pertains to HIV-testing policy. Once more, the policy of confidentiality was not recommended, but required by Western metropolitan centers. The policy, formulated in these communities with individually oriented ethics, was informed by the philosophy and policies of private individual rights and overlooked societies organized around individual rights that do not sacrifice community rights. While I do not wish to romanticize and generalize African cultures, in many the individual and the community are not defined separately. In "The People Next Door," Mercy highlights the Akan's perspective of community, underlining that

the most central idea of community is that of unity in diversity. This is represented by two crocodiles who share the same stomach. The symbol points out that it is unnecessary for people whose destinies are joined together to struggle for a larger share of available resources. . . . One's neighbor's day is one's day; one's trouble is bound to affect one's neighbor. Many proverbs, sayings and folktales underline this principle. The *Adinkra* symbol of four hearts joined together teaches togetherness in thought and deed. There is recognition that disharmony is possible in community, but the symbol and proverb relating to tongue and teeth say that although they quarrel occasionally, that is never a reason for parting company. (2004, 48)

When the required HIV & AIDS policy of testing emphasized individual rights and privacy at the expense of community rights, the African cosmology was robbed of creatively informing its own communities about the prevention of HIV & AIDS. A good example of this is when President Festus Mogae of Botswana declared HIV & AIDS a national disaster. The slogan used was "*ntwa e bolotse*," ("war is declared on the pandemic"). Although this was a national health issue, there was no attempt to engage the cultural structures of public healing, such as public divination on the causes of the disease or communal assumptions of healing. While the president equated HIV & AIDS prevention to that of national war, this declaration did not call for a *pitso* (a compulsory camp meeting of all men) to discuss and understand the enemies' strength, possible strategies, and the call for protecting the community from the enemies, in this case HIV & AIDS. Educational and information campaigns were intensified to a point where almost 90 percent of the population was held to be correctly informed about HIV & AIDS (UNDP and Botswana Government 2000, 42). Yet each year HIV infection rates have continued to escalate. The incidence of rape also rose dramatically (UNAIDS 2001, 24).

The much promoted strategy of ABC—Abstain, Be faithful and Condomize—had little effect. Young girl children who were trying to abstain would either be raped at home or on the streets, since the myth of "virgins can cleanse one of HIV & AIDS" was growing (Weinriech and Benn 2004, 34). In addition, more adult men opted for younger girls since they believed that the latter were unlikely to be infected (UNDP and Botswana Government

2000, 42). The younger girls dating older men had no advantage of age, gender or financial power to use in negotiating for protected sex. As a result, they engaged in unprotected sex and then later dated younger boys. So-called intergenerational sex became a vicious circle that defied the window of hope that young people would remain free from the infection (UNDP and Botswana Government, 2000, 3–6, 26–37; Weinriech and Bern 2004, 27–28).

Females in general had little or no control. Some widows could not abstain from sexual relations because of dispossession. While the government instituted social services for orphans, the stigma remained extremely high, leading many to resist registering with government social welfare departments and to turn to sex-work instead (Weinreich and Bern 2004, 32–34; UNDP and Botswana Government 2000, 18; UNAIDS 2001, 27–28).

Married women who were faithful were not necessarily protected since the culture declared "*monna ke poo ga agelwe lesaka*" ("a man, like a bull, cannot be contained in kraal//having multi partners among men/married males is natural and is to be expected by wives"). In fact, research showed that "all over the world, men tend to have more sex partners (as well as extramarital partners) than women, thereby increasing their own and their primary partners' risk to contracting HIV" (UNAIDS 2001, 24). As for most married women, they did not have the right to say when, where or how sex will take place (Gupta 2000; UNAIDS 2001: 23). In addition, having children is still highly valued. Indeed, marriage became one of the most deadly institutions for women due to gender inequality (UNAIDS 2001, 22), for at least single women still had some bargaining power with their partners and control over their own sexual lives.

As for condomizing, the free distribution of condoms neither protected men or women. Among men and boys, wearing a condom was an attack on one's masculinity; it was an admission that one is afraid of taking risks (UNDP and Botswana Government 2000, 32; UNAIDS 2000; 2001). Besides, the myth of "you cannot eat a wrapped sweet" reigned.

The confidentiality policy also tied the hands of medical doctors, for they had no right to test anyone for HIV & AIDS without the patient's consent, even if they could gather useful information from various patterns of persistent opportunistic infections. If and when doctors were given the right to test and a patient was found positive, the doctors had no power to insist on partner notification since this would violate the individual rights of the concerned person; similarly, informing and counseling former partners would violate the policy of confidentiality.

Given this policy, there were and still are many cases where relatives are taking care of very sick relatives, without knowing the status of their patients. The results are sometimes tragic. Thus, the testing policy of confidentiality, intended to protect individuals, began to make a heavy contribution to killing both individuals and communities by creating an unprecedented amount of HIV & AIDS stigma and discrimination (UNAIDS 2002, Visser and Mhone 2001). The policy of confidentiality spun a virtual shroud of secrecy, shame, and fear around the pandemic as something that should not be openly shared. It sent a message that seemingly said "HIV & AIDS are not diseases like all other diseases that we have had to tackle together; rather, they are the burden of an individual."

Among the infected who found themselves called to carry their crosses alone, the policy of confidentiality groomed anger, leading at times to the deliberate infection of others. In others, it groomed desperation, leading to the proliferation of deadly myths such as "virgins can cleanse a man from AIDS" (UNDP and Botswana Government, 2000, 5–6; Weinreich and Bern 2004, 27–34). Among married couples "silent fears and mistrust reigned" (Katongole 2001, 125–43). Within this process, individuals carried the unnecessary guilt of holding themselves responsible for their own infection, and the initial religious response that HIV was a punishment from God fuelled this notion. Once such a perspective was officially planted and groomed, the confidentiality policy raised fear, shame, isolation, rejection, anger, stigma, and discrimination to even greater levels of confidentiality. Not only did individuals fear that some people—family, spouses, friends, workmates, church members or their own children—would find out about their status, but people also became afraid of finding out for and about themselves. Keeping such a big secret is, in itself, an incredible burden of ill-health.

I firmly believe that an HIV & AIDS prevention program informed by the wisdom of "I am because we are, and we are because I am" would have enabled a more effective approach to prevention and care. It would have begun with the understanding that "one's trouble is bound to affect one's neighbor" and proceeded on the foundation of "we are together in carrying each others cares" and "I am because we are," thus dispelling shame, isolation, fear, stigma and discrimination. Even now, it is clear that people who have disclosed and are open about their status live longer and better lives, although some have not survived the stones and fires of death imposed by their stigma-sensitive communities (see Visser and Mhone 2001, 43–44). Furthermore, prevention strategies and programs work better when people are able to test and share their HIV status.

HIV & AIDS bring the relationship of the rights of the individual and the right of the community into critical focus. That is, what does it mean to be faithful to the ethic "I am because we are, and we are because I am," an ethic that must take both the individual and the community seriously? Given the socially driven face of HIV & AIDS, an exclusive focus on an individual's physical symptoms and treatment as a private secret of the infected and the affected aided the spread of the pandemic itself, rather than its prevention. Such an approach has not even protected the individual, let alone the community. The much chorused strategy of ABC continues to fail, because it overlooks the fact that an individual exists within relationships and, unless these relationships are revisited, scrutinized and healed, HIV will find its way through the As, the Bs and the Cs.

A community approach that looks at the existence and health of individuals as inseparably intertwined within all relationships is more suited to dealing with issues of poverty, gender inequality, child abuse, spousal and ethnic violence, racism, national corruption, international injustice, and ethnic, migrant, and sexual discrimination. This long list describes unhealthy relationships that need revisiting and healing whether we talk as family, local, national and international communities, or as individuals living in and with various communities. That is, we need to fully acknowledge that "One's trouble is bound to affect one's neighbor" and to constantly seek to cultivate the vision of *adinkra* as a space of affirmation, liberation, and healing of individuals in community.

AIR/S AND HIV & AIDS PREVENTION

AIR/s as Setho/Isintu

It is noted among well-known scholars that the term AIR/s is the creation of colonial anthropologists and African scholars (Mndende 1996, 242), since most African societies do not separate the sacred and the secular. To speak of AIR/s is, therefore, once again, a foreign-imposed framework. One does not choose to be or not to be a believer in AIR/s, although the Christian religion has introduced this concept by suggesting that when one chooses to be a Christian, a person can either choose to embrace African cultural ways of living or reject them. Rather, one is a member of AIR/s by virtue of being born into and living within African communities and by socialization through an African cosmology (Mmualefe 2004, 4–7).

It follows that the very name AIR/s is not a name that African people would appropriate for themselves to express their belief systems. In Southern Africa those who have agonized over what constitutes a more authentic naming of AIR/S have argued that AIR/S would be properly named as *Setho, Isintu, Chitu*, or the act of being a human through living within the community and in well-being and harmony according to the cosmology of *Bantu/ Batho*, an African language group that covers a vast amount of the continent. According to *Batho*, a person's humanity and existence are inseparably united and can be expressed only in relationship to respecting others and being respected by others. Hence, a person's humanity can be realized only through relationships. "Without others, one cannot be" (Mmualefe 2004, 17).

With the understanding of AIR/s as *Setho/Ubuntu*, the struggle against HIV & AIDS would certainly begin on a different note and progress at a different pace toward a different direction. "[A] process of earning respect by first giving it, and [of] gaining empowerment by empowering others" would address the spread of HIV & AIDS by revising attitudes toward unhealthy relationships that cause and uphold poverty, gender inequality, spousal violence, civil wars, child abuse, racism, ethnic cleansing, national corruption, and international injustice, which destroy individuals and communities. Through this process, the community would revisit the structures that condemn some people to poverty, thus exposing them to HIV infection. *Setho/Isintu* would force men who express their manhood through subjugating women, raping them, and infecting young girl-children to rethink their masculinity.

An approach based on *Setho/Ubuntu* would also question a culture that defines women and children as powerless subordinates, thus exposing them to HIV infection. Recapturing *batho* as "a process of earning respect by first giving it, and [of] gaining empowerment by empowering others," would be applied to all problematic relationships. Indeed, all socially unhealthy relationships that do not empower or respect some members of the society would be revisited. In other words, the concept of community, the *adinkra* paradigm, ought to and should become the cornerstone of propounding an African indigenous theology of justice and liberation by constantly revisiting "what it means to be community and to live in community," "what violates community," and "how we can live in community in our new and hybrid twenty-first century contexts." Being a community is not and cannot be a one-time thing; rather, it is a process that must be continually cultivated by its members. This approach should inform the continual assessment and review of all oppressive relationships and the re-imagination of communities that respect and empower all their members regardless of class, gender, age, ethnicity, race, sexuality, and nationality for it is only then that we can say "I am because we are, and we are because I am." The *adinkra* space of justice, solidarity, and liberation in African cosmology is highly relevant and central to the struggle against HIV & AIDS, but work must be done to implement it.

This approach is, at present, only in the realm of theory, because the approach to HIV & AIDS is not officially informed by the worldview of *Setho/Isintu*, but by a very different worldview. However, what I am saying concerning the struggle against HIV & AIDS remains a challenge and a possibility for scholars of African cosmology, who need to use their skills as scholars within, with, and for their communities in the struggle against the devastation of HIV & AIDS. The struggle against HIV & AIDS is far from over.

THE *ADINKRA* APPROACH: DIVINATION AS HEALING OF INDIVIDUALS AND COMMUNITIES

In this section, I want to dwell on what I think could ideally happen, or could have ideally happened, if programs to prevent HIV and AIDS began from a community-oriented approach to health informed by an African worldview. This is not just an ideal, but how a scholar of AIR/s could possibly be part of the solution, given that "HIV/AIDS is everybody's business" (Dube 2003a, vii). How would HIV & AIDS prevention be informed by the concept of "I am because we are, and we are because I am" or, to use a southern African saying, "*Motho ke motho ka batho, umuntu ngu muntu nga Bantu*" (One is only a human being in and through other people, or a person is always part of community, or no person is an island)? *Botho/Ubuntu*, the act of earning respect by first giving it, thus entails living respectfully and responsibly within the earth community at large. How then would *Botho/Ubuntu* inform the struggle against HIV & AIDS and especially their prevention?

First, it is important to deliberate briefly on how ill-health was approached within the Setswana cosmology of *Setho/Isintu*. I will use the example of *ngaka*, the diviner-healer. On being plagued by ill-health, one approaches the diviner-healer to consult on the causes of ill-health. The approach is communal in that the ill person is accompanied by relatives. The diviner-healer uses a divining set to consult the spiritual world concerning the causes and nature of one's illness. The diviner-healer begins by handing the divining set to the concerned person, to blow his or her breath on the set, and in so doing write his or her story on the set, which is then read communally by the diviner-healer, the consulting patient, and the accompanying relatives. In cases where the sick person cannot personally attend, consultation is carried out by relatives, who bring a piece of clothing belonging to the concerned relative (see van Breugel 2001, 234). Once the consulting person has blown her or his spirit, the diviner-healer offers a poetic prayer while shaking the divining set and then throws it down to be read for the causes of ill-health and the necessary healing.

The process of divination includes examining all the relationships of the consulting person. This includes relationships within the family and with neighbors as well as relationships with the living dead within the spiritual realm. If the diviner set indicates that some relationships are not healthy, for example, if children neglect their parents or if elders are not given proper care and respect, the consulting person is advised to work on improving those relationships. Sometimes reconciliation rituals may be needed, especially if broken relationships with the living dead are involved. Unhealthy relationships, in other words, are held to be an integral part of one's ill-health. As Seratwa Ntloedibe points out, the "failure of relationships results in the breakdown of health" (2000, 500). Physical healing of the body is thus accompanied by the healing of relationships. Consequently, healing is regarded as healing of all relationships. Health is, therefore, closely tied to healthy relationships and ill-health is closely tied to unhealthy relationships. This philosophy requires an ethic of being responsible for one's own health and for that of others through maintaining healthy relationships (Dube 2001a, 184). The healing of relationships is integral to treating physical pain.

Divination is always a participatory process. Thus, when the diviner-healer throws open the divining set for reading, it functions as a story book that only comes to life and completion with the full participation of the consulting readers. "The diviner-healer walks the consulting reader/s through each pattern and the circumstances that the set reveals, asking the consulting reader/s to confirm or deny if the patterns represent what s/he knows about his/her own life. . . . The consulting reader/s is therefore an active and, indeed, an integral participant in the reading and writing of her/his social story from and into the divining set" (Dube 2001a, 183).

Although J. W. M. van Breugel's discussion of the Chichewa language of Malawi displays many missionary and colonizing biases (see Schapera 1938, 255–56), and a surprising patriarchalization of the matrilineal society, one can, nonetheless, grasp that the role of a diviner-healer and divination form a participatory process of analysis and production of social knowledge. According to van Breugel,

> Each diviner has his own method of consulting the *ula* (divining set). But what they all have in common is that they ask those who come to consult them to supply all the necessary information, and to give the details of e.g. the illness and the relationships in the family and village. In particular the diviner is interested to know whether there have been any disputes, whether the sick man has enemies, whether there are jealousies, whether any relative has recently died. . . . The diviner is very astute in putting his questions. He is usually a master in weighing-up a situation with its strained relationships and suspicions. By his questions he usually guides and leads his clients on till the client himself formulates his own suspicions. (van Breugel, 2001, 234)

Many scholars have rightfully underlined the centrality of the diviner-healer in the community. Echoing M. Gelfand, whose study concluded that the Shona diviner-healer "is a doctor in sickness, a priest in religious matters, a lawyer in legal issues, a policeman in the detection and prevention of crime" (Gelfand 1964, 55), F. Staugard has also said that, "the traditional healer in the Tswana village . . . is a religious consultant, a legal and political advisor, a police detective, a marriage counselor and a social worker" (1985, 15). For Gomang Seratwa Ntoedibe, the "Ngaka plays a vital role in all aspects of Batswana life" and "is undoubtedly a savior and liberator among his/her people" (2000, 503–4). The diviner-healer was and still is a social analyst of relationships and is actively involved in helping members of the community to analyze the social conditions of their relationships and recreate healthy relations. Such an approach takes into consideration all the vital relationships—social, environmental, and spiritual.

While the diviner-healer's approach is holistic, many studies emphasize that divination is not solely/exclusively an esoteric practice of an individual spiritual aspect. Rather, the process of divination fully involves the consulting person/people. As such, it becomes a process of collective social analysis and production of knowledge about relationships.

Given that HIV & AIDS are symptoms of social ills, it is, therefore, more than an issue of individual morality and health; rather, it is also about the morality and health of our cultural, spiritual, social, economic, and political structures. It is about broken relationships within communities and the world. Given that AIR/s approach to health and healing is holistic and focuses on the healing of all relationships, it is clear that the African cosmology has a significant contribution to make to HIV & AIDS prevention. Prevention calls for a community-centered approach in which the whole community works for its own health and the healing of its members. Community consultation will be needed to divine the broken relationships as well as to undertake the necessary actions to mend them. I see this approach as central to the prevention of HIV & AIDS, given the pandemic's dependence on broken or unhealthy relationships, that is, social injustice. An AIR/s scholar who seeks to be part of defining and promoting a community approach to HIV & AIDS prevention must be challenged to rethink his/her pedagogical methods. In other words, an "*adinkra* approach" calls for the full involvement of AIR/s academic lecturers with the troubles of the communities. This certainly has pedagogical implications.

ADINKRA PEDAGOGICAL IMPLICATIONS: COMMUNITY TEACHING FOR HIV & AIDS PREVENTION

In general, the struggle to cultivate a *Setho*/AIR/s community-oriented approach to HIV & AIDS prevention presents a

challenge for academic AIR/s teachers. What would such pedagogy entail, and how could it proceed?

Curriculum Transformation

Community-oriented pedagogy for HIV & AIDS prevention must be preceded by a curriculum transformation that seeks
to decolonize the place, the approach and the content of the
syllabus and programs. Such an approach seeks the full realization of *adinkra*, the manifestation of *Botho/Ubuntu* in the community. AIR/s have suffered marginalization through colonization, first by colonial missionary programs of suppression and
then by colonial anthropologists' suppression by observing and
organizing the world only according to Western colonizing
perspectives. This was structurally buttressed by missionary
education, which marginalized AIR/s from the curriculum of
formal schools, while promoting the religions and values of the
colonizer.

The first indigenous African academicians, in most cases, were
members of AIR/s who had been converted and trained in Christian and biblical studies and whose minds had, in many cases,
also been colonized. Although they made significant contributions toward decolonization, they remained within the colonial
paradigm that viewed AIR/s as incomplete and awaiting the fulfillment and/or revelation of Christian religion (Ntloedibe-
Kuswani 2001b, 97–120). Further, AIR/s were structurally
marginalized as they did not have specialists, sponsors, or a place
in Western and African theological departments. A great deal of
progress has been made, but this situation still remains in place,
with many AIR/s scholars and lecturers trained primarily in Christian and biblical religions. Some successfully manage to give
AIR/s attention, but many still regard AIR/s as awaiting the revelation and fulfillment of Christianity.

Decolonizing the AIR/s curriculum calls for studying AIR/s
as a worldview complete in its own right. However, AIR/s must
be continually re-interpreted for different contexts and times.
Given the multitude of social challenges that confront the African

continent, the task of bringing AIR/s to speak to the liberation and empowerment of people is vital. Indeed, a great challenge that confronts AIR/s scholars is to analyze why the community-oriented cosmology of Africa has produced some of the most insidious national corruption, deadly ethnic wars, and rampant poverty and disease. AIR/s scholars in community should articulate for us what community is in our contemporary times and within the new and "imagined communities" called nations. How should the concept of community be re-imagined, re-created and reconstructed to empower its members to deal with poverty, civil violence, child abuse, gender inequality, national corruption, and ethnic and sexual discrimination so that the values of "I am because we are, and we are because I am" can be empowering policies.

Given that all studies indicate that diviner-healers were the multitalented icons of their societies who offered divination through a deep and wide understanding of the social relations of their communities, AIR/s programs need to struggle with educating diviner-healers. This is precisely because with colonization the diviner-healers were named as witches and structurally marginalized in both their public and political status and their religion was excluded from theological programs, which largely remained Christian and biblically oriented. Second, while pre-colonial diviner-healers operated in self-contained communities sharing the same worldview, values, and leader/s, urbanization, brought about by colonization, incorporated various ethnic groups. As a result, the task of diviner-healers became much more complex. Understanding and analyzing social relationships from all levels and within wider contexts requires more education and experience. At the same time, most AIR/s lecturers have much to learn from diviner-healers, since most lecturers are either self-trained in AIR/s or have been trained through colonized paradigms. Curriculum transformation of AIR/s requires community learning and teaching and re-interpretation of AIR/s for the understanding and implementation of AIR/s in contemporary imagined communities (nations) of the postcolonial era.

Teaching AIR/s for HIV & AIDS prevention makes additional demands. Educating in HIV & AIDS prevention is a very broad challenge because it must address economic, cultural, social, spiritual, and political fields at family, local, national, regional, and international levels. The pandemic affects all aspects of society. The study of prevention includes the study of the causes of HIV & AIDS, their impact, preventative techniques, care-giving, and ways to end stigma and discrimination. Without an in-depth understanding of the social causes of the HIV & AIDS pandemic, such as poverty, gender inequality, child abuse, youth powerlessness, and ethnic and sexual discrimination, one is likely to resort to cheap sermons on morality or the lack of it.

An AIR/s teaching scholar in the HIV & AIDS struggle must be, like a diviner-healer, a highly analytical scholar who understands the wide variety of relationships and how they affect the health of both the individual and the community. Knowledge about HIV & AIDS becomes an addition to one's field of specialty and requires additional research to inform and teach as well as to dialogue with diviner-healers on their understanding of the pandemic. The latter may very well include inviting diviner-healers to the classroom, as well as leading training sessions for them on HIV & AIDS, their causes, impact, and prevention. HIV & AIDS are a new pandemic that has challenged scientists, medical doctors, economists, priests and ministers, marriage counselors, politicians, and teachers—just about every sector of informed science and society. It has also revealed the inadequacy of human knowledge and sent everyone rushing into new research and the production of new knowledge. Diviner-healers have a vital role to play in HIV & AIDS prevention, but to do so they must fully understand the causes and impact of the pandemic. AIR/s lecturers are suited to this course.

TEACHING FOR HEALING:
COMMUNITY DIVINATION FOR HIV & AIDS PREVENTION

If it is to contribute successfully to reducing the spread of the diseases, HIV & AIDS prevention must move beyond the classroom and the university setting to involve the affected communities. The preparatory stage of such a move would have to begin with intentionally transforming the curriculum. The syllabi would have to seek to understand the causes of HIV & AIDS and the methods of prevention as much as possible for the lecturer, students, and diviner-healers. It would also focus on an in-depth understanding of health from the perspective of African cosmology and how that cosmology can inform HIV & AIDS prevention and care. The second preparatory step would be to mobilize the community by means of consultations and public divinations. Such meetings and consultations would be held with HIV & AIDS educators' project managers, policy makers, social workers, activists, health officers, legal persons, various community leaders, and the main community leader, the *kgosi*, to prepare for public divination on the causes and prevention of HIV & AIDS. The aims would be stated as clearly as possible—namely, to undertake a public divination in order to understand the causes of HIV & AIDS and to arrest a national disaster through a communal recommendation of healing broken relationships.

Following the preparatory meetings of various stakeholders, the stage would be set for public divination. Under the leadership of the community leader/s *(di/kgosi)*, who has the mandate to call for public divination in the event of national disaster, a public community meeting would be called. The community and all the stakeholders would gather together for divination, including various other community leaders, the designated diviner-healer, the HIV & AIDS activists, social workers and project managers, policy and law makers, the AIR/s lecturer, students, and the community. Because our communities have now lived with the pandemic for more than two decades, observed its symptoms and impact and sought healing, I would say that the responsibility of naming HIV & AIDS in African languages is a must. In this participatory setting, the community can review the several unofficial names that have already emerged and weigh the most appropriate name to be officially adopted. Adopting a name informed by their own experiences and from their own languages would help affected communities to understand and own the pandemic as something that is taking place within their communities.

The second stage, that of divining for the causes, can then follow. At the invitation of the community leader, the diviner-healer would be invited to come forward and open the divination set for diagnosis. The infected and affected community would constitute the consulting readers. The diviner-healer would proceed in the normal style of first throwing open the divining set for reading and then asking appropriate questions that bring the community to provide data and to analyze relationships and how they facilitate the pandemic. This participatory process of the infected and affected community and specialists (HIV & AIDS educators/project managers/activists, social workers, spiritual leaders, health specialists, policy and law makers) would lead the community in writing its own diagnosis. I expect that such a process in which all members of the community participate would highlight the link of HIV & AIDS with the unhealthy relations of poverty, sexual violence against women and girl-children, gender inequality, youth powerlessness, national corruption, international injustice, racism, and ethnic and sexual discrimination. Different members of the community will be able to relate how they have experienced the entry of the pandemic into their families and neighborhoods. The input of HIV & AIDS on educators, activists, social workers, medical health specialists, and policy and law makers would counter ill-informed analysis through this process of open dialogue. Divination will thus serve as an open communal space of participatory analysis into the causes of the pandemic and public mobilizing of the energies of prevention.

Once the causes have been identified, the third stage of divination would then follow, that of divining for the appropriate healing of both relationships and the physical body. I expect that members of the community at this point would question the cause of poverty and how it can be eradicated. This question can lead to interrogating the social systems and the management of national resources as well as undertaking poverty-reduction projects. Members who are particularly prone to infection through poverty would be given appropriate references for registration and access to social welfare systems.

A second important question would be to interrogate the causes of gender inequality and how we can best empower both men and women. These questions should lead to revisiting our cultural constructions of man and woman and their possible re-interpretation to ensure that we remain as a community shaped by "I am because we are, and we are because I am." The latter should counter masculinities that sponsor the spread of HIV & AIDS as violations of individual and community rights and health.

In this participatory fashion of seeking healing, I expect no rock to remain unturned. Such questions as what causes child abuse and how can we protect children rights should be asked. Who must act? What causes ethnic violence and national corruption and how can we stop them? And who must act? What causes HIV & AIDS stigma and how can we stop it? As mentioned earlier, consulting diviners, in this case the infected and affected community, will carry the full responsibility of healing broken relationships. Once all unhealthy relationships have been identified and responsible groups have been challenged to create healthy relationships, then the issue of physical healing can be addressed. Collaboration with participating HIV & AIDS educators and health specialists' recommendations would be made. For example, the ART (African Religions Teacher) clinics could be named as places to collect medication. Family members could also be asked to assist in monitoring the adherence of their relatives to ARVs as well as to manage expected any side effects. Moreover, in the public space of divination, spiritual healing would also be addressed.

ADVANTAGES: AN *ADINKRA* COMMUNITY IS A HEALING COMMUNITY

The first and major contribution of public divination on the cause and prevention of HIV & AIDS pertains to its potential for breaking both stigma and discrimination. A community that is gathered and which publicly identifies itself as infected/affected— as a sick community, one which is seeking divination under its community leader/s—would be openly acknowledging a "corporate ownership of the pandemic." This communal ownership will be the healing energy for individual bodies and the community as a whole. Further, it will signify the departure from the private and confidential policy toward the policy of *Setho/Isintu* and its worldview *"motho ke motho ka batho/umuntu ngu muntu nga Bantu."* ("One's trouble is bound to affect one's neighbor"). Cultivating such a public space of communal ownership gives way to an *adinkra* salvation—a community of hearts that are bonded together in joy and pain thereby becoming a healed and healing community. As HIV & AIDS research and documentation attest, breaking the stigma in and of itself goes a long way in allowing prevention and care programs to become more effective.

Second, a public divination will go a long way in helping the community confront and reconstruct some of its most harmful cultural perspectives. It will become an educational space. In the public forum of divination, where everyone speaks and gets listened to, unhealthy relationships and cultural practices will come under careful scrutiny for destroying both individuals and communities. Such practices as widow inheritance, tolerance of multisexual partners for men, the rape of virgins in search of HIV & AIDS healing, witchcraft accusation, widow cleansing, and dispossession of widows and orphans will be named as erroneous and unacceptable to community building. Men would be called to a different form of manhood, one which is characterized *botho*— the ethic of earning respect by first giving it. The diviner-healers themselves, would be brought to book against gender-biased divinations (see Maluleke 2001: 247), through educational empowerment and open interaction with the whole community as they voice their reservations towards the diviner-healers reading of the divining set, which sometimes fuels witchcraft accusation and widow dispossession. Women would have their views heard and be backed by other members of the community. Individuals would be provided with public legal protection against such practices. Public divination, in other words, would be participatory public learning for all the members of the society as they interrogate the causes of the spread of HIV & AIDS, and as they map out ways of healing relationships and becoming a community of life.

Finally, another advantage to public divination and prevention of HIV & AIDS is that it would be a decolonization of the AIR/s (see Mndende 1996: 242, 251), and the minds of African communities and structures—for the collapse and lack of effectiveness of African cosmology does not lie in the poverty of ideas. Rather, it lies in the fact that AIR/s/*Setho* exist as a dismissed, submerged, unofficial, marginalized or suppressed worldview, with the Western perspectives often functioning as the official standard. Be that as it may, salvation in the HIV & AIDS era, and from all other social ills, lies in the African communities striving to live out the message of the *adinkra* symbol—the message of "four hearts joined together." Salvation, liberation and healing is, therefore, a process of continually revisiting and re-articulating what it means to live in community and as community, "where I am because we are, and we are because I am." For this, we have a model from Mercy herself, who for years has labored to build a Circle of Concerned African Women Theologians as the *adinkra* community, struggling for justice and empowerment of African women from all that denies their full humanity in their specific communities and cultures (Kanyoro 1997: 7–27; Oduyoye 2004: 4–6). For this legacy—the legacy of the most illustrious African woman—"*the precious black bead*"—Mercy Amba Ewudziwa Oduyoye, to you I say, the struggle for *adinkra* communities in Africa continues: *A luta continua!*

NOTES

[1] According to Kofi Asare Opoku (1997: 113), "The Akan use the *adinkra* symbols to convey knowledge and intangible truths and ideas about life and meaning."

[2] Throughout this paper, I will use HIV & AIDS instead of the generic HIV/AIDS. This is because People Living with HIV & AIDS (PLWHA) have problematized the latter as equating all HIV+ people with having AIDS. Since these two are very different conditions, in this paper I will respect the perspective of PLWHA on insisting upon the separation of the two.

[3] Throughout this essay, I will use African indigenous religion/s (AIR/s), to note that there are different schools of thought. Some prefer African religion, others African religions and others African indigenous religion/s (AIR/s). I have added the stroke, "/s", (AIR/s) to accommodate different perspectives. As other scholars have noted, I am not sure if the category of "religion" is the best concept by which to define African cosmology.

REFERENCES

Amanze, J. N. *African Traditional Religion in Malawi: The Case of the Bimbi Cult.* Blantyre: Kachere, 2002.

Botswana Government. 1996. *Vision 2016: The Long Term Vision for Botswana.* Gaborone: Government Printers.

Dube, M. W. 1996. "Readings of *Semoya*: Batswana Women Interpretations of Matt. 15:21–28." *Semeia* 73. Atlanta: Scholars Press, 111–129.

———. 1999. "Consuming a Colonial Cultural Bomb: Translating *Badimo* into 'Demons' in Setswana Bible." *Journal for the Study of the New Testament* 73, 33–59.

———. 2001a. "Divining Ruth for International Relations." In *Other Ways of Reading: African Women and the Bible.* ed. Dube, M. W. Atlanta: SBL, 179–198.

———, ed. 2001b. *Other Ways of Reading: African Women and the Bible.* Atlanta: SBL.

———, ed. 2003a. *HIV/AIDS and the Curriculum: Methods of Integrating HIV/AIDS in Theological Programs.* Geneva: WCC.

———, ed. 2003b. *AfricaPraying: A Handbook of HIV/AIDS Sensitive Sermons and Liturgy.* Geneva: WCC.

———, and R. A. M. Kanyoro. eds., 2004. *Grant Me Justice: HIV/AIDS and Gender Readings of the Bible.* Pietermaritzburg: Cluster Publications.

Gelfand, M. 1964. *The Witchdoctor.* London: Harvill Press.

Gupta, Geeta R. 2000. "Gender, Sexuality and HIV/AIDS: The What, the Why and the How." *Plenary address.* XIII Internatonal AIDS Conference. Washington: ICRW (International Centre for Research on Women).

Kanyoro, R A M. 1997. "Keynote Speech." In *Transforming Power: Women in the Household of God.* ed. Oduyoye, M. A., Accra: Sam Woode Ltd, 7–27.

Katongole, E. 2001. "Christian Ethics and AIDS in Africa Today: Exploring the Limits of a Culture of Suspicion." *Missionalia* 29 (2), 125–143.

Lutheran World Federation. 2002. *Crises of Life in African Religion and Christianity.* Geneva: Lutheran World Federation.

———. 2003. *For the Healing of World: Study Winnipeg*, Lutheran World Federation 12th Assembly, Canada 21-31 July.

Maluleke, T. S. 2001. "African 'Ruths' and Ruthless Africa: Reflections of an African Mordecai." In *Other Ways of Reading: African Women and the Bible*, ed. Dube, M W. Atlanta: SBL.

Maluleke, V. E. 2004. "Nobody Ever Said AIDS." In *Nobody Ever Said AIDS: Stories and Poems from Southern Africa.* eds., Rasebotsa, N., M. Samuelson, and K. Thomas. Cape Town: Kwela Books.

Mbiti, J. 1991. *Introduction to African Religion*. Gaborone: Heineman.

Mmualefe, D. O. 2004. "Towards Authentic Tswana Christianity: Revisting Botho." Unpublished master's thesis. Eden Theological Seminary, Missouri.

Mndende, N. 1996. "Ancestors and Healing in African Traditional Religion." In *Groaning in Faith: African Women in the Household of God.* eds., by Kanyoro, M. and N. Njoroge. Nairobi: Acton, 242–252.

Moila, M. P. 2002. "Health, Sickness and Healing." In *Crises of Life in African Religion and Christianity*. Lutheran World Federation. Geneva: LWF, 35–46.

Ntloedibe, G. S. 2000. "Ngaka and Jesus as Liberators." In *The Bible in Africa: Transactions, Trajectories and Trends*. eds., West, G O. and M. W. Dube. Leiden: Brill, 498–510.

Ntloedibe-Kuswani, S. 2001a. "Translating the Divine: The Case of Modimo in Setswana Bible." In *Other Ways of Reading: African Women and the Bible*, ed. Dube, M. W. Atlanta: SBL, 78–100.

———. 2001b. "The Religious Life of an African: A God-given Prepartio Evangelica." In *Talitha Cum! Theologies of African Women*. ed. Dube, M. W. Pietermaritzburg: Cluster Publications, 97–120.

Oduyoye, M. A. 1985. *Hearing and Knowing: Theological Reflections on Christianity in Africa*. Maryknoll, New York: Orbis Books.

———. 1995. *Daughters of Anowa: African Women and Patriarchy*. Maryknoll, New York: Orbis Books.

———. 2004. *Beads and Strands: Reflections of An African Woman on Christianity in Africa*. Maryknoll, New York: Orbis Books.

Opoku, K. A. 1997. *Hearing and Keeping: Akan Proverbs*. Pretoria: UNISA.

Peek, P. M. ed. 1991. *African Divination System: Ways of Knowing*. Indiana: Indiana University Press.

Rasebotsa, N., M. Samuelson, and K. Thomas, eds. 2004. *Nobody Ever Said AIDS: Stories and Poems from Southern Africa*. Cape Town: Kwela Books.

Schapera, I. 1938. *A Handbook of Tswana Law and Custom*. London: Frank Cass.

Staugard, F. 1985. *Traditional Healers: Traditional Medicine in Botswana*. Gaborone: Ipelegeng Publishers.

Thairu, K. 2003. *The African and the AIDS Holocaust: A Historical and Medical Perspective*. Nairobi: Phoenix Publishers.

Trimiew, D. M. 2004. "Ethics: Moral Evolutions from Customary Societies to Atomistic Individuals." In *Handbook of US Theologies of Liberation*. ed. by de La Torre, M. A. St Louis: Chalice Press, 101–109.

UNAIDS. 2000. *AIDS Epidemic Update*. Geneva: UNAIDS

———. 2002. *A Conceptual Framework and Basis for Action: HIV/AIDS Stigma and Discrimination*. Geneva: UNAIDS.

———. 2003. *AIDS Epidemic Update*. Geneva: December.

UNICEF. n.d. *People, Sexuality, Gender and HIV/AIDS*. Gaborone. Unpublished report.

UNDP and Botswana Government. 2000. *Botswana Human Development Report 2000: Towards an AIDS-Free Generation*. Gaborone: UNDP.

van Breugel, J. W. M. 2001.*Chewa Traditional Religion*. Blantye: Kachere.

Visser A. and H. D. Mhone. 2001. *Needs Assessment Report. People Living with HIV/AIDS in Botswana*. Gaborone: COCEPWA.

Weinreich, S. and C. Benn. 2004. *AIDS: Meeting the Challenge*. Geneva: WCC.

Wimbush, V. ed. 2000. *African American and the Bible: Sacred Text and Social Textures*. New York: Continuum.

8

Women as Healers

The Nigerian (Yoruba) Example

Dorcas Olubanke Akintunde

Women within traditional Nigerian Yoruba society, as in other cultures, play the roles of caregivers. They not only bear life, but they nurse, they cherish, they give warmth, and they care for life because all humanity passes through their bodies. And, yet, the important contribution that such women bring to these roles has either been grossly undervalued or often overlooked. Happily, there are exceptions. The work of Mercy Amba Ewudziwa Oduyoye is notable among these, particularly in her research on the Akan women of Ghana. Utilizing something of her methodology, I dedicate this present study on Nigerian Yoruba women and their role as healers and health care practitioners to Mercy. She has set a wonderful example for us through her founding and nurturing of the Circle of Concerned African Women Theologians.

This essay will explore the impact and meaning of health in the context of women as caregivers within traditional Yoruba society. My main argument will be that women are the mothers of all living human beings (see Gen. 3:20). This compels them to bring health to all those under their care, even though sometimes this is done at the expense of their own health and well-being. This is particularly important in African societies where life is lived for the good of the whole community.

Women have gone beyond being domestic caregivers, as their impact outside the boundaries of the home have often shown. In writing about the care-giving role of the Akan women of Ghana, Mercy notes that some traditional Akan proverbs confirm these qualities in women. For example, "a hen might step on her chick, but not with the intention of killing it"; "the tortoise has no breasts, and yet she feeds her young ones"; and "when you catch the mother hen, the chicks become easy prey" (Oduyoye 1995, 59). Mercy further notes that the proverbs about the hen speak of the role of the female in birthing and nurturing the continuance of the species. Mothers feed and protect their young. As in Akan culture, Yoruba culture places the welfare of children and the home above everything else. This is true of other African clans. It is an attribute that was exhibited in the past as well as within contemporary African society. Nothing else takes precedence. Hence the proverb, "when one's mother or child lies dying, one does not pursue disputes" (Oduyoye 1995, 60). Mercy observes further that it is an aberration if a woman acts to the contrary.

In an article co-authored with Elizabeth Amoah, Mercy narrates the story of Eku, the matriarch among the Fante clan. In their journey to their present home in southern Ghana, the Fante crossed vast tracts of waterless plains and became exceptionally thirsty. Fante lore says that although their agony was very great, their leader, Eku, did not despair. She spurred the people on in the midst of their plight. Encouraging them forward, they dragged themselves to a pool of water, yet none dared to drink. Having suffered much treachery upon their journey, the Fante were highly suspicious that their enemies may have poisoned the pool. Nevertheless, Eku, drank the water and gave some to her dog. The people waited patiently for any sign of sickness or death, but none came upon either Eku or her dog. Jubilant, they fell into the pool and drank to their fill as they shouted, *"Eku aso!* Eku has tasted, Eku has tasted on our behalf, we can now drink without fear of death" (Amoah and Oduyoye 1989, 36). This is the extent to which women go to provide care for not only their immediate family members but for society at large.

There is no doubt that within Yoruba society, care-giving roles have been reserved exclusively for women. This has caused much debate. Women are often regarded as caring too much about relationships or being too involved in the care and nurture of children to be capable of higher moral considerations. Feminist theologians have acknowledged the difference between what are "biologically essentially" women's roles (such as breastfeeding) and what are socially constructed roles (such as food preparation and housework). Hence, men can also be caregivers. Visits to hospitals and maternity centers have shown that in situations where the mother is in full time employment, fathers have assisted in care-giving. One could also argue that the "economic crunch" felt in many parts of Africa has compelled some women to become breadwinners, thus forcing men into care-giving roles.

HEALTH AMONG THE YORUBA

Among the Yoruba, it is true that *ara lile ni oogun oro* (Health is wealth) and *Alaafia ni oogun oro* (Good health is the magic of wealth). All is in vain without good health and nothing can be achieved through ill health. When two people meet, their greeting is the question *Se alaafia ni?* (Are you in good health?) or *Se daadaa ni?* (I hope all is well?). People in good health can fulfill their social functions as well as their moral obligations, hence the saying *Alaafia lo ju, ilera loro, eni ti o ni alaafia lo ni ohun gbogbo* (Health is paramount, health is wealth, whoever is in good health has everything). The absence of good health is sickness or illness *(aisan* or *amodi)*. Illness among the Yoruba is understood in three particular ways. First, it is natural or physical, such as poisoning, pain, diarrhea, cough, and so on. Second, it is supernatural, preternatural, or spiritual, including attacks by witches or wizards. Third, it is mystical. This final category is attributed to spirits, divinities, or ancestors for punishment of offences against them.

To the Yoruba, the degree of seriousness depends on the duration of the illness and the individual's response to therapeutic measures. If a person remains ill for some time and does not respond favorably to treatment, then the illness is deemed serious. This will be referred to as *ako aisan*, which is a severe illness defying solution. Such an illness can be hereditary or of natural causes or it can result from supernatural or preternatural forces. But the cause must be related to the host factor. It has been argued that host factors play an important role in the etiology and manifestation of illness. This can be likened to the Yoruba concept of *ibode*. If one's head receives *ibode* (is cursed), it means that the illness will defy cure. A common prayer among the Yoruba is *Ori mi ko ni gba abode* (My head or my being will not be attacked or cursed or susceptible to sickness that defies cure.) Not all disease results in illness, unless one's head is cursed. Thus one's *ori* (head) could resist sickness or resist all misfortune as noted in the 207th verse of the Odu Ifa Ogundatatura:[1]

> *Ori rere ni isegun ota,*
> *Ori aisan l'ota I di ni adipa.*
> (It is a good head that overcomes the enemy;
> it is the defective head that the enemy renders
>   impotent permanently.)

Diseases and illnesses can be grouped as major or minor. Minor illnesses include headache, cough, fever, nettle rash, running stool, whitlow, gonorrhea, rheumatism, ulcers or sores, cholera, hernia, tetanus, and bedwetting. Major illnesses are madness, small pox, and illnesses associated with children and babies such as thrush, disease of the umbilical cord, the swelling of glands, and so on.

In all of these and many others, women have proved their mettle as traditional healers and have employed their culture and knowledge and the community's norms and values to explain the cultural, social, magical and the physical environment of the patient in order to hasten the cure.

Three types of healing can be identified among the Yoruba. First is the healing that is spiritually based upon ritual, incantations, and the mental application of certain understood natural laws. A second type of healing is physically based upon the use of herbs without any ritual element or incantation. The third kind of healing is a combination of spiritual and physical healing.

WOMEN AND HEALING

In what ways do women serve as agents of healing? There are women priests and women healers. Osun is adept at herbal healing and is the giver of babies and the custodian of the safe delivery of infants (Oduyoye 1998, 112–20).

Healing restores a person both physically and spiritually. Nigerian women, and Yoruba women in particular, feature prominently in providing and makes use of health care. The cultural construction of their patriarchal society has stipulated that it is their responsibility to provide child and family care by way of growing and preparing food. At an early age Yoruba women are socialized into folk medicine and are expected to be proficient in the diagnosis, prognosis, and treatment of simple ailments. The burden of maintaining a family environment that is clean and healthy physically, spiritually, and emotionally is constantly upon them. In sum, women more than men are custodians of health.

Medicine women offer healing services in their capacities as healers and cultic functionaries, especially in the area of childcare. Like their male counterparts, women healers either learn or inherit their knowledge of herbs. Both involve the observation and memorization of the names of herbs and their use from the *onisegun* (those who deal with medicine). They can also be regarded as botanists as they deal with plants, trees, and the bark of trees. These categories of women offer consultation services for sick people who need either spiritual or physical healing or both. According to Yoruba beliefs, these roles had been denied to women in the past, being reserved solely for men. It is gratifying to realize that women healers are now more commonly accepted. In all the references to diviners, herbalists, and traditional healers by Awolalu, the use of "he" is noticeable, which implies that men had always dominated in these areas (Awolalu 1979, 122–23). For clarification, I will describe the functions of Yoruba female healers in seven different categories.

Yoruba Women as Traditional Gynecologists

Women are traditional gynecologists. Before the introduction of orthodox (Western) medicine, Yoruba women were involved in gynecology. They counseled when to have intercourse and how a threatened abortion could be avoided. Pregnant women were advised not to move around between 1:00 and 3:00 in the afternoon in order to avoid the heat of the sun. Likewise, they were to refrain from going out after 7:00 in the evening in order to avoid confrontations with evil spirits that might endanger their lives or those of the baby. The belief was also held that the baby could be changed to a "monster" by those evil spirits roving around at nightfall. They also gave counsel on the type of food suitable for pregnant women and nursing mothers. As no formal school taught these things, knowledge was transferred from mother to female offspring, from one generation to the next.

Yoruba Women as Traditional Birth Attendants *(Agbebi)*

Some Yoruba women are traditional birth attendants. Women in this category are found in rural areas where Western health care delivery systems are not available. Plants, roots, and herbs were discovered for the pre- and post-natal care of women and infants. Though the efficacy of these herbs is a matter for debate, they were important to traditional medicine and provided a psychological feeling of well-being. These traditional birth attendants in contemporary society are trained in missionary houses and most reside in maternity centers attached to churches.

Yoruba Women as Pediatricians

In the old days, common everyday remedies were always home made. Women made tonics, cough syrups, laxatives, liniments, and ointments. Mothers would always identify the nature of the illness and the medicine to use. Ordinarily, the mother would pour the medicine, usually in liquid form, into the mouth of the baby lying across her knees. At any given time, a baby may have more than five different kinds of medicine, both for washing and for drinking. At this stage, a baby would be given herbs by infusion, as well as breast milk.

Yoruba Women as Circumcisers

It is the practice among the Yoruba to circumcise every child, both male and female. At one time this procedure was the exclusive domain of men. In recent times, however, women have been involved as circumcisers, but still not as much as men. In some localities, they move around early in the morning before the sun rises. It is the belief among the Yoruba that clotting of blood will be faster before the sun rises than when the temperature becomes hot and humid.

Female circumcision is an issue that has generated much debate at both local and international levels. While some people regard it as archaic and barbaric, the practice still goes on because some Yoruba people are still married to their culture. Some of the reasons given for encouraging the practice include the belief that it will reduce sexual urges in girl children. However, some research has shown that circumcised females become more promiscuous, due to their sexual desires that are never met. In my opinion, it is a practice that must be eradicated as it reduces libido and does more harm than good. It is gratifying to note that presently non-governmental organizations, in cooperation with the Nigerian government, have been campaigning against this practice through both the electronic and print media.

Yoruba Women as Traditional Orthopedists

Yoruba women specialize in traditional orthopedics as evidenced from the various uses of herbs and elements. As with traditional circumcisers, this role was previously limited to male traditional healers. In contemporary society, female traditional healers take advantage of modern technology by advertising their expertise on radio and television. A case in point is Sisi Mama Iya Akure, a mother from Akure, who advertises regularly on local radio and television stations.

Yoruba Women as *Babalawos* (*Ifa* Diviners)

To say that this role had been a preserve of the male among the Yoruba would be an understatement. As the name implies, *baba* among the Yoruba is "father." Hence, to find a woman as "father" or "father of *awo*" (mystery) would be an aberration. Nevertheless, McClelland, who researched the cult of *Ifa* among the Yoruba, came across a female *babalawo*, that is, one endowed with the gift of divination (McClelland 1982, 88). It is also on record that a female Ifa priestess visited David Hinderer, a pioneer missionary to the Yorubaland in Igbore township in 1850 (McKenzie 1997, 409). These women's performance as diviners was stellar.

Yoruba Women as Priests

As priestesses, women offer sacrifices and hold "mysterious conversations" with the spiritual entities that are members of the cult. In the Yoruba worldview, a great majority of Yoruba witches are believed to be women and thus represent the bad aspects of the mother or the female. Nevertheless, male traditional priests consult them during periods of crisis, hence the saying, *O d'owo eyin iya mi* (I am leaving everything to you, my mothers). The "*osos*" are their male counterparts, but they are not in the majority according to the Yoruba.

UNDERSTANDING WOMEN AS HEALERS

Women are believed to be powerful metaphysically, hence people consult the *aje funfun* (white witches) among the Yoruba. *Aje funfun*, unlike the *aje dudu*, are benevolent spirits. They cure rather than harm or cause illness. In times of national or tribal crisis, the *aje funfun* are consulted, as it is believed that solutions to the turmoil befalling society lie with them. Some women even claim to have been blessed with children by the *aje funfun*. As healers or diviners, women consult and placate the tutelary spirits in order to receive from them the power to heal or for divination (Onwuka 1998, 45–56; Olunlade 1999, 44–54).

In the history of women healers among the Yoruba, a case in point is that of a prophetess, Akere, a healer among the Egba in 1855. She was a priestess of Yemoja, a water goddess whose domain extends to the rivers, lakes, lagoons, and the wide expanses of the sea. Yemoja is a fertility goddess who represents the place of origin and the maternal source of human, animal, plant, and divine life. Among the Orisa, she is the symbol of motherhood. Akere is a kind and nurturing yet stern mother. As a priestess of this great Orisa, Akere's healing ministry was therefore targeted toward the barren. Barrenness is not only considered a curse, but the one who is barren is also considered a curse. It is every woman's desire to be fruitful. Thus comes the Yoruba saying *Omo ni yoo sin mi* (I will be buried by my children).

Akere had a stable location or a fixed center of healing. She operated near a small stream not far from the Ogun River (McKenzie 1997, 396). Her ministry was to cure diverse sicknesses and "render all barren women prolific." Akere was said to have been commissioned by Yemoja to provide such barren women with six hundred thousand children. McKenzie describes her healing method as follows:

> The client kneels in the presence of the priestess, a calabash of cold water, about a bottle full or more taken from the priestess's water pot is . . . delivered to the individual to be drunk. . . . After this he/she is directed to wash in a small stream that is close by with a calabash, which is filled with water to be carried home, after which virtue is communicated by the priestess dipping her hand in it. All the applicants for this purpose have to place their calabashes on the ground in two rows on the right and on the left till virtue is

conferred, after which it is taken home to be drunk according to direction. More than a hundred calabashes at once are placed on the ground in this way waiting for her to impart virtue to the water. (McKenzie 1997, 396)

This method is similar to the practices of the Aladura churches in Nigeria. Worshipers throng the church with different sizes of containers in order to receive "blessed water" for healing and other therapeutic purposes. Within the Christ Apostolic Church, when the water is being prayed for, the congregation is to sing *Jesu Olomi iye re o* (Jesus, the source of living water is here). In the Cherubim and Seraphim Church and the Celestial Church of Christ, the rod being held by the apostle or leader is dipped into the water brought by the congregation in the belief that power has been transferred to it. The Yoruba believe that when a person prays or speaks into the water it receives power, for there is power in words and the water, after being imbued with spiritual power, is no longer ordinary.

THE DIFFERENT HERBS AND ELEMENTS FOR HEALING

The healing of sick people among the Yoruba takes different forms. The commonest is the use of herbs, fruits, tree bark, roots, animal parts, or bodily waste. The concoctions depend on the nature of the illness. Healing can also be appropriated by means of incantation. To the Yoruba, everything in nature has its special name, including people and some diseases. Thus, it is believed that the patient will be cured by calling those names during incantation. Incantation is also used to cure snakebites. When the spot is cut and some incantations are recited, the poison is said to flow out of the wound. Through incantation, the snake is brought back to the spot and killed. As part of the cure, the victim may be asked to eat a raw snake after the head and tail have been cut off.

The Yoruba medicine woman uses among other things, egbogi (roots of trees), *agbo* (concoctions of roots, barks, and leaves), *agunmu* (powdered medicine to be drunk), *epa* (lotions or antidotes), *ero* (balm), *ogede* (incantations), *ofo* (spells), *ase* (verbal commands), *sigidi* (medical image), *igbadi* or *saworo* (waist girdle, anklets), *onde* (waist girdle), *aje ara* (preventive/preemptive dose), *gbere* (medicated incision), and *etutu* (balm or appeasement) (M. Oduyoye 1998, 55–70). Other natural objects used in healing include *obi* (kolanut), *omi* (water), *orogbo* (bitter kola), *ataare* (alligator pepper), *epo* (palm oil), *oti* (wine), *oyin* (honey), *eja* (fish), and *iyo* (salt). These elements are also provided during a marriage or naming ceremony.

Recently, there has been a revival in Nigeria in the use of traditional medicine. Radio and television stations have been instrumental in supporting the "back to traditional medicine" campaign. Such drugs and potions should, however, be certified by the National Agency for Food and Drug Administration and Control (NAFDAC). It is also gratifying to note that a woman, Dr. Dora Akunyili, the director general of NAFDAC, has been assigned the role of monitoring this organization, which has succeeded in impounding counterfeit drugs and other consumable items in the country. In December 2003 alone, NAFDAC intercepted bogus and expired drugs totaling 408.2 million naira.

WOMEN AND HEALTH-CARE PROVISION IN CONTEMPORARY NIGERIA

Within contemporary Nigerian society, the activities of women as health-care providers are noteworthy. Women serve as medical doctors and there are numerous women's groups and associations involved in the health-care delivery system. The Catholic Medical Missionaries of Mary Sisters in Nigeria is one example. These Sisters have established hospitals throughout Nigeria where people of different religious backgrounds can receive medical attention (Johnson-Bashua 1999, 141–46). The Sisters have also established a facility for the care of lepers and built homes for those with disabilities and they have also provided spiritual healing to the sick through their counseling programs. Known as pastoral church workers, they counsel patients and discuss edifying texts from the Bible. Similarly, women in other denominations are not left behind in the provision of health care. The Good Women Association of the Christ Apostolic Church has established "Faith Homes" for the women in the assembly and in other denominations. The Women Missionary Union (WMU) of the Nigerian Baptist Convention is also involved in health-care services.

CONCLUSION

I have attempted to show how Nigerian women have been significantly involved in the health-care delivery system. I have also demonstrated that within the Yoruba society women have always practiced medicine and healing. Though their contributions have often been overlooked because women typically practiced within a domestic setting, some were not limited to the home. As traditional healers women serve as priests, doctors, nurses, circumcisers, and medicine women. Although men have always been involved in these roles, it has been discovered that some women have broken with the status quo and become involved. Finally, I have briefly examined the role of women as health-care givers within women's Christian organizations in Nigeria, which has inspired other women to get involved in providing health care.

Although this essay has shown that the provision of health care by women is linked to their biological ability to conceive and bear children, it should also be emphasized that, due to the modern life style and the pursuit of the fullness of life, this role has to be shared with men. After all, the process of conception is a joint venture between men and women. It makes sense therefore that both men and women should be involved in the provision of care that brings healing to humanity.

NOTE

[1] This is one of the Ifa Corpus among the Yoruba.

REFERENCES

Awolalu, J. Omosade. 1979. *Yoruba Beliefs and Sacrificial Rites*. London: Oxford University Press.

Amoah, Elizabeth and Mercy Amba Oduyoye. 1989. "The Christ for African Women." In *With Passion and Compassion: Third World Women Doing Theology*. Edited by Virginia Fabella and Mercy Amba Oduyoye. Maryknoll, New York: Orbis Books.

Johnson-Bashua, A. O. 1999. "Religion and the Changing Roles of Women: The Activities of the Medical Missionary of Mary's Sister." In *Religion and Family: A Publication of the Nigerian Association for the Study of Religious Education*. Edited by G. Aderibigbe and D. Ayegboyin. April, 141–45.

McKenzie, Peter. 1997. *Hail Orisha! A Phenomenology of a West African Religion in the Mid-Nineteenth Century*. Leiden/New York: Brill/Koln.

McClelland, Elizabeth M. 1982. *The Cult of Ifá among the Yoruba*. London: Ethnographica.

Oduyoye, Mercy Amba. 1995. *Daughters of Anowa: African Women and Patriarchy*. Maryknoll, New York: Orbis Books.

Oduyoye, Modupe. 1998. "The Medicine Man, the Magician and the Wise Man." In *Traditional Religion in West Africa*. Edited by E. Adeolu Adegbola. Ibadan, Nigeria: Sefer Books.

Onwuka, S. C. 1998. "I Was a Juju Priest." In *Traditional Religion in West Africa*. Edited by E. Adeolu Adegbola. Ibadan, Nigeria: Sefer Books.

Olunlade, T. 1999. "Ipa Ti awon Obinrin ko ninu eewo to jeyo nipa Asayan Oriki at Orile Yoruba." *Yoruba: A Journal of the Yoruba Studies Association of Nigeria* 1: 44–54.

Olajubu, Oyeronke O. 2003. *Women in the Yoruba Religious Sphere*. Albany: State University of New York Press.

Protus, K. 1996. "Women, Health Development and Theological Education." In *Women, Culture and Theological Education*. Edited by K. Protus and Mercy Amba Oduyoye. Enugu, Nigeria: SNAAP, 116–29.

PART IV

AFRICAN WOMEN'S EXPERIENCES OF HEALTH AND HEALING, ENDURANCE, AND PEACEMAKING

9

Women, Poverty, and HIV in Zimbabwe

An Exploration of Inequalities in Health Care

Sophia Chirongoma

The writing of this essay was inspired by reflections on my own family life. I have experienced suffering, pain, frustration, and despair, combined with a debilitating sense of hopelessness, when faced with illness because of a lack of resources. During the past few years, I have lost close relatives and loved ones, mostly from HIV-related illnesses; watching helplessly as they lay dying, I wished I had the financial means to assist them in accessing medication. This pain was made even greater due to the realization that some of their ailments could have been treated, or at least be temporarily relieved, through pain-relieving medications.

DEMOGRAPHICAL STRUCTURE OF ZIMBABWE

According to the on-line version of the *Encyclopedia Britannica*, the current population of Zimbabwe numbers around 11.4 million people. Of this number, around one-quarter of the population, mostly men of working age, live in urban centers, with most

173

of the older people, women, and children remaining in the rural areas. This chapter, which I dedicate to Mercy Amba Ewudziwa Oduyoye, concentrates on the rural lifestyle of women living in Masvingo Province. Although women are responsible for most of the production and processing of food crops, men control the means of production, land, cattle, and reproduction. Hence, although women provide their labor, the financial benefits are enjoyed mainly by men. This situation seriously jeopardizes women's financial security and their ability to pay for health care. Women's waking hours are spent on such back-breaking activities as weeding, harvesting, or collecting animal fodder or fuel, all of which have a direct effect on the productivity of agriculture (Pearson 1992, 292). During the farming season in particular, women work fifteen hours or more per day. In contradistinction, their male counterparts—especially those in urban areas—usually work for about eight to nine hours a day, and the work is not as exhausting as domestic and agricultural work.

The urban communities have better living conditions, transport systems, and sanitation. There are better health facilities and all medical facilities are centralized. Members of the urban communities, especially the middle and upper classes, have medical insurance and thus have good access to health care. Of the estimated 326,000 people who live on communal lands and the 209,179 in new resettlements, none have access to health-care facilities (Poverty Reduction Forum 2002). Furthermore, without sanitation and access to clean, potable water, rural women spend most of their time and energy fetching water from unsanitary and distant sources. Most rural areas in Masvingo Province do not have access to clean, potable water; instead they rely on streams and rivers. All these shortcomings expose the rural communities to intestinal and other diseases and add the care of the sick to the already overburdened tasks of women. Most rural women suffer harsher extremes of poverty than low-income men within their communities. They also lack access to resources for development, such as credit facilities and the attention of extension workers. Such gender inequalities produce barriers to these women's equal social participation (Mosse 1993, 218).

AVAILABILITY AND ACCESSIBILITY
OF HEALTH FACILITIES TO THE COMMUNITIES

Health is one of the most important social concerns of the Zimbabwean people. Major gains were achieved in the health sector during the 1980s by joint and complementary action between the health sector and communities. The health system of Zimbabwe used to compare favorably with most other countries in sub-Saharan Africa. Upon independence in 1980, the government invested heavily in education and health. There was an expansion of health care to the rural areas and urban poor. During the 1980s, infant mortality fell from 86 to 61 per 1000 births, immunization increased from 25 to 80 percent, and the crude death rate dropped from 10.1 in 1982 to 6.1 in 1987. Life expectancy increased from 55 to 59 years. A health infrastructure was constructed and there was greater access to health-care facilities. Qualified personnel entered the system and more emphasis was placed on preventive and simple curative care such as immunization campaigns, health information in the areas of family planning, mother-child health care, environmental health, and the treatment of communicable diseases (Chibanda 1996, 218).

Following the cumulative effect of HIV/AIDS and World Bank/IMF-imposed structural adjustments, real cuts in the budgets for health care and welfare services and a decrease in household incomes reversed all these gains. This severely compromised the quality of health care, demoralized personnel and their clients in the health care sector, and led people to solve their health problems in ways that were not always effective for their own health or for the long-term health needs of the nation. In 1980, the Ministry of Health was reported to be providing 71 percent of health expenditures (Ministry of Health Child Welfare 1984, 35). By 1994, this figure had fallen by 29 percent, with 31 percent coming from individual direct payments and 12.2 percent from donor financing (Loewenson 1998, 14). User fees were instituted for health and education, and food subsidies were eliminated. The result was a disaster for the people of Zimbabwe, especially for the poor majority. The previously stable attendance rates at medical facilities plummeted after the introduction of user fees. The situation was further exacerbated by the mass exodus of the qualified health personnel from the public sector as they sought better working conditions elsewhere.

Rural communities have been hardest hit and the majority of rural clinics have closed due to lack of staff. The few that are still operational are run mostly by unqualified staff and are bedeviled by shortages of drugs and equipment. There is a critical shortage of staff in the medical field. Currently, about 24 percent (2,360) of posts lay vacant in all the provinces. Since January 2000, about 7 percent of qualified health personnel have left the health services, with a loss to nursing of 12 percent, to medical practitioners of 13 percent, and to pharmacists of 18 percent (Loewenson 2000). Most of the facilities are isolated, especially in Masvingo Province, and sometimes patients are too weak to walk to the nearest clinic. Due to transportation problems, there are several cases of pregnant women delivering their children enroute to the clinic, which is detrimental to the health of both the mother and child. Some children born under such circumstances have been named *Chenzira*, meaning "on the roadway." Others simply resort to delivering at home with the assistance of *nyamukuta* (traditional birth attendants). Sometimes sick people are carried on a wheelbarrow to the clinic or even on a scotch-cart pulled by donkeys, which is both unsafe and uncomfortable.

In my rural home in Masvingo, two clinics service the area, the government-owned Mashenjere Clinic (10 kilometers away) and the African Reformed Church-operated Shonganiso Clinic (8 kilometers away). Both have become "white elephants" because of shortages in medications of even the most basic drugs. Most people have simply given up visiting the clinics because, after having struggled to travel the long distances and paying consultation fees, nurses simply examine them and direct them to the nearest referral center that is 70 kilometers away. Most poor people cannot afford the bus-fares to these referral centers or the higher user fees that they charge. There are agonizingly long queues at these hospitals and sometimes people collapse or even die in the queue. They also experience acute staff shortages.

I still painfully remember my cousin Christine who died in child-birth at Morgenster hospital in 1996 because she went into labor during the weekend and suffered complications that required a caesarean section. Due to shortages of doctors over the weekend, not a single doctor was available as doctors only make occasional visits during the week. My sister had been in labor since Friday and by Saturday she was in a coma. Sunday night, in great pain, she passed way. This is only one example of the many patients who die because there are no qualified personnel to attend to their health-care needs.

A UNICEF report has noted that during a relatively short period of time the quality of health services fell by a colossal 30 percent. Twice as many women died in childbirth in Harare hospitals after 1990 than before. Bed occupancy rates at Harare hospitals fell from 5,766 in December 1990 to 4,795 in December 1991 (Ministry of Education, Zimbabwe 1994: 28). The scenario of the health sector in Zimbabwe after 1990 was aptly depicted by a visiting newspaper reporter as a "death trap." The report went on to state: "Not only do these hospitals face critical drug, equipment and staff shortages, they are becoming extremely expensive for the ordinary worker who is battling to make ends meet" (*Daily News*, 8 November 2000).

Service providers are so insistent about prior payment that the significance of saving lives seems no longer a priority. Personally, I had a very painful experience at Gweru General Hospital on 17 February 1999 when I was admitted temporarily to undergo a caesarean section to deliver my son, Tadiwanashe. My ordeal started when I was moved from the private hospital where I had been admitted, as it had no surgical facilities. I had left all my belongings at the private hospital, including my money and purse. When it came to prepare me for surgery, I was asked to pay a fee for the anesthesia that would be administered. I tried to explain to the service provider that I had no money with me and would pay afterward, but he could not be persuaded. He probably feared that I might die during surgery and he would not be able to recover his money. Despite the fact that I was in so much pain that I could barely speak, he kept pressurizing me, with little or no concern that I had been in labor for two days and the baby was now in distress. The anesthesia was administered only after my relatives had been called and had paid for the service. If the fee had not been paid, in all probability, my son and I would have died.

The entire health-care system has become so materialistic that those without sufficient resources cannot hope to survive. Even being admitted to a hospital is a nightmare. Most people fail to be admitted because they cannot afford to pay the admission fees; others seek an early discharge or even abscond to save money. In some hospitals, mothers are held hostage in the maternity ward and are not discharged until their bills have been paid, because staff fear that once patients are discharged, they will not return to settle their accounts.

THE IMPLICATIONS OF ECONOMIC STRUCTURAL ADJUSTMENT POLICIES ON WOMEN AND THE POOR

As the crisis in Zimbabwe deepens, budget items are eliminated and the available share of our ever-shrinking financial resources is particularly felt by women and girl children. In times of such shortages, the food intake of women and girl children is sacrificed so that men can be allocated more food. Even with health care, a male family member has first priority. Because most families do not value women, they do not feel obliged to spend valuable resources seeking medication for women. The situation of women is even more difficult because women, from their concern for the family's welfare, commit most of their time to working at home (often as a real sacrifice), even when ill, and endure their illness, seeking medication or care only when they become seriously ill (Phiri 2003, 9). This often jeopardizes their chance for a full recovery.

As governments struggle with economic structural adjustment policies (ESAP) and IMF/World Bank-imposed austerity cutbacks on welfare services, the work of women is increased. As long as family care remains the sole responsibility of the woman, they will continue to bear a disproportionate share of the costs of structural adjustments. As Chauke (2003, 135) reiterates, all people feel the economical burden; however, the burden is doubled on girl children and women because Zimbabwean society places women on the lowest step of the human ladder. For most women in rural and urban communities, adjustment has meant ever increasing workloads and falling living standards as they struggle, often unsuccessfully, to maintain their standard of living and to ensure the basic survival of their households (Dube 2003, 76–77).

The financial squeeze on family budgets has been so tight that it has pushed the children of poorer families out of school prematurely (Hill 2003, 90). It is mainly the girl child who is the first to be sacrificed. Available statistics show that 80 percent of all females undergoing education attend primary schools; 19 percent are at a secondary level; 0.8 percent are in vocational, industrial, or teacher training; and 0.2 percent attend universities. Recurrent expenditures on primary and secondary education where women are concentrated have declined by more than 30 percent during ESAP, while those for higher education increased by 1 percent in the 1994/95 fiscal year above its 1990/91 level (Chisvo and Munro 1994, 24). While ESAP reduce government spending, the most negatively impacted are women, who as teachers, health workers, and public-sector workers, often take the brunt of cuts in employment. This results in women being trapped in a vicious cycle of poverty and deprivation since it is men who enjoy a better financial standing.

THE VULNERABILITY OF WOMEN AND THE POOR TO HIV/AIDS INFECTION

The high incidence of HIV/AIDS and the recurrent droughts since 2000 have impacted heavily on women and poor households. Improper diets and poor nutrition, due to an inadequate food supply, have jeopardized the correct regimen for most medications, resulting in a failure to properly treat TB, sexually transmitted infections (STIs), and malaria. Two results are drug-resistant strains of viruses and the continued transmission of infections. People who live with HIV are precipitated into AIDS if faced with poor nutrition and stress, which shortens their life expectancy and diminishes their quality of life. Children and HIV+ breast-feeding mothers are sometimes given low priority in food distribution, leading to a rapid decline in health. Families of people living with HIV become more vulnerable due to their diminished labor capacity as women spend more time caring for their sick relatives. Diminished agricultural productivity and the ability to work for cash leads many families to sell their assets and reduce levels of childcare, leading to an ever-increasing cycle of poverty and deprivation.

The negative results of ESAP further deepen insecurities, placing people under pressure and stress, which leads to their adoption of risky survival strategies. This makes them highly vulnerable to HIV infection and AIDS. Some survival strategies include cross border trading, gold panning, and informal trading. Hence, when HIV/AIDS was first identified in Zimbabwe in 1985, it found "fertile ground" in the form of a social environment conducive to its spread. This social environment was generated by a historical template characterized by rapid social and economic change, changing morals, high mobility, gender inequalities, and widespread and deepening poverty. In its latest national HIV estimate reports (2003), the Zimbabwean Ministry of Health and Child Welfare details an adult HIV prevalence rate of 25 percent. Although the epidemic is generalized, commercial farming and mining areas, border posts, and growth points are special areas that best illustrate development vulnerabilities in the population (Gomo 2003).

Farming communities have a higher prevalence of HIV infection than the general population. Workers' compounds on large farms constitute small and closed communities that have few social and recreational facilities other than the ubiquitous beer outlets (Gomo 2003). Very low wages and harsh working conditions cause males and females alike to drown their frustrations in alcohol and unsafe sexual activities.

The situation is similar in the mining areas, with an increase in the number of illegal gold dealers popularly known as *makorokoza*. The dealers have access to vast amounts of money, but the work is done by poor people, who become even more vulnerable. Because minors historically work under very dangerous circumstances that often result in death or serious injury; they spend their money recklessly and are unconcerned about protected sex, openly exchanging sexual partners, which results in a high rate of infection. Female casual mine workers who are poorly paid become an easy prey to *makorokoza* and to male mine workers whose wives cannot live with them in the single-sex accommodation complexes. Consequently, men contract the infection and pass it on to their wives back home. This is reminiscent of the situation at Renco Mine in Masvingo South, where most people from my rural home go in search of employment. When they return home they are said to have been *akarohwa nematsotsi* (attacked by the thugs). This is the euphemism that my people use when referring to HIV-related symptoms.

Border posts are another haven of commercial sex work, especially the Beitbridge and Plumtree border posts to South Africa and Botswana. Long-distance truck drivers and corrupt customs officials take advantage of women who do not possess legal travel documents and are desperate to cross the border to trade. Some women will also be desperate to avoid paying high custom and excise duties on imported items. They fall prey to corrupt men who are capable of twisting rules and regulations, demanding that the women pay "in kind" with their bodies. These women have no other recourse since cross-border trading is their only source of income.

Intergenerational sex also plays a pivotal role in the persistence of major HIV epidemics. A UNAIDS report highlights the "feminization of AIDS" reflected in the fact that in South Africa and Zimbabwe more than 75 percent of HIV+ youth aged 15 to 24 are female. African women are being infected at an earlier stage than their male counterparts (UNAIDS, August 2004). Of the two million Zimbabweans living with HIV/AIDS, 1.2 million are women. The HIV prevalence rate among women aged 15 to 24 years ranges from 25 to 40 percent, compared with 10 to 15 percent for men of the same age. Most poor and desperate young women often have two types of partners: an older man who has accumulated assets and is able to provide money and gifts, and a slightly younger man being cultivated as a potential husband. Married women are more likely to become infected as men dominate when it comes to sexual matters. Thus, even if a husband is unfaithful, wives are powerless to negotiate for safer sex. Statistics reveal that a woman who gets married doubles her risk of infection the day she marries because she loses the cultural and religious right to protection, which is the condom, because she now needs to conceive (UNAIDS August 2004). Kala clearly depicts how the transmission of HIV/AIDS in heterosexual relationships is mainly caused by a refusal to change cultural traditions (1994, 16). HIV/AIDS makes life harder for women, it deepens poverty, and it increases a need for resources that do not exist.

THEOLOGICAL REFLECTIONS

This essay has attempted to explore the inequalities that prevail among women and men in urban and rural communities within Zimbabwe when it comes to accessing resources, especially health-care facilities. The exposed discrepancies call for an urgent course of action. Women suffer the most, and the challenge is upon the women of Zimbabwe to stand up and reclaim the rights and privileges enjoyed by some and yet denied to the majority. We have to be active agents in changing our circumstances (Phiri 2004, 41). Throughout the ages, women have been groaning and mourning for the loss of their children, like the biblical Rachel, whose voice was heard in Ramah and who refused to be comforted. It has been agonizing to watch our children and loved ones die of HIV/AIDS and other opportunistic infections. Our voices should not only be heard above our mourning, but as Christians and members of the academy we need to raise these concerns high, since God desires that all enjoy the fruit of the earth.

In order for all to have life in abundance, the whole community must cooperate. Mercy Oduyoye has defined wholeness of life as all that makes for fullness of life and makes people celebrate life. . . . [It] implies the possession of the powers, graces or attributes that call for the celebration of life, and demonstrates the integrity of the human body, good eye-sight, hearing and speech and the wholeness of mind and limbs. (Oduyoye 2001, 34)

The church must play a pivotal role in addressing issues of poverty, inequalities, and inaccessibility of health care, which mainly affect the poor, women, and children. The church must be guided by the concept of *shalom* and address human problems in a holistic manner. Shalom cannot be achieved if health, wholeness, and well-being are lacking (Oduyoye 2002, 40). The wholeness of life demands release from poverty and physical ailments such as HIV/AIDS. Mercy Oduyoye concurs that Jesus, the anointed one of God and a source of wholeness, was

empowered and sent by God to show humanity what it means to live fully the image in which we are made. Living fully has come to mean resisting oppression, transforming potential death into life and believing that the resurrection happens every time we defeat death and begin a new life. (Oduyoye 2001, 64)

Women and all those who suffer from deprivation should find encouragement and consolation in Jesus as the caring compassionate healer who is outraged by the injustices of poverty, violence, inequality and sickness.

The church needs to be reminded that its first and foremost task is to serve the body before saving the soul. There are many churches in Masvingo that appear not to be actively involved in addressing these fundamental community needs. Hence, the challenge is upon all Christians and the whole community to fight against all the forces that keep humanity locked in poverty, malnutrition, deprivation, and ill-health. Churches must join hands and commit themselves to the cause of the hungry, the needy, the sick, and the dying. The Roman Catholic Church in Zimbabwe has been instrumental in providing food and health care to most needy communities. Catholic Relief Services (CRS) has established community-based programs that help those infected or affected by HIV/AIDS and that address the underlying causes of HIV/AIDS. It has also established home-based care programs to provide networks of support for the infected and affected. Such efforts should be emulated by other churches. Churches can make a difference by ensuring that they have active ministries to the sick and the dying, providing HIV/AIDS drop-in centers, and establishing church and primary health-care clinics, especially within rural communities.

Most Christians rely on their congregations as a support system. If their congregations fail to assist them at their time of greatest need, they often have nowhere else to turn. If the church is a united institution, oneness in Christ should be exercised by sharing one another's burdens and by seeking corporately to correct injustices that deny access to health care or food security for the poor.

The churches can also address issues of poverty by initiating income-generating projects that will economically empower the poor. Even though most rural women are uneducated and lack access to resources, they can still benefit from projects initiated by churches, such as the manufacture of peanut butter, poultry production, craft work, and gardening. Such projects can empower poor people financially and protect them from the vulnerability of adopting risky survival strategies that further expose them to HIV infection.

REFERENCES

Bond, Patrick and M. Masimba. 2003. *Zimbabwe's Plunge: Exhausted Nationalism, Neoliberalism and the Search for Social Justice*. Pietermaritzburg: University of Natal Press.

Chauke, E. 2003. "Theological Challenges and Ecclesiological Responses to Women Experiencing HIV/AIDS: A South Eastern Zimbabwe Context." In *African Women, HIV/AIDS and Faith Communities*. Edited by Isabel Apowa Phiri, Beverley Haddad and Madipoane Masenya. Pietermaritzburg: Cluster Publications.

Chibanda, S. 1996. *Adjustment and Women's Health in Zimbabwe: The Current Financial Crisis.* Unpublished Report prepared for the Women Action Group, Harare.

Chisvo, M. and L. Munro. 1994. *A Review of the Social Dimensions of Adjustment.* Harare: UNICEF.

Dhliwayo, R. 2001. *The Impact of Public Expenditure Management under ESAP on Basic Social Services: Health and Education.* SAPRI.

Dube, Musa W. 2003. "Talitha Cum! Calling the Girl-child and Women to Life in the HIV/AIDS and Globalization Era." In *African Women, HIV/AIDS and Faith Communities.* Edited by Isabel Apawo Phiri, Beverley Haddad, and Madipoane Masenya. Pietermaritzburg: Cluster Publications.

Gomo, E. 2003. "Highlights of the Zimbabwe Human Development Report 2003: Redirecting Our Responses to HIV/AIDS." Harare: 6 May. http://hdr.undp.org/reports/view-reports.cfm/ (accessed 16 July 2004).

Hill, Geoff. 2003. *The Battle for Zimbabwe: The Final Countdown.* Cape Town: Zebra Press.

Kala, Violet. 1994. *Waste Not Your Tears.* Harare: Baobab.

Koenig, Harold George. 1999. *The Healing Power of Faith: Science Explores Medicine's Last Great Frontier.* New York: Simon & Schuster.

Loewenson, Rene and D. Saunders. 1988. "The Political Economy of Health and Nutrition." In *Zimbabwe's Prospects.* Edited by Colin Stoneman. London: Macmillan.

Loewenson, Rene. 1988. "Labour Insecurity and Health." *Social Science and Medicine* 27 (7): 733–41.

———. 1989. *Health in Zimbabwe: Community Perspectives.* Monograph 98. Harare: TARSC.

———. 1998. *Public Participation in Health: Making People Matter.* Harare: Paper prepared for collaboration between the Training and Research Support Centre (TARSC) Zimbabwe and the Institute of Development Studies (IDS), United Kingdom.

———. 2000. "2001 Health Budget: Enough to Make You Sick." *Herald* 21 November. Harare: Government Printers.

——— and M. Chisvo. 1994. *Transforming Social Development: The Experience of Zimbabwe.* Unpublished Report Prepared for UNICEF, Harare.

Masenya, Madipoane. 2004. "Struggling with Poverty/Emptiness: Rereading the Naomi-Ruth Story in African-South Africa." *Journal of Theology for Southern Africa* 120: 46–59.

Ministry of Education, Zimbabwe. 1994. *Think About It: An AIDS Action Program for Schools Form 1 Students' Book.* Harare: Ministry of Education/UNICEF Harare.

Ministry of Health and Child Welfare, Zimbabwe. 1984. *Planning for Equity in Health.* Harare: Government Printers.

————. 1997. *National Health Strategy for Zimbabwe, 1997–2007.* Harare: Ministry of Health and Child Welfare.

Mosse, J. C. 1993. "Why Development Is a Gender Issue." In *Changing Perceptions—Writings in Gender and Development: Half the World Half a Chance: An Introduction to Gender and Development.* Edited by T. Wallace and C. March. Oxford: Oxfam.

Nicolson, Ronald. 2003. "Why Religious Health Assets Matter: A Response." African Religious Health Assets Program Colloquium Report. Pietermaritzburg, August.

Oduyoye, Mercy Amba. 2001. *Introducing African Women's Theology.* Sheffield: Sheffield Academic Press.

————. 2002. *Beads and Strands: Reflections of an African Woman on Christianity in Africa.* Akropong-Akuapem: Regnum Africa; Maryknoll, New York: Orbis Books.

Pearson, R. 1992. "Gender Matters in Development." In *Poverty and Development in the 1990s.* Edited by Tim Allen and Alan Thomas. Oxford: Oxford University Press.

Phiri, Isabel Apawo. 2003. "African Women of Faith Speak Out." In *African Women, HIV/AIDS and Faith Communities.* Edited by Isabel Apawo Phiri, Beverley Haddad and Madipoane Masenya. Pietermaritzburg: Cluster Publications.

————. 2004. "A Theological Analysis of the Voices of Teenage Girls on 'Men's Role in the Fight against HIV/AIDS' in KwaZulu-Natal, South Africa." *Journal of Theology for Southern Africa* 120: 34-54.

Poverty Reduction Forum. 2002. "Stakeholder Workshop on the Food Situation in Zimbabwe: Mapping a Way Forward." University of Zimbabwe, Institute of Development Studies. October. http://www.sarpn.org.za/documents/d0000093/ (accessed 29 June 2005).

Shorter, Aylward. 1985. *Jesus and the Witchdoctor: An Approach to Healing and Wholeness.* Maryknoll, New York: Orbis Books

UNAIDS. 2004. "Poverty and Women's Oppression." August. http://www.hdnet.org/ (accessed 19 July 2004).

Vambe, T. M. 2003. "HIV/AIDS, African Sexuality and the Problem of Representation in Zimbabwean Literature." In *Journal of Contemporary African Studies* 21 (3).

10

Women and Peacemaking

The Challenge of a Non-Violent Life

Susan Rakoczy, IHM

The media brings home the daily reality of war: death, destruction, soldiers and civilians blown up by bombs, the torture of prisoners, homes destroyed, women and children fleeing. The places of war seem endless: the Middle East, Iraq, Darfur in the Sudan, Burundi, and the Democratic Republic of Congo. The question is where the next war will be, since we know from bitter experience that there is always a "next war."

The visuals of war are mostly male. Certainly the decisions to go to war are made overwhelmingly by men. During the weeks in early 2003, leading up to the second war in Iraq, it was men, dressed in suits, of many nationalities, who debated the war in the United Nations. The one exception was Condoleezza Rice, at that time national security adviser to President George W. Bush; she argued for war as strongly as any of her male colleagues. These men held the fate of a country, a region, and the world in their hands. And while American women soldiers have been implicated in the torture of Iraqi prisoners, war and destruction are still mostly a male occupation.

Dorothee Soelle, a German theologian, asserts that "The women's movement has repeatedly uncovered the connections between male dominance and war, between maleness and self-identification with the warrior, between lust and violence" (Soelle 1990, 9). The violence of war and the violence of rape are one.

How would the world be different if women were fully involved in making decisions on how nations and people relate to each other? Occasionally there are events in which women take a central role in making peace. One very important occasion occurred in the Philippines during 1985, in which women's non-violent demonstrations helped to end the oppressive Marcos regime. And on 9 August 1956, twenty thousand South African women of all races marched peacefully on the South African government's Union Buildings to protest the pass laws. Because women are so seldom part of the peacemaking process, it is hard to judge how their presence in significant numbers in government and the United Nations would change relationships between nations. But we can argue that things could not be any worse than they are now, and so we can hope that the presence of women would make a crucial difference in international relations.

This essay will explore peacemaking from the perspective of women and the implications of a spirituality of non-violence. What resources do we find in the Christian tradition for this demanding commitment? The witness of two women, Evelyn Underhill and Dorothy Day, both pacifists, give an existential grounding to these reflections. Two examples of non-violent actions by South African women show that non-violence is practical and possible. The reflections of a group of women in South Africa on peace and non-violence in their own lives also demonstrate how women approach these life and death issues. The gospel of Jesus includes the challenge to live a non-violent life each and every day.

RESOURCES FOR A SPIRITUALITY OF NON-VIOLENCE

A Gospel Vision

Dorothee Soelle wrote, "In Jesus Christ, God disarmed himself. God surrendered himself without protection and without arms to those who keep crying for more and more protection and arms. In Jesus Christ, God renounced violence. And of course, he did this unilaterally, without waiting for us to lay down our arms first" (quoted in Dear 2003, 58).

One of the greatest tragedies of our times is the complicity of religion in violence and war. The aftermath of the terrorist attacks upon the United States on 11 September 2001 clearly exposed this rhetoric. President George W. Bush used "crusade" language, recalling the wars in the Holy Land during the European Middle Ages, while the language from some Muslim leaders was that of jihad (holy war).

Yet no world religion, including Christianity, worships God as one who is violent and full of hatred for humankind.[1] John Dear, an American pacifist, asserts that "non-violence is at the heart of every religion, because first and foremost, non-violence is at the heart of God" (Dear 2003, 59). For Christians, the gospels provide many resources for a life of non-violence and peace. Jesus taught the challenge of forgiving our enemies (Matt. 5:43–47, Luke 6:27–30), forgiving a brother or sister seventy times seven times (Matt. 18:21–22) and of being peacemakers (Matt. 5:9). As he prepared to go to his own death, Jesus entrusted the gift of God's own peace to his disciples (John 14:27).

Through his life, ministry, and death, Jesus reveals God as the God of love, peace, and compassion, one who suffers with those who experience violence. Our images of God as being "on our side" in war and conflicts (large and small) are projections of our own feelings of anger, mistrust, jealousy, and the desire to do revenge. As Christians, we are embarrassed when we read about the crusades and the battle cry "God wills it" as European kings and warriors made the land where Jesus lived run with blood when they murdered their Muslim enemies. But the violence in our own hearts and writ large in our world today is the same.

Non-violence and peacemaking are sacred duties of faith, not optional hobbies for a few. Since we are all sisters and brothers of the one God who is love, not hatred, we are bound together in a shared humanity. All of life is a gift of God, thus all life, including the lives of those I name as "enemies," is sacred. How can we kill those who are members of our human family?

Yet our hearts are violent. We know this from our own experience every day of dislike, hatred, and anger. We divide people, including other nations, into "friends" and "enemies." The world has an incredible number and kinds of weapons to kill others, but within our own heart are the same weapons. Thus, to be nonviolent means to begin to disarm our own hearts and to meet others as friends, not enemies. The witness of Nelson Mandela, who offered the hand of reconciliation to the whites of South Africa—the architects and the beneficiaries of apartheid—was striking because it is so rarely seen. Our armed hearts say, "Destroy those who have hurt you" but the gospel says, "Bring peace to all."

We are called to create communities of non-violence, to recreate the church in the image of Christ the peacemaker. The family, the local church community, and church leadership structures are challenged by the gospel to live the same non-violence as Jesus did, to reach out the hand of reconciliation and friendship to anyone, in any place, who seems to be an "enemy" to us.

WITNESSES FOR PEACE:
EVELYN UNDERHILL AND DOROTHY DAY

But is this simply a beautifully sounding theory or soft religious language? Are there Christians who have lived such lives? The witness of two women, Evelyn Underhill and Dorothy Day, are striking examples of the power of the gospel of non-violence.

Evelyn Underhill

Evelyn Underhill, an English Anglican (Episcopalian), is a unique and significant person: a married woman, writer, and spiritual director whose adult life in the twentieth century included a commitment to pacifism from the 1930s until her death in 1941. Underhill was born in Wolverhampton, England, on 6 December 1875, the only child of Arthur Underhill, a distinguished barrister, and Alice Lucy Ironmonger. She was baptized and confirmed as an Anglican, but her family was disinterested in religion.

She was educated at home and at a private school, and later at the Ladies Department of King's College, London. On the eve of her seventeenth birthday she wrote, "I believe in God and think it is better to love and help the poor people around me than to go on saying that I love an abstract spirit whom I have never seen" (Cropper 1958, 5).

Raised in a nominally Anglican family, she gradually began to be attracted to Roman Catholicism. But her husband-to-be, Hubert Stuart Moore, opposed her conversion and she decided to delay her entrance for a year. They were married on 3 July 1907 and later that year Pope Pius X published the encyclical on modernism, *Pascendi Dominici Gregis*. She considered herself a modernist and realized that she could not intellectually compromise herself by becoming a Catholic. In the early 1920s she became a regular Anglican communicant.

As a married woman of her time she supervised a large London house and entertained her husband's business colleagues and their mutual friends. On the surface she was the model of an early twentieth-century dutiful wife. But the reality was quite different, for Evelyn Underhill exercised great influence through her writings, the most important of which is the classic study *Mysticism: A Study in the Nature and Development of Man's Spiritual Consciousness* (1911);[2] through her ministry as a spiritual director; and through her leadership of retreats. After her death in 1941, Archbishop Michael Ramsey said that "she did more than anyone else to keep the spiritual life alive in the Anglican Church in the period between the wars" (Greene 1991, 5).

Underhill's writings describe a mysticism of love as surrender to the mystery of love who is God. Such surrender is active and practical, involving the whole person. Mysticism is a real experience of both head and heart, for the person is transformed through union with the living God. The fruits of this union include a non-violent, pacifist life. During the 1920s Underhill became ever clearer about the relationship between one's life of prayer and one's commitment to active charity, but she was very reluctant to be associated with specific political or religious causes.

This changed dramatically to a pacifist commitment in the 1930s as the war clouds first gathered over Europe and then burst forth in 1939. She had supported Britain's involvement in World War I as an expression of her patriotism, and she worked in the office of Naval Intelligence for Africa as a translator and writer of guidebooks.

But in the 1930s her position changed. By 1932 she was supporting European disarmament and in 1936 she became a member of the Peace Pledge Union and the Anglican Pacifist Fellowship. Her patriotism was now expressed as a commitment to pacifism and most of the writing that she did in the last few years of her life concerned the Christian's response to war.

Evelyn Underhill made a pacifist commitment and urged other Christians to do so because she came to understand that pacifism in the face of violence is the proper way to express the love of God. To love God means to give ourselves completely in love. She wrote, "The doctrine of non-resistance is after all merely a special application of the great doctrine of universal charity. . . . It is a courageous affirmation of Love, Joy and Peace as ultimate characters of the real world of the spirit; a refusal to capitulate to the world's sin and acquiesce in the standards of a fallen race" (Underhill 1988: 205–206).

She was truly disturbed by the church's response to World War II and saw the faith of the church as very weak in the face of such great evil as the war. Its life of faith was so feeble and ineffective that it sought to please people, especially those in power, not God, and was afraid to risk and to suffer. She wrote, "We are forced to the bitter conclusion that the members of the Visible Church as a body are not good enough, not brave enough to risk everything for that which they know to be the Will of God and the teaching of Christ" (Underhill 1940).

Pacifism, she wrote, can only be sustained by a supernatural faith that "love is the ultimate reality and must prevail" (Underhill 1943, 1989, 288). She wanted every Anglican who believed that Christianity had a commitment to peace to join the Anglican Pacifist Fellowship. Her pacifism had an eschatological vision, for the pacifist was the forerunner and precursor of a world yet to come.

Some of the very last things that Evelyn Underhill wrote were prayers for a prayer service on peace in the time of war. She died

on 15 June 1941, in the midst of World War II in Europe and
before the war had spread to the Pacific area and the atomic bomb-
ing of the Japanese cities of Hiroshima and Nagasaki and the
post-war revelations of the Holocaust. Her own journey from
patriotic support of World War I to a strong pacifist commitment demonstrates that the spirit of peace can and does change
hearts and lives.

Dorothy Day

Dorothy Day was born on 8 November 1897 in Brooklyn,
New York to Grace Satterlee Day and John Day. She was the
middle child of five siblings. Her father was a sports writer, and
when Dorothy was six, the family moved to Oakland, California,
so that he could take up a new job. But the newspaper plant was
destroyed in the San Francisco earthquake of 1906 (an event that
she remembered all her life) and the family moved to Chicago.

Like many American families of the time, the Day family were
nominally Protestant, but seldom attended church. When Dorothy was ten she began to sing in the choir of the local Anglican
Church, and was then baptized and confirmed.

Her family valued reading, education, and writing, and she inherited her parents' love of literature and her father's writing tal-
ent. As a teenager, she began to read accounts of the class struggle
in the United States and England, and Upton Sinclair's novel *The
Jungle*, which described the conditions in the stockyards in Chicago where she was living at the time. As a university student, she
wrote for a local paper and began to observe the social conditions
of the times and the gap between the rich and the poor. Her profound social conscience was growing and she joined the Socialist
Party at the university. Her years of formal academic study ended
when she was eighteen since her family moved to New York. She
began to write for the *New York Call*, a socialist newspaper. In
1917 she was arrested for the first time when she joined a suf-
fragist protest at the White House in Washington, D.C.

Her next years were a time of searching, drifting, and relationships that turned sour. Friends remembered that she talked

of God and, indeed, seemed "haunted by God" (Allaire and Broughton 1995, 17). She lived a common-law marriage with Forster Batterham. Although they had similar political views, he was upset by her growing interest in religion. To her joy, she became pregnant, but Forster was upset, since he opposed having children (his own, and those of anyone else). Day had become increasingly interested in Catholicism, which deepened the conflicts between them, especially since she had decided to have their child baptized. Their daughter, Tamar Teresa, was born in 1926.

The tensions increased between Dorothy and Forster and he left her in 1927. She was then conditionally baptized and entered the Catholic Church. After a few years of traveling in California and Mexico, she eventually returned to New York. It was 1932 and the Great Depression had descended upon the United States.

A Prayer Answered

In December she was sent on an assignment by the Roman Catholic journal, *Commonweal*, to cover a hunger march in Washington, D.C., organized by the Communists to call for legislation to combat the growing social injustices that the Depression was unveiling. As she watched the marchers, she felt the distance which her conversion had brought into her life: "I could write, I could protest, to arouse the conscience, but where was the Catholic leadership in the gathering of bands of men and women together, for the actual works of mercy that the comrades had always made part of their technique in reaching the workers?" (Day 1952, 165).

After the march finished on 8 December, she went into a church and prayed in desperation an entreaty, "There I offered up a special prayer, a prayer which came with tears and anguish that some way would open up for me to use what talents I possessed for my fellow workers, for the poor" (Day 1952, 166).

When she returned to New York, Peter Maurin was waiting for her at her apartment. Her true call in life was about to unfold.

The Catholic Worker Movement

Maurin, born in France, had been a teacher, an itinerant worker in Canada, and a caretaker at a boys' camp. He was convinced that the social teachings of the Roman Catholic Church had the power to change the social order and to remake society. He thus introduced Day to the riches of the Christian tradition on economic and social issues. In one sense, everything that Dorothy Day did from that day in December 1932, when she met Peter Maurin, to her death on 29 November 1980, was simple and all of one piece: editing and writing for *The Catholic Worker* newspaper; founding houses of hospitality where the poor could be fed and housed; running soup and bread lines; writing books and articles; protesting the social injustices of each decade, from the Depression to the struggles of the farm workers in the 1970s. She lived a pacifist commitment during World War II and throughout her life, protesting nuclear weapons in actions that included some time in jail. The fruits of her intense life of prayer were clearly shown in her life.

The values that are at the heart of the Worker's vision—voluntary poverty, community, love for all especially the least, personal responsibility, pacifism and non-violence—are woven from the "sincerity and seamlessness of her life" (Roberts 1984, 5).

A Pacifist Commitment

The most controversial dimension of Dorothy Day's vision was her complete and total pacifist commitment. It has been said that "before Dorothy Day there was no Catholic pacifist theology" (Riegle 2003, 43). She built her position strictly on gospel principles: Jesus was non-violent and thus every Christian is called to be the same. She rejected the "just war" theory, dating from Augustine of Hippo, which set down conditions under which war could be waged.

This was a consistent position throughout her life as the challenges of war and injustice changed: opposition to the Spanish

Civil War, to World War II, to civil defense drills in the 1950s, to the Vietnam War. The Catholic Worker movement supported those who refused to serve in any way. During the Vietnam War the issue was not whether the war was unjust (that was manifestly clear to her), but how to resist it, including burning draft cards and raids on government offices.

Day took her pacifist position "to the streets on picket lines and in jail and to the common man and woman through her writing and public speaking" (Krupa 2001, 194).

Her commitment of non-violence extended beyond opposition to war as she engaged with the major situations of injustice in American life. She protested the lynching of black Americans when others were silent. She housed striking workers in Catholic Worker houses in order to affirm their right to strike for better working conditions. She recognized the horrors of the Holocaust long before others and denounced the German policy of extermination of the Jews (Krupa 2001, 195). In the pages of *The Catholic Worker* she condemned the incarceration of Japanese-Americans in prison camps during World War II. Her final jail sentence was in 1973 when she was arrested in California for demonstrating in favor of striking farm workers led by Cesar Chavez.

When questioned about her unflinching commitment to peace and non-violence she replied, "We believe that Christ went beyond natural ethics and the Old Dispensation in this matter of force and war and taught non-violence as a way of life" (Krupa 2001, 196).

WOMEN'S WITNESS FOR PEACE

The lives of Evelyn Underhill and Dorothy Day present a striking witness for peace and non-violence. Both affirmed pacifism as the only moral response of Christians to war and violence. Pacifism should not be interpreted simply as a refusal to declare war and participate in war, but as an effective means to change minds and hearts, to oppose policies that violate gospel principles, and to actively change situations that make war and violence possible. These women challenge all people to reflect on why they support violence (direct and indirect), and how they are called to incarnate Jesus' way of non-violence every day.

During the years of the struggle against apartheid, and to the present, South African women have used many non-violent strategies to witness to the need for justice, equality, and peace. Two have been chosen as exemplifying many others. The demonstration against the pass laws on 9 August 1956 and the work of the Black Sash both speak of the power of women's collective, peaceful action. These are not pacifist responses but certainly represent strong and effective non-violent strategies.

Opposition to the Pass Laws

One of the most oppressive parts of the apartheid system was the pass laws and the restrictions on residence and travel they imposed. In September 1955, the government announced that passes were soon to be issued to women. A month later the Federation of South African Women organized their first march on the Union Buildings in Pretoria to protest this new law. They were led by four women, representing the racial complexity of South Africa: Lilian Ngoyi (African), Helen Joseph (White), Rahima Moosa (Asian), and Sophie Williams (Colored). Other demonstrations soon followed: 6,000 in Port Elizabeth, 2,000 in Johannesburg, and smaller groups in Durban, East London, and Cape Town (Walker 1982, 91). Annie Silinga of the ANC Women's League declared that "intimidation does not frighten us and we women are prepared to fight these passes until victory is ours" (Walker 1982, 191). Women resisted the pass laws because of the threat they posed to their homes and children.

When the government began to issue passes to women, they focused on smaller towns. Resistance began to develop in the farming town of Winburg in the Free State. Here the first pass-burnings were held in 1956. More protests followed throughout the country. It is estimated that in the first seven months of 1956 "approximately 50,000 women took part in 38 demonstrations against the pass laws, in 30 different centers" (Walker 1982, 193).

The largest and most famous demonstration, which took place on 9 August 1956 at the Union Buildings in Pretoria, was organized by the Federation of South African Women. It is estimated that 20,000 women participated. They came from all over the country.

> Many of the African women wore traditional dress, others wore the Congress colors, green, black and gold; Indian women were clothed in white saris. Many women had babies on their backs, and some domestic workers brought their white employers' children along with them. Throughout the demonstration, the huge crowd displayed a discipline and a dignity that was deeply impressive. (Walker 1982, 195)

Albertina Sisilu recalled that momentous day,

> As we marched, we collected women. We arranged to meet at Pretoria Station. Our men walked beside us to support us, Nelson (Mandela) and Walter (Sisulu), they accompanied us. When we arrived, the police announced from a loudspeaker that our march was banned. However, we decided to have our meeting. Instead of marching as a group, we walked in ones, twos and threes to the Union Building. I couldn't believe what I saw when I arrived. There was a sea of women, a huge mass, oh, it was so wonderful. (Magubane and Lazar 1993, 39)

Prime Minister J. G. Strijdom refused to meet them. A protest song composed for the demonstration asserted, "Strijdom, you have tampered with the women, you have struck a rock" (Walker 1982, 195).

This powerful act of non-violent protest against an unjust law did not overturn it, which would not happen for many decades, but it asserted boldly and courageously that the women of South Africa knew their rights as human beings and so stood together in peace and solidarity. South Africa remembers their non-violent protest in the celebration of National Women's Day on 9 August each year.

The Black Sash

In 1955 a small group of predominantly English-speaking, white, middle-class women formed the Women's Defense of the Constitution League, later called the Black Sash. These women were outraged at the government's attempts to circumvent the constitution and force through the elimination of the common voters' roll for the "colored population." They developed a common pattern of demonstration: "silent, orderly stands and all-night vigils by women outside public buildings in the main urban centers" (Walker 1982, 174). As a symbol of mourning what was happening in the country, they wore black sashes draped across one shoulder, hence their name. The sight of white women demonstrating against the government enraged many, since "not only were they defying the government, they were also defying a set of unwritten rules about what was seemly and proper conduct for women" (Walker 1982, 174).

After the Separate Registrations of Voters Act was passed in 1956, the Black Sash survived an identity crisis and shifted its focus to become a forceful presence of protest throughout the years of apartheid. In 1977 the Black Sash national conference committed itself to support universal suffrage for all South Africans. In 1983 it stated, that through non-violent and peaceful means, it was committed to:

- Promote justice and the principles of parliamentary democracy in South Africa;
- Seek constitutional recognition and protection by law of Human Rights and Liberties for all;
- Further the political education and enlightenment of South African citizens and others;
- Undertake whatever other activities may further the objectives of the organization (Nash 1983, inside front cover).

For decades, the Black Sash has run advice offices to assist people in dealing with the government and securing the benefits to which they are entitled. This valuable work continues ten years after democracy. The Black Sash has been multi-racial for many years.

PRACTICAL PEACEMAKING

What are the dimensions of peacemaking and non-violence in ordinary life? In a focus group discussion, twelve women representing Lesotho, Namibia, Scotland, South Africa, Uganda, and the United States of America discussed issues relating to leading a non-violent life.[3]

Disarming the Heart

It is a daily challenge to "disarm our heart" and interact with people peacefully. The women shared phrases in their various languages that are deemed violent and offend others. A popular expression in South African English is "battle," as in "I battled to find a parking space." Another violent expression is "I could kill him (her)" as an expression of anger and frustration. This is sometimes said among friends, but one woman commented that if said to others, it can be devastating. The phrase "I could kill for it" means that one really wants something. People insult each other in many ways such as saying "You are brain-damaged" or "You are brain dead."

There are phrases in other languages, such as Sotho, that insult others and are used in daily conversation. The word *bliksem* in Afrikaans means "I hit you" and *voetsak* ("get out of here") is used to chase a dog away, but when said to persons, becomes most insulting. The women were reluctant to say some of the phrases in their mother tongues because they are so abusive, but used English translations as a way to soften and yet convey the violence in some expressions, such as "I will beat you, go to hell with you."

In the discussion, the women recognized how ordinary so many expressions of violence are and how language thus shapes relationships. When I say to a person "I could kill you," this reveals a great deal about the violence in my own heart. Why not use a softer phrase such as "I totally disagree with you"?

The Violence of War

The Ugandan woman had known violence directly and personally. One of her brothers was a soldier in Yoweri Kaguta Museveni's National Resistance Movement during the 1980s in his struggle to gain political power. She said that they knew he could be killed at any time. This brother continues to serve in the Ugandan army, while another brother was "abducted, killed and never buried." She recalled how one time she wanted to go and fight but her father told her, "One gun in the house is enough." Her family was often under threat and they had to stay in the bush at night and decide where to run. Even today she does not like to watch TV newscasts that contain violent scenes, as they trigger painful memories. A South African woman who spent her early years in Kenya remembered the Mau-Mau uprising of the 1950s and how scared she was at night. The white settler community was filled with fear.

This led to a discussion of the causes of war in Africa, which sees seemingly unending conflict. The women spoke of the liberation movements in Africa that sought to end colonialism and bring freedom to the people. Often violence was used. Wars and other conflicts are caused by ethnic differences, the struggle for power in political parties, jealousy, and fear. One of the women from Lesotho commented that poverty is also a cause of violence and that in her country people steal sheep and cattle with guns. Her own family has lost many animals in this way. Religion and ethnicity are causes of war as the situation in Darfur in the Sudan poignantly illustrates, and the equally menacing way that the Rwandan genocide speaks to the power that hatred has in destroying the lives of others.

Does the violence of war achieve anything? The Ugandan woman said that after the war ended in 1986, living conditions got better. For example, her family had electricity restored after being without power for six years. But wars beget wars, and in northern Uganda the Lord's Resistance Army (LRA) uses the abduction of children as a key part of its violent tactics. Here a cycle of revenge and violence continues since children are brought up to revenge families who had members killed and/or raped. Children learn that violence is "effective" and sometimes they too are only too willing to kill and rape. Nigeria has its religious tensions between Christians and Muslims that are often ignited by small incidents.

The litany of wars in Africa goes on and on and on. How will the people of Angola, Burundi, the Democratic Republic of Congo, Ivory Coast, Liberia, Rwanda, Sudan, and Uganda be healed?

Women and Conflict

The women shared some experiences in which women can resolve conflicts non-violently. In Zulu culture, women have traditionally been able to stop fights by falling over the person being beaten. One of the women mused that this may be due to respect for women as "the persons who bring children," the life-givers, although this respect is somewhat diminished today. This tradition is also known among the Sotho people and in Uganda. A Sotho woman described how her brother was being beaten up by several men. A woman heard the noise, stepped into the fray, put a blanket over her brother, and probably saved his life.

In Swaziland the king imposed his brother as a chief over the people. The women indicated their opposition by showing their backsides to the chief. The killing and deporting of people stopped. The men said, "We gave the women permission." Namibian women supported the war for independence by cooking for and aiding the soldiers. The Namibian woman said that without the women's efforts "there would be no independence." The women commented that in Africa, women are generally seen as symbols of peace.

Peacemaking at the Personal Level

The influence of one person to halt wars is minimal, to say the least. But all persons find themselves in conflicts with others over important or trivial matters. The discussion surfaced some very practical strategies for making peace and resolving conflicts.

Timing is important. Do not approach the other person when you are still very angry, but wait until you are less agitated. The other person also has to be ready to speak. When you do talk with the other person, focus on the behavior of the person; do not accuse her or him personally. Do not blame the other person. This leads to defensiveness, and the spiral of violence, especially in verbal forms, will continue. Express your feelings and apologize for your role in the conflict.

If the issue is very serious and emotional, perhaps a third party is necessary to help the two persons talk to each other. The discussion included descriptions of how the air can be poisoned in families, in hospitals, in church communities, and in religious congregations through conflict. Conflicts between parents, such as those over money, spill over into the lives of the children and sometimes they are forced to take sides.

Peacemaking challenges us in very ordinary experiences. Commenting on South Africa's dangerous drivers, one woman said that her strategy is to "leave it and smile" at drivers who nearly cause accidents.

Learning to Be Peacemakers

The women shared a number of scripture texts that help them to be peacemakers. The example of Abraham and Lot dividing the land peacefully (Gen. 13:8–9) shows that contentious issues of possession and greed do not have to be solved violently. The Beatitudes challenge us to be peacemakers (Matt. 5:9) and this is possible because Jesus has given us his own gift of peace (John 14:27).

The New Testament contains a number of strategies for resolving conflicts. Reconcile with the person who has offended you (Matt. 5:21–25), be willing to forgive even your enemies (Matt. 5:44–46), and do this many times a day. The gift of love makes this possible (1 John 4:7–12). The prayer attributed to St. Francis of Assisi, "Lord, make me an instrument of your peace," also provides inspiration.

Effective Peacemaking

Real peacemaking begins from within since we must be at peace within ourselves in order to bring this gift to others. This emanates from a life of prayer and reflection. One woman commented that "when you meet someone who is truly peaceful, there is an 'aura of peace' around them."

In order for women to be peacemakers, they must be respected in their societies, and the women commented that this is often not the case. A clear sign is the increasing level of violence against women since often men see women as objects for their use and not as real human beings.

Women must be united to be effective peacemakers. An example was cited of the support around the world for the Nigerian woman who was to be stoned to death for adultery. Women's (and some men's) voices spoke loudly of her plight. But often women are afraid to speak because they fear a lack of support.

The group stressed that women bring very important gifts to peacemaking. They are generally more compassionate and so societies expect them to try to achieve peace and unity. They are seen as striving for unity, especially in the family, where the mother tries to bring everyone together without taking sides, and also in many situations of daily life where there is dissension and a breakdown of relationships.

Peacemaking is daunting because it demands so much courage, but without peacemakers every level of society, including the church, falls deeper into unending spirals of physical and psychological violence.

A VOW OF NON-VIOLENCE

A number of years ago, Pax Christi USA, an international Christian peace organization, wrote a "Vow of Non-violence" to assist persons in disarming their heart and becoming peacemakers. Persons make this vow after a time of prayer and reflection; generally it is made for one year and then usually renewed. The text of the Vow reads:

Recognizing the violence in my own heart, yet trusting in the goodness and mercy of God, I vow for one year to practice the nonviolence of Jesus who taught us in the Sermon on the Mount:

"Blessed are the peacemakers, for they shall be called the sons and daughters of God. . . . You have learned how it was said, 'You must love your neighbor and hate your enemy;' but I say to you, 'Love your enemies, and pray for those who persecute you. In this way, you will be daughters and sons of your Creator in heaven.'"

Before God the Creator and the Sanctifying Spirit, I vow to carry out in my life the love and example of Jesus:
    by striving for peace within myself and seeking to be a peacemaker in my daily life;
    by accepting suffering rather than inflicting it;
    by refusing to retaliate in the face of provocation and violence;
    by persevering in nonviolence of tongue and heart;
    by living conscientiously and simply so that I do not deprive others of the means to live;
    by actively resisting evil and working nonviolently to abolish war and the causes of war from my own heart and from the face of the earth.
    God, I trust in Your sustaining love and believe that just as You gave me the grace and desire to offer this, so You will also bestow abundant grace to fulfill it. (Pax Christi USA, n.d.)

CONCLUSION

It is much easier to make war than to make peace. Violence is often the first human response to insult and injury, perceived or real. But the gospel calls Christians to something far different: a non-violent life. The pacifist witness of women such as Evelyn Underhill and Dorothy Day challenges us to examine how much violence there is in our hearts. The efforts of South African women to use non-violent action in the face of injustice are important chapters in the history of the struggle against apartheid. Peace-making is not only for the international stage; it is needed daily, since we all meet so many situations in which we have the choice to respond with anger and violence, or with the gentleness and forbearance of Jesus. The decision is ours.

NOTES

[1] All world religions have iconic figures of peacemaking: Thich Nhat Hanh (Buddhism); Dorothy Day and Martin Luther King, Jr. (Christianity); Mohandas Karamchand Gandhi (Hinduism); Abdul Ghaffar Khan (Islam); Abraham Joshua Heschel (Judaism); The Baha'i, Jains, Quakers, Shinto, Sikhs, and the indigenous religions of Africa, North America, and the Pacific Islands all witness to peacemaking (see Dear 2003, 59).

[2] Evelyn Underhill was a prolific writer. In addition to her three novels, she produced forty books, editions, and collections, and more than three hundred and fifty articles, essays, and reviews (see Greene 1991, 37). *Mysticism* is her best known work. She also translated and edited critical editions of some of the mystics: *The Cloud of Unknowing* (1912), Richard Rolle's *The Fire of Love* (1914), Jan Van Ruysbroeck, *The Adornment of the Spiritual Marriage, The Sparkling Stone, The Book of Supreme Truth* (1916) and Walter Hilton's *The Scale of Perfection* (1923). Her last major work was *Worship* (1936).

[3] This discussion was held on 6 May 2004 among a group of women students and lecturers at St. Joseph's Theological Institute, Cedara, KwaZulu-Natal, South Africa.

REFERENCES

Allaire, James and Rosemary Broughton. 1995. *Praying with Dorothy Day*. Winona, Minnesota: Saint Mary's Press/Christian Brothers Publications.

Cropper, Margaret. 1958. *Evelyn Underhill*. London: Longmans, Green and Co.

Day, Dorothy. 1952. *The Long Loneliness*. San Francisco: Harper and Row.

Dear, John. 2003. "Our God Is a God of Non-Violence: Peacemaking Religion in a War-Making World." *Grace and Truth* 20 (2): 58–68.

Greene, Dana. 1991. *Evelyn Underhill: Artist of the Infinite Life.* London: Darton, Longman and Todd.

Krupa, S. T. 2001. "American Myth and the Gospel: Manifest Destiny and Dorothy Day's Non-Violence." In *Dorothy Day and the Catholic Worker Movement.* Edited by William J. Thorn et al. Milwaukee: Marquette University Press, 184–200.

Magubane, Peter, and Carol Lazar. 1993. *Women of South Africa: Their Fight for Freedom.* Boston: Bullfinch Press; Little, Brown and Co.

Nash, M. 1983. *Law Without Justice: A Dangerous Prospect.* Johannesburg: Black Sash.

Pax Christi USA, n.d. "Vow of Non-Violence."http://www.paxchristiusa–.org/news_events_more.asp?id=55 (accessed 9 June 2004).

Riegle, Rosemary G. 2003. *Dorothy Day: Portraits by Those Who Knew Her.* Maryknoll, New York: Orbis Books.

Roberts, Nancy L. 1984. *Dorothy Day and the Catholic Worker.* Albany: State University of New York Press.

Soelle, Dorothee. 1990. *The Window of Vulnerability: A Political Spirituality.* Translated by Linda M. Maloney. Minneapolis: Fortress Press.

Underhill, Evelyn. 1940. *The Church and War.* England: Anglican Pacifist Fellowship.

———. 1943, 1989. *The Letters of Evelyn Underhill.* Edited by Charles Williams. Westminster: Christian Classics.

———. 1988. *Evelyn Underhill: Modern Guide to the Ancient Quest for the Holy.* Edited by Dana Greene. Albany: State University of New York Press.

Walker, Cheryl. 1982. *Women and Resistance in South Africa.* London: Onyx Press.

11

Stand Up and Walk,[1]
Daughter of My People

Consecrated Sisters of the Circle

Sr. M. Bernadette Mbuy Beya

INTRODUCTION[2]

In some African countries the birth of a girl-child is still considered to be bad luck. This is an enduring example of deeply engrained sexism. We long for this to change. Our entry into the third millennium does not seem to be a triumphant one. Can we tell God that our birth into the world is a happy event? We often remain powerless when witnessing the victory of evil over good. It is not only in old ways and traditions that this is apparent; it sometimes seems as if human beings seek to harm and destroy themselves by using ultramodern technology. Today, because of technology and highly advanced communication, one cannot ignore the troublesome realities such as drug and alcohol abuse, pedophilia, and pornography. The way the world tackles questions that relate to sickness, suffering, euthanasia, death, abortion, homosexuality, marriage and family life cast trouble in our hearts. This moral crisis is an issue for everyone, even those of us living in community. We all saw the shocking images on television of American soldiers torturing Iraqi prisoners. Yet, ironically, the American government still pretends to be the champion of democracy as it tries to police good governance and human rights for the rest of the world. Clearly, change in the world does not always promote the humanity of every human being.

Many people are afraid of the cycle of violence that we are witnessing. The state of the world leads us to ask desperate questions. Is our world a heartless world without mother and without God? What of those who are different from us? Do we have to accept with impunity that they have no right to live? As consecrated women of the church, is not our role to give heart to society? But, how can we do this?

Realizing that the humanization of the world lies in the hands of women, I have recently been involved in a leadership training program for women. Since we women give life, it is also our duty to protect it. We have this duty, despite the fact that the role of women may seem outdated in light of the current medical technological developments in reproductive health and the growing illiteracy among women in some two-thirds world countries. The aim of this program[3] was, "To promote the emergence of new female leadership ready to make a difference, capable of setting up and leading the whole society (men and women) towards a social alternative based on justice, peace, forgiveness, reconciliation, responsibility (at all levels) and solidarity, the fruit of which should be universal fraternity (and sorority!)."

I first met Mercy Amba Ewudziwa Oduyoye in Mexico in December 1986 during a gathering of the women members of the Ecumenical Association of Third World Theologians (EATWOT). We were shocked by the silence imposed upon African women and by their resignation to it. Together we began to formulate an idea of how to help African women stand up for themselves. According to my matrilineal line, I am descended from a great chief. As a result, my mother never wanted me to adopt a servile attitude. My mother always required that I make my presence known, in the house and elsewhere.

Today, it is not only a matter of standing up, it is also necessary to begin taking steps toward our own liberation as women created in the image and the likeness of God. As Jesus instructed his disciples, "You give them something to eat" during the dividing of the loaves and the fishes (Mark 6:37), his call is addressed to us also, in terms of the hunger that the African woman suffers: for food, personhood, and freedom. By placing us in the midst of the world, the founder of our Institute of Sainte Angèle invites us to bring the newness of the gospel into daily reality.

THE SECULAR CONSECRATED LIFE
WITHIN A SOCIETY IN CRISIS

I am not going to risk trying to define a secular consecrated life here, but I would like to share my journey as a consecrated woman in the Circle of African Women Theologians. In August 1988, together with eight other African women members of EATWOT, I was invited by Mercy, then Deputy General Secretary of the World Council of Churches, to a meeting in Geneva to examine the possibility of launching a biennial institute of African women concerned about culture and religion. The principal theme was "Arise, African Woman." This was subdivided into six sub-topics: African woman and sexuality; marriage in Africa; Christianity and African rites; African women and the Bible; women's participation in the life of the church; and Jesus Christ and women's liberation.

Participants at this meeting were given the responsibility of developing one of the sub-topics with the aim of mobilizing as many women as possible for the inauguration of such an institute, which was to take place in Accra, Ghana, 23 September to 1 October, 1989.

Nearly eighty women from twenty-four African countries attended the inauguration of the Biennial Institute of Women in Religion and Culture. The objective was clearly defined: "To confront the scarcity of religious literature about women by African women" (Oduyoye 1990, 4). Men and women from outside the continent had written about African women as subjects, but at that stage, the authentic voices of African women were silent. African women theologians were invited to go back to their sources and include African women at the grassroots level in their theological reflections. It was agreed that no barrier would be insurmountable, whether it be language, culture, or religion.

Without going into the details of this conference,[4] suffice to say that many books have been published since the Circle's launch in 1989. Mercy's great achievement has borne much fruit, calling African women, including Roman Catholic sisters, to take common cause with other women of conscience in building a broad, yet strong coalition of solidarity. In her book, *Circle Thinking: African Women Theologians in Dialogue with the West* (2003),[5] Carrie Pemberton expresses appreciation for the contribution of Roman Catholic sisters as women and mothers in the Circle.

My particular vocation as a consecrated woman of the church is to make Christ present within daily life. It is a call that resembles that of a mother or a single woman in other societies. The major difference is that I have chosen to express this call by a complete engagement in the service of the church and of the world, as yeast in dough. The meaning and importance of consecration is explained in *Repartir du Christ* (Eucharistic Presence of Christ), a document that describes in detail the role of consecration in a secular world. As it states, "There exists in the present world an urgent need for a prophetic witness based on the primacy of God and the good to come" (Tequi 2002) The crux of its argument concerns seeking God through faith and inviting other human beings to draw near to God. "The hidden and prolific presence of the consecrated, men and women, who have the experience of old age, loneliness, sickness and suffering, is too significant" (Tequi 2002).

It is important to consider the difference between the commitment of the consecrated and the good deeds of humanitarians. In his book *L'Illusion Humanitaire*, Bernard Debré thoroughly criticizes the plethora of global humanitarian organizations that have misappropriated liberalism for purposes not even vaguely humanitarian. As a result, women and men have lost their sense of compassion, solidarity, and even a proper work ethic! (Debré 1997, 8). What this means is that such organizations give an impression of maintaining and promoting conflicts to legitimate their presence.

The consecrated life itself is questioned in a secular society. The consecrated have to courageously face problems such as growing old and the widening of the generation gap, something that affects the whole of society. There is also the problem of fewer and fewer young people choosing to take up religious vocations; hence the average age of individuals in religious communities has become much higher.

There are other pressing problems facing society at large. The use of birth control since the 1960s has not solved the problem of a radically increasing global population. There is also a high incidence of neglect of the aged, who should receive respect. This was tragically exemplified during 2003, when a severe heat wave in the Congo caused the death of many elderly people living in unacceptable conditions. In some cases, families did not arrange for their funerals, leaving it to the public services to take responsibility. We are also confronting the phenomenon of street children. In light of all of these tragic social ills, one could ask, "What has become of the African family?" In times gone by, Africa was proud of its familial system in which each member had respect for the other. According to that system, abandoned children and elderly people without support did not exist. Children used to receive education in their families, where they learned the meaning of community, how to take care of one another, and a healthy respect for tradition. Little remains of this education, following the devastation of HIV/AIDS and the destruction of economies by corrupt political systems.

While the European Union represents opportunities for its member countries, it remains a threat to the survival of the poor, particularly those in developing countries. Africa is facing the immorality of poverty, created in part by modernization and a globalized economy driven by greed and consumption. Meanwhile, there is an urgent need for investment in scientific research to fight HIV/AIDS and other diseases and to provide generic medicines to the poor. Our call as consecrated women enjoins us in the fight for the equitable sharing of land resources, for economic justice, and for human rights.

Africa had a keen sense of family, the sacred, life, and living in community. Our ancestors lived in a world where their culture was protected from Western realities. Today, across Africa, there are endless wars whose principal victims are women and children. The tragic testimonies of women who have been displaced by war are overwhelming. Women and children are used as shields of war. This is an example of the defilement of the sacred, of women, and of life itself. We are reluctantly immersed in this modernity and, yet, many hesitate to relate to the positive African traditions.

A striking example of the move away from positive African traditions is apparent at some funeral ceremonies. It is too often the case that widows are seen to be part of the goods to be distributed among the family members of the deceased. Sometimes the widow is sent back alone to her own family (that she left many years before), without her children and empty-handed. Despite the sad evidence of such dehumanizing practices (see Nwachukwu 1992), little concern is voiced. It seems as if being African justifies this lack of dignity for the living, and for the dead.

The system of living in community inherited from our ancestors, though very positive, tends to become a prison when it comes to challenging some traditions that need to be changed. A characteristic example of this is the preference of peasants to work on the farms of rich farm owners from the city, rather than cultivate their own lands, lest the community view their self-assertion and motivation unfavorably.

Our profound instability comes from the fact that received values are no longer respected. In days gone by, one could not imagine that questions about corruption, financial mismanagement, same-sex marriage, divorce, and so forth would be discussed in the public arena in so-called Christian or civilized countries. In the Congo these issues are not discussed at all, even by churches.

Fratricidal wars that take place in the Democratic Republic of Congo are encouraged and even revived by manufacturers and arm dealers who benefit from such conflicts. Not only does this endanger the population, but it is also continuously impacting the standard of living of the poor. What is most ironic is that these merchants of death pretend to be the ones demonstrating democracy and peace. All Congolese are conscious that it is necessary to end this escalating violence of which women and children are the principal victims. What we are missing is the true will for peace and the support of the international community and its institutions that have the ability to provide peaceful solutions to such conflicts.

All kinds of violence are present in the world today. Not a single day passes when the television does not show images of murder, suicide missions, hostage taking, and religious intolerance. The twenty-first century is bringing tears and sorrow. Who will wipe the bloody tears of the Israeli and Palestinian mothers who spend their time burying their dead, victims of the escalation of violence initiated by the second *intifada*? Other mothers in Buenos Aires, Argentina, meet at the Place of Mary to keep alive the memory of those who have been kidnapped or killed because of their opposition to a totalitarian regime. It seems that there is a category of people who do not have the right to live in peace because of their caste, religion, family, tribal group, or political convictions. There is another category of people—a minority—who claim all the rights and privileges and hold the rest of humanity hostage. This constitutes a real challenge to our faith.

We must ask ourselves some difficult questions in order to offer a radical and healthy alternative. What kind of training is needed for consecrated people living in such a context of violence, oppression, and exploitation, where there is such a lack of respect for life and overwhelmingly pervasive negative values? And how can we implement it?

WHAT THE CIRCLE BRINGS
TO THE CONSECRATED LIFE

In our countries, where there are limited opportunities for training, it is a good idea to send candidates into institutions of spirituality or to send lay people engaged in the church to colleges that offer science of religion courses. But all training requires the payment of tuition fees, which is an obstacle to some of our candidates. In my experience, the Circle has revealed itself to be a place of excellent training for concerned women. I have gained the strength and courage needed to be involved in society and in the church. Thanks to the Circle, I have learned to identify those forms of violence that victimize women and to develop appropriate strategies of resistance. We must scrutinize the church as well, because it constantly needs to be reclaimed as a source of justice, liberation, and of internal peace.

One of the strengths of the Circle lies in the guidelines that it offers toward an orientation of freedom and the empowerment of women. The Circle provides us space to be true to ourselves, despite the fact that this initiative is rendered difficult by a socioeconomic context of immense poverty. This is further complicated by a majority of people who desire to live an easy life without risk or effort. But the Circle refuses failure in its task and it confronts head-on the absence of human values, morals, spirituality, and ethics in a society in crisis.

One of the principle tasks of the consecrated life is to free women's speech and to help women become aware of the reality in which they find themselves. The Circle has succeeded in this difficult task because of Mercy's courage and determination. The challenge she launched in 1989 has been well sustained.

The organization of the "Women of Katanga" in the Democratic Republic of the Congo (DRC) has been very active in mobilizing women—including consecrated women. It organized a march in early 2004 with the theme of "Fighting Sexual Violence Because It Victimizes Women and Children." This was an opportunity for consecrated women to demonstrate our solidarity with the survivors of domestic violence. There is no possible compromise where rape is concerned and there is no time to waste. Too many have already suffered.

The consecrated woman is sometimes unaware of the power she possesses. Because she has the privilege of living at the rockface of misery and because she possesses the ductility for working efficiently, she possesses a particular vocation to work toward the eradication of violence against women and children. Consecrated women have a significant role to play in the world. Due to their training and their social position, the consecrated are called to Christianize their own families and their neighborhoods. They can challenge the rites that affect women's lives and play a critical role in peaceful conflict resolution in the home and at the national level. They can encourage dedicated lay people to engage in all sectors of political and social life. Little by little, they should be engaging in all places where women live and fight for their survival, refusing to allow themselves to be swallowed up by their surroundings or their immediate problems so that they can become a source of abundant life.

In our institute, each member is engaged in a particular sector (according to her capacities and her personal charisma) in the promotion of women and in the struggle against poverty and misery. Because we live in the midst of and with the people of God and because we work together in the same institutions to earn our living, we are as concerned as the community about the fight for justice and peace. In my capacity as a member of the Circle, I participate in diverse political activities concerning women. Our religious house, which is called Bonne Espérance (Good Hope), is a refuge for people in difficulty. We organize all Circle meetings in this house in order to encourage women's oral and written expression skills. We have brought together women from different backgrounds and circumstances to facilitate dialogue and sharing. Consecrated women should not only console and reassure, we must also question and denounce all practices contradictory to the gospel and testify to our fidelity to Jesus Christ.

The secular consecrated life in Africa is still attempting to carve out a new identity. There is no model available for a single woman who lives alone but wants to live like other women in her community. She is criticized and discouraged because her celibacy appears to be nonsensical, particularly since the myth of fidelity within celibacy has been exploded by HIV/AIDS, which has killed priests and nuns alike. This is a concern of many communities in Africa. We had the opportunity to discuss the issue of HIV/AIDS and its effects on the life of religious communities during a seminar entitled "Sister-to-Sister" at the May 2003 All Africa Conference. Organized by the religious sisters in Nairobi, it was specifically convened to discuss this pressing issue.

What we drew from this was a deep sense of solidarity between the sisters of South East Africa. We determined that we must not judge, but rather attempt to have a vision of chastity that puts us in a position of hospitality, and openness to others. We recognized that a deep chasm sometimes exists between what we would like to be and what we are in reality. We also recognized that we can only be transformed by and through the grace and mercy of God.

What can we do in order to resist all the pressures that are placed upon us? On the one side, we have wealthy politicians who think they are capable of buying even the heart and soul of the religious community and, on the other, clergy who are tired of celibacy. The rape of nuns by priests is a phenomenon we must denounce wholeheartedly. But we must also address the issue in terms of dedicated laypersons who are not protected by the structures of community life. Catholics for Free Choice sent us a document that relates to this question. During our 2004 Mission House Annual Retreat, we chose to confront this difficult issue in order to educate and protect ourselves. The Circle is a network of women that has given strength to many African women as it promotes good and strong relationships and solidarity as we deal with this and other complicated real life crises.

We live in a world where plunder goes without punishment. In the DRC, a U.N. report has revealed an overwhelming list of the dignitaries in power and foreigners who unscrupulously plundered the riches of the country while the majority of people live in misery. The work of the consecrated, therefore, is to fight corruption and bring back moral values. Raising and shaping consciousness becomes an imperative in a context where there is tendency to rationalize everything (Valadier 1997, 28).

In August 2002 we attended the Pan African Conference of the Circle in Addis Ababa to talk about AIDS in a concrete and realistic manner. A woman from Togo shared with us about circumcision in Africa. Having given weight to her presentation, she showed a terrible video where we saw a very young girl being circumcised without anesthesia. The film showed a collective circumcision of adult women with the same unsterilized implement.

Following the conclusion of the video, there was a stunned silence in the hall. Those who were more sensitive simply began to cry. But crying is not a solution; rather, we must seek ways of putting an end to a practice that mutilates and humiliates women. Fortunately, in the Congo this practice is virtually nonexistent. But we must express our solidarity with African women who are experiencing circumcision and fighting against it.

Consecrated women should not live on tiptoe at the periphery of the world to which they too belong. They must commit themselves to work toward the coming of a better world. Their hope can give them the necessary boldness to venture off the beaten track so that they can tackle the future with a new outlook as they demonstrate the tenderness and mercy of God within a broken world.

CONCLUSION

The consecrated feminine life is a gift from God to the churches in Africa. For the sake of survival, many international congregations have opened their doors to African girl children from the beginning of the Second Vatican Council. One of the tasks of religious life in Africa is to Christianize those rites that affect the lives of women. Sr. Ephigenia Gachiri of Kenya fights hard for the abolition of circumcision of women, which is also called female genital mutilation. African women who are subjected to this practice are affected deeply because they are denied their sexuality and therefore their humanity. Unfortunately, the tendency to self-reification (which touches many African women) does not spare nuns who, under the pretext of obedience, risk missing their duty of caring and struggling for the dignity of women.

The African nun is a woman and mother. She is called to give life and to protect the life of her people. Her virginity is not synonymous with sterility and her celibacy is not a protection from using her God-given charisms. On the contrary, it is her liberation toward greater self-sacrifice. As a consecrated woman, my engagement as a theologian on the ground has true meaning.

My vocation is not separate from my constant concern for the liberation of African woman. It is a type of concern that resembles that of a hen, brooding over her chicks.

The hope of the better world that was promised through the resurrection of Christ is not an excuse to fold one's arms. On the contrary, this hope should give us the courage to improve, without delay, this world in which we live. Our hope gives us the certainty that good will eventually triumph over death and evil. Even though we experience the pain of conflicts all around us, we are convinced that the way of dialogue, pardon, and reconciliation always remains possible. "So when you are offering your gift at the altar, if you remember that your brother or sister has something against you, leave your gift there before the altar and go; first be reconciled to your brother or sister, and then come and offer your gift" (Matt. 5:23–25).

Consecrated women, as well as other women, must denounce in loud and clear tones violence against women and children and learn to conquer their fear and guilt. Maybe one day we will be constrained to take the whip in our hand so that the temple of the Spirit may once again be respected. We must become true disciples of Christ in the battle for women's liberation, rights, and justice.

The practice of evangelical councils is made very difficult because of our socio-economic and cultural context, but it is not impossible. The consecrated woman must dissociate herself from the struggle for power and have her own unique ambition to bring the gospel and humanity into her neighborhood and workplace. She must shine through the testimony of a sober life generously given so that there may be justice, sharing, love, peace, and prayer in this secularized world.

The Circle has offered a space where women have found the power and the force to appropriate their own history, and to express its content in their own words. Thank you very much, Mercy, for giving your life to this noble cause. The lack of women's rights has killed more women than any physical malady; hence, you have made an immense contribution to improving the health and life of the African woman.

NOTES

1 Taken from Matthew 9:5.
2 This text is a sharing of my own life experience as a Catholic theologian and consecrated woman of the church.
3 Program of Training at the Institute of Spirituality, Maria Malkia.
4 See Chapter 1 for a fuller description.
5 It should be noted that Pemberton's book has posed problems for some Circle members, including Mercy Oduyoye.

REFERENCES

Amoah, Elizabeth. 1997. *Where God Reigns: Reflections on Women in God's World.* Accra: Sam-Woode Ltd.
Debré, Bernard. 1997. *L'illusion Humanitaire.* Paris: Editions Plon.
Gachiri, Ephigenia W. 2000. *Female Circumcision with Reference to the Agikuyu of Kenya.* Nairobi: Paulines Publications Africa.
Mbuy Beya, M. Bernadette. 1998. *Woman, Who Are You? A Challenge.* Nairobi: Paulines Publications Africa.
Nwachukwu, Daisy N. 1992. "The Christian Widow in African Culture." In *The Will to Arise: Women, Tradition and The Church in Africa.* Edited by Mercy Amba Oduyoye and Musimbi R. A. Kanyoro. Maryknoll, New York: Orbis Books.
Oduyoye, Mercy Amba. 1990. "Introduction." In *Thalitha Qumi: The Proceedings of the Convocation of African Women Theologians.* Edited by Musimbi R. A. Kanyoro and Mercy Amba Oduyoye. Ibadan, Nigeria: Daystar University Press.
————. 1997. *Transforming Power: Women in the Household of God.* Accra: Sam-Woode Ltd.
Oduyoye, Mercy Amba and Musimbi R. A. Kanyoro, eds. 1992. *The Will To Arise: Women, Tradition and the Church in Africa.* Maryknoll, New York: Orbis Books.
Pemberton, Carrie. 2003. *Circle Thinking: African Women Theologians in Dialogue with the West.* Leiden: Brill.
Tequi, P., ed. 2002. *Repartir du Christ: Un Engagement Renouvelé de la Vie Consacrée au Troisième Millénaire Editions.* http://www.vatican.va/roman_curia/congregations/ccscrlife/documentsrc_con_ccscrlife_doc_20020614_ripartire-da-cristo_fr.html/ (accessed 22 June 2005).
Valadier, P.1997. *Des Repères pour Agir.* Paris: Editions Desclee/Bellarmin.

12

From Mere Existence
to Tenacious Endurance

Stigma, HIV/AIDS
and a Feminist Theology of Praxis

Denise M. Ackermann

FRAGMENTS FROM TWO WOMEN'S LIVES

"Thembi" died silently in a backroom of one of Johannesburg's suburbs at the age of 29. Her health began to deteriorate; she grew thin, lost her appetite, and then became too weak to get out of bed. "I asked my mother to come from the Transkei to nurse me because my boyfriend had gone back to Maputo. I cannot tell my mother that I have the 'new sickness.' She thought I had been *toored* [bewitched] and sent for the *sangoma* to rub me with herbs to chase the demons out. Nothing helps. Now I am afraid that Sisi is also sick. What will happen to her? I can't tell my church. They will judge me." Thembi died two weeks later. Her boyfriend arrived in time to bury her. Her daughter Sisi now lives with her grandmother and she is showing signs of being infected with HIV.[1]

Rose (age 30) tested positive in 1999 when she was pregnant with her second child. In 2002 the father of her children died of an AIDS-related disease. "He knew he was infected long ago but he thought being with me would cure him. He lied when I confronted him. He blamed me, even when he was dying. Thank God, my child is negative. The nevirapine helped. I want to make a life for my children. And there are so many others who have nothing. . . . So I thought, How can I help the orphans around me and earn a living at the same time? A friend who is active in the Treatment Action Campaign[2] helped me. We got a small grant and I formed a support group. I now have seven children that I look after. I grow my own vegetables. We have enough to eat and some to sell. Sometimes the church helps us with clothes. My crèche is clean, the children are happy, and God helps me to keep going. Next year we are starting a training program for support groups in my area and I am going to be a trainer and a counselor. We need to learn to speak out about HIV/AIDS and to get proper treatment. I have a life to live for all my children."

These fragments are but two among the myriad of stories of suffering and triumph and they have been chosen to illustrate the concepts of "mere existence" and "tenacious endurance" in the title of this essay. Life in the midst of a pandemic defies the statistics that fill the pages of our newspapers. The ever present specter of sickness and bodily deterioration, the calamitous effects of stigma and judgmentalism, the weekly funerals, the plight of orphaned children, and the deadly combination of poverty and HIV/AIDS are, in a sense, beyond quantifying, except to say that hundreds of people are dying daily of AIDS-related diseases and the very fabric of our society is coming apart.

This essay is dedicated to a woman whose life personifies tenacious endurance. Mercy Amba Ewudziwa Oduyoye has been an initiator, a mentor, and a visionary for all women struggling to reflect theologically on how to champion women's well-being in Africa. Her ability to endure with tenacity and courage is indeed cause for celebration and much gratitude. In this essay I will first explore the meaning of the terms "mere existence" and "tenacious endurance" and the nature of stigma. After setting out what is understood by a feminist theology of praxis, the essay concludes by exploring how stigma can be countered in communities of faith by this theological perspective.

EXISTENCE AND ENDURANCE

The *Oxford Dictionary* defines "existence" *inter alia* as "life, especially under adverse circumstances." I qualify the term by describing it as "mere existence," that is, life that is sometimes brief, sometimes more prolonged, either after being tested and found positive or after the first onset of illness. Mere existence can also mean simply struggling to hold on to life in its last phases. The word "mere" emphasizes the reality that such a life is in stark contrast to a life that is affirming and even transformative.

Mere existence also describes the condition of those people who know that they are HIV+ but who dare not disclose their status and who live in fear and loneliness in their communities. Unable to tell the truth about her condition, Thembi only survived her self-imposed silence for a short while, a tragedy that could have been avoided had she been able to receive appropriate care. Thembi's story raises the problem of silence and stigma that nourish this pandemic. Stigma breeds a stubborn multilayered silence commonly called "the denial" that has characterized this pandemic since its beginning. The reasons for this silencing stigma are complex and raise many questions. Is it about a social acceptance of death in our culture? Is it a reflection of cultural restraints imposed on discussing matters that may in any way relate to human sexuality? Is it related to shame or guilt that comes from religious convictions and social mores? What is clear is that silence and stigma are bed-mates. They do not encourage meaningful survival.

Tenacious endurance is somewhat different than mere existence. Here I am acutely aware of the pejorative meaning of the word "endurance" in feminist circles where it is seen as describing women's lot, a condition of simply having to endure abuse and violation. The *Oxford Dictionary*, however, puts a different emphasis on the word, defining endurance as "duration or continued existence in time; an ability to last, long-suffering, patience, to bear hardship or pain without giving way." This definition introduces the idea of "continued existence," "the ability to last without giving way."

Moreover, the term "endurance" (*hypomone*) occurs in the New Testament, one of the better known instances being in the Letter to the Romans (5:3). Here Paul writes about hope. He states, "And not only that, but we also boast in our sufferings, knowing that suffering produces endurance, and endurance produces character, and character produces hope." Some biblical scholars feel that Paul may have borrowed the term from the Greek Stoics. Others acknowledge that it features prominently in the "martyr" theology of Judaism, reflecting the "double sense of fortitude under suffering and trust in God for ultimate deliverance" (Byrne 1996, 170).[3] I need to admit to an immediate knee-jerk reaction to this verse. "Boasting in suffering" is off-putting in a context such as mine. Furthermore, a favorite ploy of male pastoral caregivers is to counsel women "to endure" situations of abuse in relationships, as if it will make better people of them. Clearly the term "endurance" needs to be rescued from these limited understandings.

For Paul, endurance is a necessary requirement of Christian life and not just a quality that enables people to deal with suffering. Endurance is vital in the cultivation of hope in situations that offer scant grounds for hope. Such hard-won hope can permeate the life of a believer confronting pain and tragedy. We know now that stories of those living with HIV/AIDS are not all stories of silence, stigma, and death; they are also stories of endurance under very difficult circumstances. In these circumstances, endurance does not mean "putting up with suffering." It means bearing suffering with fortitude, courage and tenacity *without giving way to it.*

The odds were stacked against Thembi, robbing her of her ability to endure, as life ebbed from her in her loneliness. Rose's story is more one of tenacious endurance. She has endured because she has come to terms with her condition and has found a vocation that has given meaning to her life. She has experienced solidarity and huge relief from living the truth of her condition. She has found courage to speak the truth, shattering the bonds of silencing stigmas, and she shows a determination to live the life she has to its fullest. She is not "giving way" to her illness, and her determination to help others appears to bolster her ability to endure.

Mere existence, as I have defined it, does not describe life that is lived fully and truthfully or life that affirms our human dignity and worth. It describes a kind of existence in conditions that rob people of their autonomy, and where the daily struggle to deal with stigma, shame, deteriorating bodily functions, discomfort, pain, and fear is overwhelming.

Tenacious endurance, in contrast to mere existence, promises some opportunity, and I repeat some, for human beings to take control of their lives, even in dire circumstances. This affords dignity and meaning to a life despite the fact that it might be infected with the HIV virus. Admittedly, such human autonomy has its limits. Undoubtedly, the ability to use medical means to counteract the effects of the virus immediately promises a better quality of life. There are, however, many South Africans, although HIV+ and not on anti-retroviral treatment, who nonetheless have, by adopting a healthy life style, changed their lives for the better. Such measures clearly have limits, but with determination, courage, the rejection of stigma, and the insistence that life can have meaning, many South Africans are creating fragile, temporary pockets of human endurance.

A FEMINIST THEOLOGY OF PRAXIS

The term "feminist theology" is contestable. There is no one feminist theology just as there is no one male theology.[4] Generally speaking, however, feminist theologies take a special interest in the lives of women, their stories, their hopes, their beliefs, and their experiences of oppression and liberation. Christian feminist theologies want to bring women's lives into the "drama of the Christian message and explore how Christian faith grounds and shapes women's experiences of hope, justice, and grace as well as instigat[ing] and enforce[ing] women's experiences of oppression, sin, and evil" (Jones 2000, 14). Feminist theology in my context takes all women's experiences of oppression and discrimination very seriously, and it extends its concern to include all people who find themselves on the margins of our society and who know the violating effects of discrimination, either on grounds of gender, race, class, ability, sexual orientation, disease or whatever, by remaining continually vigilant about the nature of the interlocking of systems of domination that contribute to such oppression.

A *feminist theology of praxis* requires further explanation. The term "praxis" points to intentional social activity. Rebecca Chopp (1996, 221) describes praxis in Christian feminism as bringing together "a stress on the interconnectedness of historical existence and normative concerns of freedom on the one hand, and responsibility to change oppressive conditions into possibilities for human and planetary flourishing [on the other]. . . ." A feminist theology of praxis seeks not only to reflect on praxis but also seeks "actively to be a *form of praxis* (*emphasis added*) to shape Christian activity around the norms and visions of emancipation and transformation" (Chopp 1996, 222). It is always alert to the experience and place of women in its reflection. "Praxis as a starting point emphasizes the importance of everyday life and human bodiliness, as well as holistic anthropology, in order to overcome the dualisms of private-public (individual-community), and body-soul (matter-spirit)" (Vuola 2002, 98). Christian praxis is based on the willingness to be God's hands in the world, alleviating oppression and forming communities of endurance and hope and new understandings of what constitutes human flourishing. The vision of a world in which God is at home, in which love, justice, freedom, equality, and peace thrive needs more than the prayer "May your kingdom come." It requires the willingness of those who utter this prayer to translate it into deeds. Praxis is a central interpretative lens for my theology.

Feminist theologians have defined the conditions for their praxis. These conditions are first, *accountability*, which means that theologies of praxis are done in the interest of groups of people who experience oppression and discrimination. Second, praxis is conceived in *collaboration* with others whose aims are similar and with other disciplines. Third, all research, learning, and teaching begin with our own *lives-in-relation*. We cannot do theology as isolated individuals but rather as members of particular communities. Knowledge is born in dialogue with others and is contingent on the difference it makes to our lives and to others. Fourth, the *diversity of cultures* is a condition for feminist theological praxis. No theology can be applied universally, as women learned when men's experiences were given universal significance. The last condition is *shared commitment*, because feminist theological praxis is strategic and action-orientated (Cannon et al. 1988, 23-27).

A feminist theology of praxis is explicitly concerned with the ethical when issues such as sexuality and reproduction, violence against women and children, relationships between men and women, and relationships between human beings and nature are pursued. Theology that is explicitly ethical and contextual speaks from specific situations; names experiences; identifies suffering; and articulates possibilities of hope and transformation, testing them within a given moral and ethical framework. The relationships between knowledge, power, and interests are of ethical concern. This makes a feminist theology of praxis self-consciously contextual and historical, and it knows that difference and particularity run throughout its deliberations. Epistemologically, such theology is grounded in a method that in its most profound sense is understood as the unity of knowledge as activity and knowledge as content.

In summary, a feminist theology of praxis begins with the critical analysis of given contexts and a particular focus on how gender roles are understood and lived out. It then seeks to engage contextual situations with liberating and transformative praxis in order to encourage human flourishing, undergirded by the belief that such theology is done in service of furthering God's reign on earth.

STIGMA–A DEADLY MILLSTONE

There is one aspect of the AIDS pandemic that, in my view, is essentially its most explosive aspect, and that is stigma. The social, cultural, and political responses to HIV/AIDS are characterized by the meshing of collective denial and high levels of stigma. When Peter Piot, the executive director of UNAIDS, addressed the tenth meeting of the agency's Program Coordinating Board in December 2000, he described the need for a "renewed effort to combat stigma" as the most pressing item on his agenda for the world community.

In his now classic work, *Stigma: Notes on the Management of a Spoiled Identity* (1963), Erving Goffman defined it as an attribute that significantly discredits a person and that, in the eyes of society, reduces the dignity of the person who possesses it. Such a person lives with an "undesirable difference," one that is often understood as "deviance" or what Goffman describes as a "spoiled identity." Goffman's insights on stigma were groundbreaking. They do, however, require further formulation when applied to the AIDS pandemic. Stigma is not just some kind of "thing" that confers a "spoiled identity" on an individual. Neither is it a static concept. Stigma in the HIV/AIDS context can ultimately be understood only in relation to power and domination, gender and social inequality, and deeply embedded cultural and religious concepts of what it means to be a sexual human being. Stigma never arises in a social vacuum. It always has a history that shapes the form it takes. It is also vital to understand how stigma is used by communities, individuals, and the state to produce social inequality and how this relates to the political and social economy of a community. Rapidly accelerating processes of social exclusion, for example, feed the present radical restructuring of the world economy. They are linked to what is called "informational capitalism." These combined factors have a polarizing effect, particularly on those who live in the developing world. Previous inequalities are reinforced as the gap grows between those who know and those who have and those who do not have access to

information and who live below the poverty line. The poor continue to be stigmatized.

To return to stigma and HIV/AIDS. From the beginning of
this pandemic a series of powerful metaphors have been mobilized around the disease. Richard Parker and Peter Aggleton
(2002, 16) mention the following: AIDS as death, as horror, as
punishment, as crime, as war, as other(ness), as shameful. Parker
and Aggleton (2002, 17-19) also note that the production of
AIDS-related stigma can be associated with 1) class divisions
(AIDS is a disease of the rich or a disease of the poor); 2) gender-
related divisions (AIDS is a woman's disease or a disease caused
by men); 3) race divisions (AIDS is a black plague or AIDS is an
African disease); and 4) sexual relations and divisions (AIDS is a
gay plague). Sexual stigmatization has indeed often been linked
to gender-related stigma and further exacerbated by notions of
sexual promiscuity. Societies have their own ways of describing
disease transmission. Many may be highly scientific and rational
and others may be illogical and unreasonable. Whatever they are,
they are usually fiercely held and difficult to contest. Once HIV/
AIDS is understood as life-threatening, people become afraid.
HIV/AIDS is then linked to behaviors already stigmatized and
often seen as caused by moral fault rather than a virus.

Before concluding this all too brief excursion into the nature
of stigma, it is relevant to add that stigma can be experienced at
different levels. First, there is the societal level where laws, rules,
policies, and administrative procedures have important consequences for HIV/AIDS-related stigmatization. In South Africa,
compulsory testing is not allowed, but there are frequent instances
where people with HIV are excluded from certain occupations
and forms of employment. The South African government's well-
documented negative response to the provision of medication
and its lack of political leadership both contribute to the stigmatization of AIDS sufferers. Second, stigma is also experienced on
an individual level. When it is extended to family, friends, and
faith communities, it is inevitable that those who are HIV+ will
withdraw into silence in order to protect themselves, as Thembi's
story so graphically illustrates. Third, stigma is also internalized.

Cultural and societal understandings, family attitudes, and personal experiences of shame and guilt are deeply absorbed, hindering life-giving responses to stigma.

Finally, in Parker and Aggleton's (2002, 22) words:

> Perhaps the greatest tragedy of all is that HIV and AIDS-related stigmatization causes much of the energy that could be useful to prevent infection to be displaced. People are victimized and blamed, social divisions are reinforced and reproduced, and new infections continue to take place so long as people continue to systematically misunderstand the nature of the epidemic and its causes.

DEALING WITH STIGMA–
FEMINIST THEOLOGICAL PRAXIS IN CONTEXT

Many concerns arise from reflecting on the stories of Thembi and Rose. I shall single out a few that touch on the issue of stigma to illustrate how a feminist theology of praxis can offer pointers for countering the effects of stigma in communities of faith. Critical solidarity with the suffering, a praxis of care for the sick, advocating for treatment for the affected, caring for the needy by providing nourishment and nursing, and taking up the challenge of promoting the care and education of orphans are all vital in combating this pandemic. These tasks cannot be avoided. But for feminist theologians there is also a duty to use the limited space we have within theological discourse. I suggest that a feminist theology of praxis that makes the countering of stigma within faith communities a central focus can, in a context such as mine, contribute to the embracing of tenacious endurance rather than of mere existence for those who are suffering. How might this happen?

The Praxis of Story-Telling

Human beings cannot survive without a narrative identity (Dube 2003, 107-8; Phiri, Govinden and Nadar 2002, 3-12). Our stories are our lives. Telling stories is intrinsic to claiming our identity and, in the process, finding impulses for hope. For those living with HIV/AIDS there is a need to claim and to name their identities in order to move away from the victim status often thrust upon them. Telling our stories also has a sense-making function. The act of telling the story assists the narrator in making sense of her or his experiences in an often chaotic world. Whether stories are revealing in shaping identities or whether they are making sense of situations that call for understanding, they should be heard in churches.

Narrative is the life-blood of a feminist theology of praxis. "Story is the articulation of one's experience in verbal narrative . . . in song, poetry, fiction, (auto)biography, liturgy and sacred texts. . . . The hearing, telling, naming and inclusion of women's stories is necessary to doing our theology; without our stories there is not feminist theology" (Eilts 1996, 278). In Nelle Morton's (1985) memorable phrase, when women are "heard to speech," new images of relationship with the divine and with one another emerge. Might Thembi's circumstances not have been different if her story had been heard while she was still able to tell it? Fortunately Rose's story is an affirmation of the ability to find hope and meaning, which is inspiring to others who carry the virus. Story-telling is, however, not without risk. AIDS claimed its first martyr in South Africa when Gugu Dlamini was stoned to death in her village for telling her story and revealing her HIV status.

Are our faith communities offering opportunity and space for those who are infected to tell their stories and to be heard with respect and compassion? Thembi's experience seems to indicate the opposite. Raising awareness that HIV/AIDS is a disease and not a moral failure is vital to the respect with which these stories should be treated and disseminated. Feminist theological praxis suggests that telling and listening to the stories of those who are suffering, discriminated against, or oppressed is an essential starting point for counteracting silence, denial, and stigma. The stories told in this chapter raise the question of the power of narrative: who speaks, who hears, who interprets what is said, and in whose interest? Caution is called for, as well as respect for the complexity of the life of the narrator, knowing that what is revealed is but a fragment of a life. A feminist theology of praxis is interested in the praxis of listening. Such listening is deliberately empathetic, eschewing the contestable notion of impartiality and practicing listening that speaks of care and solidarity in situations of suffering. It is participative, since the listener may enter the conversation, allowing both the story being told and her (or his) own story to interact and in this process to change. The praxis of listening is linked to an ethic of listening that respects confidentiality, respects anonymity, respects cultural differences, and, when given permission, uses such narratives in the interest of resistance to stigma and discrimination. Lastly, listening requires discernment that is in essence sensitive to the context, to the place and plight of the narrator, and that is aware of other narratives, some of which may paint very different pictures.

The Praxis of Gender Analysis

Stigma is a powerful tool of social control. These women know. A feminist theology of praxis uses gender analysis both to understand and to counteract the dire effects of stigma. This is no easy task. However, a thoughtful feminist analysis of millennia of male-centered traditions and practices, which have discriminated against women, show that their effects have been dire for this pandemic. Gender stereotyping results in ascribing limited cultural identities to both men and women that stigmatize their abilities and roles in society. "Masculinity" is identified with reason, action, and the capacity to rule, while "femininity" is associated with gentleness, passivity, and being auxiliary to men. The effects of traditions and practices based on this sexist understanding of human nature have dire consequences for relationships between men and women. Moreover, sexism is expressed in personal, interpersonal, cultural, economic, legal, and political terms and it is part of an entire social and cultural system with a long history. When sexism in our religious traditions reinforces cultural sexism, women are subjected to male cultural and religious hegemony. This in turn buttresses the disordered relationships between men and women that lie at the heart of this pandemic.

AIDS is in fact a gendered pandemic. As such it requires gender analysis to unravel the complex relationship between culture, gender, and religion and how this unholy trinity contributes to fuelling the pandemic. Women's questionable status in society and in their religious institutions, combined with high incidences of rape and poverty, demonstrate the disordered gender relations that are feeding this pandemic. The combination of poverty and sexism is lethal for poor rural women living in patriarchal societal structures as much as it is for single women struggling to survive in shacks on the outskirts of South African cities. It is not surprising that poor rural women—who have little education and who live in traditional patriarchal relationships—generally lack the skills and the power needed to negotiate safe sex practices. Strategies to deal with HIV/AIDS have failed these women because they insist on preventative behavior that they, the women, have little power to implement. HIV/AIDS too often means rejection, abandonment, exclusion, and shame. African theologian Teresa Okure, in addressing an AIDS symposium in Pretoria in 1998, pointed to the shocking fact that in many African countries being a married woman carries the highest risk of HIV infection. In summary, a gender-based analysis of the roots of stigma is essential. A more insightful understanding is needed of how gender relationships are influenced by cultural and religious traditions and how they can empower women to make different decisions when we choose to enter into relationships.

The Praxis of Mutual Relationship

There is no more central concept in feminist theologies than relationship. It is found at the heart of feminist theologies, feminist ethics, and feminist theory. The nature of the importance of relationship is explored by feminist theologians in, among others, parenting and sexual relationships and relationships at the workplace. Contemporary ecologies and reconstructed cosmologies also tell us that everything in the world is interdependant and interconnected. Our interrelatedness carries with it our responsibility for one another. In the words of Elizabeth Johnson (1994,

184): "Stress on the interrelatedness of all creatures with each other provides the context for responsible attention to the needs of others inclusively, especially therefore those who are most deprived."

However, the moment we affirm the primacy of relationship, we need to ask what it means to be an individual person. Our individuality arises from and is shaped and tempered by our being in relationship with others. We are a mixture of attachment and autonomy; we are both connected yet independent to varying degrees. And there is a tension between our need to relate and the reality of our oneness. Johnson (1994, 226) describes women's challenge in this regard as follows:

It is the emphasis on freedom in personal relation that must not slip from view in the search for right speaking about God and the world. While emerging feminist ontology is articulating the insight that no reality can be construed apart from its constitutive network of relationships, feminist wisdom also emphasizes the importance for every woman of centering herself, affirming herself, and choosing her own life's directions.

This tension is creative when we understand that our personhood comes out of loving relationships with others and that it grows and is nurtured because it is summoned into such loving relationships. We are beings always in the process of becoming more ourselves through our relationships with others.

A feminist theology of praxis, like feminist theological ethics, embraces relationship as a central concept. It begins, on the one hand, with a critique of the historical forms in which relationship has been realized. Such critique focuses on the inequality of power and the unfair patterns of economic sharing that have dogged sexual relations, parental responsibilities, and political systems. Given the gendered nature of the HIV/AIDS pandemic and the disordered nature of relationships in systems that believe that women are men's property, such a critique is timely. On the other hand, a positive understanding of relationship stresses mutuality and interrelatedness. Positive relationships are by nature two-way affairs and interrelatedness implies mutuality between and responsibility for one another. We come to know ourselves by being in relationship with others.

The present blight of HIV/AIDS, greatly exacerbated by denial and stigma, calls for the vigorous affirmation of not only the individuality and dignity of all sufferers, but the fact that being in mutual relationship is at the core of being a human being. Persons living with HIV/AIDS are too often labeled and ostracized. Their individuality is denied as they are identified by the victim status thrust upon them. Sufferers simply become a statistic, an "HIV+" person. Their potential for relationship is cut off at the root when they are evicted by their families, or when women, on revealing their status to their partners, themselves often the cause of the woman's infection, are rejected together with their children and land up on the streets, bereft of support and unable to sustain themselves or their offspring.

Granted the primacy of relationships, the nature of such relationships will determine whether they will result in mere existence or rather contribute to tenacious endurance. HIV/AIDS is often the consequence of relationships gone awry. Morbid and disordered relationships that fester on the abuse of power, sexism, stigma, and betrayal characterize much of the suffering in this pandemic. According to Margaret Farley (1996, 239), what is needed is a new paradigm for human relationships, marked by "equality of power, mutuality of freedom and responsibility, love that is other-centered yet neither neglectful nor destructive of the self, and fidelity."

Body of Christ Praxis

There are a number of metaphors in scripture for the gathering of believers. In his writings, Paul describes such an authentic community in a particularly organic metaphor, the Body of Christ (1 Cor.10:17; 12:2-27; Rom. 12:4-5). Emphasis is laid on the unity of the Body, while acknowledging the multiplicity of its members.

"[W]e who are many, are one body, for we all partake of the one bread" (1 Cor.10:17). According to Jerome Murphy-O'Connor (1982, 179), Paul "saw the Body of Christ not as a functional unity but as a unity on the level of being." The physical body suggests to Paul "the idea of *coexistence* in the strict sense of that much abused term because this conveyed perfectly his understanding of authenticity" (Murphy-O'Connor 1982, 179). The church as the Body of Christ has many limbs, all sharing a common existence because they are related as integral parts of the single whole. To amputate a limb destroys its being and its function; to stigmatize a limb deprives it of its authentic role in the Body; to shame a limb so that it becomes limp and impaired in its functioning contributes to the whole no longer being what it is destined to be. As Murphy O'Connor (1982, 179) puts it so strikingly: "The animation of life has given place to the stillness of death."

Today the Body of Christ is the church with AIDS. We are a body of sick people, invaded by a deadly virus. We diminish the true nature of the church as the Body of Christ when stigma, shame, and judgment characterize our reactions and our relationships with one another. Thembi could not trust the church with her sickness. Her fear of being shamed overpowered her need for care in her last days. When mutual care and trust among members of the Body of Christ are destroyed by the desire to judge and shame, the functioning of the Body is undermined. Every member of the Body has worth and a role to play (1 Cor.12:4-26). The Body of Christ is in grave danger when it does not affirm the value and the role of every single one of its limbs, no matter their HIV status or any other affliction.

The Eucharist is, among others things, a celebration of God's unconditional acceptance of human beings in a world that practices stigma and exclusion. In holy communion the risen and exalted Christ is present, the One whom God sent to redeem the world. In Christ we are reconciled to God and to one another as we are freed from sin—sin as guilt and power—that enslaves us (Welker 2000, 101). The announcement "Glory to God in the highest, and peace on earth among humans on whom God's favor rests" is realized in the holy meal.

There is also a fathomless link between the bodies of Thembi and Rose and millions of other sufferers and the crucified and resurrected body of Jesus Christ whom we remember and celebrate in the bread and the wine. Deep inside the Body of Christ, the virus lurks. As we remember Christ's sacrifice, we see in his very wounds the woundedness of his sisters and brothers who are infected and dying. In Robert Jenson's incomparable phrase, "God deep in the flesh" draws us all into the Body of Christ. Christ is the one who takes the church as his bride, makes it his Body, and through this act sets before us the possibility of relationships in love that are the antithesis of those that deny human flourishing.

After eating the bread and drinking the wine, we pray that we may be sent out into the world in the power of the Holy Spirit "to live and work to your praise and glory." In the context of the HIV/AIDS pandemic, the parable of the Good Samaritan is unequivocal about how we might live and work. We are told to love God, ourselves, and our neighbors (Mark 12:29-31). In this parable we are shown how to minister to those in need. The priest and the Levite are traditionally seen as prime examples of narcissistic self-love—what is mine is mine—while the Samaritan shows true neighborly love—what is mine is yours. The Samaritan is described as "having compassion." Outside the original parables of Jesus this quality is not used of women and men. It describes a divine attribute. Yet in at least three of Jesus' parables it occupies a central place and denotes a human quality. Compassion is shown to be "the basic and decisive attitude in human and hence in Christian acts" (Moessner 1991, 203). Does this parable not mirror an object lesson on a human scale of what the reign of God's grace will be like? It seems to speak of the authentic self-sacrifice that stands at the core of the Christian gospel. What could it mean for all its members if the Body of Christ were to be moved to compassion toward those affected by the pandemic? Should the church not at least be attempting to hasten—if not to mirror—God's reign on earth instead of judging and shaming those in need? Is Rose's care of AIDS orphans not a compelling example of "having compassion"?

Embodied Praxis

This pandemic is all about bodies. A feminist theology of praxis emphasizes the *embodied* nature of our humanity. HIV enters, lurks, and then makes forays into the immune system until ultimately it destroys the body. Suffering, disease, and death are our contextual bodily realities. In Musa Dube's (2001, 59) arresting words:

> Still bleeding and searching for healing, Mama Africa has been struck by a new disease: HIV and AIDS. She is now a nurse. She runs home-based care centers for her dying children and people. She washes them, feeds them, holds them in her arms, and rocks them, singing a little song, while she awaits their death. And when they finally die, she rises to close their eyes, to wrap them and bury them. Mama bears in her own flesh the wounds of their suffering.

Our bodies are more than skin, bone and flesh. Our bodies encompass the totality of our human experience: our thoughts, our emotions, our needs and memories, our ability to imagine and to dream, our experiences of pain, pleasure, power, and difference, as well as our beliefs and our hopes. Our social reality is an embodied reality. The church is an embodied reality. It is also a community of sexual beings. A distorted understanding of human sexuality bolstered by centuries of Christian sexual ethics that have done little more than teach the "don'ts" about human sexual behavior has also contributed to the stigmatization of HIV/AIDS. This pandemic has a great deal to do with how people live out their sexuality. It is simply not good enough merely to preach fidelity and abstinence in sexual relations. This message cannot be heard, understood, or followed as long as it is communicated without a properly constructed debate on what constitutes moral community. If this debate does not take place in religious institutions, if it is silenced by cultural taboos and centuries of Christian moral teaching that has shown little understanding of embodiment, human sexuality will continue to be seen by many as something shameful, and sexual behavior will automatically be stigmatized.

For HIV/AIDS infected women and children whose bodies are in pain, hungry, abused, or rejected, the body is at the center of all political, social, and religious struggles. Paula Cooey (1993, 108) summarizes these struggles as follows:

> Our share in the process of making up a better world, and making it real in the flesh, begins with a mighty groan in protest against the violation of the body—its starvation, its malnutrition, its sexual and vocational exploitation, its imprisonment and torture, it murder, and its use as a battleground for establishing the control over many by a few. For the body has served and still serves as a symbolic and actual focus for much that has been oppressive in patriarchy.

It is vital for the church to embrace an embodied theological anthropology. Otherwise the injunctions of the gospel remain pleasant-sounding theological theories that are not rooted in embodied acts of love and care.

CONCLUSION

In my context, tenacious endurance is possible if those infected with HIV/AIDS can experience the Body of Christ as being in solidarity with them, eschewing stigma, and practicing mutual relationship. A feminist theology of praxis can tackle the question of stigma by embodying the ethical demand for theology that is praxis-oriented. By this I mean that theology, done at arm's length from the reality of the context in which we seek to speak theological words is not worth the paper it is written on. Theologians have to engage the messiness of life by trying to nurture gospel practices in the midst of tribulation. After all, the notion of practice is at the heart of living the gospel. Christians act so that realities are transformed, transfigured, revolutionized, and converted (Forrester 2000, 27).

In the letter attributed to James (1:22-25), the author cautions the faithful:

> But be doers of the word, and not merely hearers who deceive themselves. For if any are hearers of the word and not doers, they are like those who look at themselves in a mirror; for they look at themselves and, on going away, immediately forget what they were like. But those who look into the perfect law, the law of liberty, and persevere, being not hearers who forget but doers who act—they will be blessed in their doing.

An authentic feminist theology of praxis must take its engagement with the "doing of the word" as the measure by which its integrity and its authority will be judged in the community of faith and in the public square. Perhaps then it can contribute to the struggles of those faithful people who seek to endure in daunting circumstances. In this endeavor we would be wise to draw on the example set for us by the life and work of Mercy Oduyoye.

NOTES

[1] Thembi's true name is not revealed to protect her child from being stigmatized in her community.

[2] A non-governmental organization devoted to the treatment and rights of those infected with HIV/AIDS, headed by Zackie Achmat.

[3] Job is regarded as a striking example of the quality of endurance.

[4] The *Dictionary of Feminist Theologies* edited by Letty M. Russell and J. Shannon Clarkson (Louisville: John Knox/Westminster Press, 1996) demonstrates this with its eight different entries for feminist theologies.

REFERENCES

Byrne, Brendon. 1996. *Romans*, Sacra Pagina Series Vol. 6. Collegeville, Minnesota: The Liturgical Press.

Cannon, Katie G. et al. 1988. *God's Fierce Whimsy: Christian Feminism and Theological Education*. New York: Pilgrim Press.

Chopp, Rebecca. 1996. s.v. "Praxis." In *Dictionary of Feminist Theologies*. Edited by Letty M. Russell and J. Shannon Clarkson. Louisville, Kentucky: John Knox/Westminster Press.

Cooey, Paula M. 1993. "The Redemption of the Body." In *After Patriarchy: Feminist Transformations of the World Religions*. Edited by Paula M. Cooey, William R. Eakin, and Jay B. McDaniel. Maryknoll, New York: Orbis Books.

Dube, Musa W. 2001. "Fifty Years of Bleeding: A Storytelling Feminist Reading of Mark 5:24-43." In *Other Ways of Reading: African Women and the Bible*. Edited by Musa W. Dube. Atlanta, Georgia: Society of Biblical Literature.

———. 2003. "Social Location as a Story-telling Method of Teaching in HIV/AIDS Contexts." In *HIV/AIDS and the Curriculum: Methods of Integrating HIV/AIDS in Theological Programs*. Edited by Musa W. Dube. Geneva: World Council of Churches Publications.

Eilts, Mitzi N. 1996. s.v. "Story." In *Dictionary of Feminist Theologies*. Edited by Letty M. Russell and J. Shannon Clarkson. Louisville, Kentucky: John Knox/Westminster Press.

Farley, Margaret. 1996. s.v. "Relationships." In *Dictionary of Feminist Theologies*. Edited by Letty M. Russell and J. Shannon Clarkson. Louisville, Kentucky: John Knox/Westminster Press.

Forrester, Duncan B. 2000. *Truthful Action: Explorations in Practical Theology*. Edinburgh: T. and T. Clark.

Goffman, Erving. 1963. *Stigma: Notes on the Management of a Spoiled Identity*. New York: Simon and Schuster.

Johnson, Elisabeth A. 1994. *She Who Is: The Mystery of God in Feminist Theological Discourse*. New York: Crossroad.

Jones, Serene. 2000. *Feminist Theory and Christian Theology: Cartographies of Grace*. Minneapolis, Minnesota: Fortress Press.

Moessner, Jeanne Stevenson. 1991. "A New Pastoral Paradigm and Practice." In *Women in Travail and Transition*. Edited by Marine Glaz and Jeanne Stevenson Moessner. Minneapolis, Minnesota: Fortress Press.

Morton, Nelle. 1985. *The Journey Is Home*. Boston: Beacon Press.

Murphy-O'Connor, Jerome. 1982. *Becoming Human Together: The Pastoral Anthropology of St. Paul*. Good News Series II, Second Rev. Ed. Wilmington, Delaware: Michael Glazier.

Nelson Mandela Medical School/HSRC. 2002. *Study of HIV/AIDS. South African National HIV Prevalence, Behavioral Risks and Mass Media*. Cape Town: HSRC.

Parker, Richard and Peter Aggleton. 2002. *HIV and AIDS-related Stigma and Discrimination: A Conceptual Framework and Implications for Action*. Rio de Janeiro/London: ABIA/TCRU.

Phiri, Isabel Apawo, Deverakshanam Betty Govinden, and Sarojini Nadar. 2002. "Introduction." In *Her-Stories: Hidden Histories of Women of Faith in Africa*. Edited by Isabel Apawo Phiri, Deverakshanam Betty Govinden, and Sarojini Nadar. Pietermaritzburg: Cluster Publications.

Piot, Peter. 2000. "Report by the Executive Director to the Program Coordinating Board. Joint United Nations Program on AIDS." Rio de Janeiro, 14-15 December.

Soyinka, Wole 1993. *Art, Dialogue and Outrage: Essays on Literature and Culture*. New York: Pantheon Books.

Russell, Letty M. and J. Shannon Clarkson, ed., 1996. *Dictionary of Feminist Theologies*. Louisville, Kentucky: John Knox/Westminster Press.

Vuola, Elina. 2002. *Limits of Liberation: Feminist Theology and the Ethics of Poverty and Reproduction*. Sheffield: Sheffield Academic Press.

Welker, Michael. 2000. *What Happens in Holy Communion?* Translated by John E. Hoffmeyer. Grand Rapids, Michigan: Eerdmans.

13

Navigating Experiences of Healing

A Narrative Theology of Eschatological Hope as Healing

Fulata Lusungu Moyo

NAVIGATING HEALING: INTRODUCTORY NARRATIVE

The twentieth-century closed with a number of personal and family-related unanswered questions, questions that both challenged and redefined my theological thinking on health, healing, and wholeness. 1999 had ushered in a number of pressing situations that only God could answer. My family always believed that God is the one who sustains life holistically. In cases of sickness and ill-health, we believed that God heals. For us, the methods and nature of healing were always God's issue.

I invite you to make a circle with me as I tearfully sing my song of pain; first as a wife and caregiver to a dying husband, Solomon Moyo, and then as a widow. Though it is a song of a Malawian Tumbuka-Ngoni Christian Reformed widow navigating the meaning of health, blend in the voices of your own songs so that together we theologize hope in an otherwise hurting and "dying" continent. In honor of Mercy Amba Ewudziwa Oduyoye, I propose to use a narrative theology approach to tell my story and reflect on it so as to heuristically find meaning and healing (Oduyoye 2001, 10). Telling our stories helps us bring about a fourfold yield: 1) engaging in dialogue with others helps us relate personal hurt and search for healing with academic reflection; 2) it will provide other perspectives that will enrich our own; 3) singing our own songs and reflecting on them in dialogue with existing songs by others will help us shift from positions of help-lessness as victims to being agents who make a contribution to theologies of life and wholeness; and 4) the act of narration is in itself therapeutic. In other words, the telling of painful stories helps us embark on the process of "narrative therapy" for health (Phiri, Govinden, and Nadar 2002, 6-8).

My song has two stanzas. The first narrates my husband Solomon's ill health, my Christian community's messages of hope, and my care-giving experiences.[1] The second stanza includes my theological reflection on issues of health and healing that ema-nate from my experience. These reflections are sung in two cho-ruses beginning with the phenomenon of health and closing with healing as a notion of eschatological hope. They will be framed within the dialogical space that lies between liberation theology and pastoral theology, in what Chopp and Parker call "doing of theology" since "both theologies are committed to being a way of ongoing reflection in and on praxis as ways of discerning" (Chopp and Parker 1990, 4).

THE GOD OF A "THIRD-WORLD CHILD": MY STORY AND MESSAGES OF HOPE

In March 1999, following a two-month course of medication for stomach ulcers, my husband Solomon was diagnosed with liver cancer.[2] As Ngoni-Tumbuka Reformed Christians, Solomon and I believed in the healing work of Jesus. Before the diagnosis, as third-world children, neither of us had heard of liver cancer. When we were eventually confronted by it, we nevertheless believed that

God would bring healing. During the six-week course of chemotherapy administered both at the hospital and at home, many Christians visited and prayed for Solomon's healing.

In her poem "I Know Some Women" (Oduyoye in Amoah and Martin 2001, 10) Mercy chants the praises of women and their strength that holds the world together and brings hope. When Solomon became sick, out of my love for him and my sense of duty to safeguard my family's welfare,[3] I solicited prayers for healing from the global Christian community. Although I saw his health deteriorating in the weeks that followed, I still continued to believe in faith that the mountain of sickness could be removed by God's power "for nothing will be impossible for you" (Matt. 17:20).

The Messages of Hope

To keep the fires of hope burning, I opened a small diary in which those who could not visit Solomon personally could write their messages of hope and spiritual comfort. Between 20 March and 22 April 1999, 174 such messages were written. Of this number, due to the limitation of space, I include only fourteen messages, selected on the basis of their contribution to seeking a miraculous cure, the place of faith, and their underlying theology of hope. The first message to Solomon expressed the aim of this diary, "to keep a record of God's work in your life, your friends' prayers, . . . your favorite verses."[4]

1. Solomon, our God is an awesome God. God reigns, heals and wants wholeness. We are with you in prayer.

2. God's grace and healing is all we have and trust. God's healing is all evident to us always. May the Lord speedily accomplish this healing in you. For God's praise and glory.

3. Doctors can think it is difficult, but the God we believe in . . . gives answers because the battle is God's. We believe that faith as small as a mustard seed can move mountains, and the united faith

that we have together in our situation adds up to something bigger. God cannot neglect us.

4. This sickness will not end in death. It is for God's glory so that Jesus may be glorified (John 11:4).

5. "And God said to Abraham 'Why did Sarah laugh? . . . Is anything too hard for God?'" (Gen. 18:13-14). Jesus said, "with people this is impossible, but with God all things are possible" (Matt. 19:26).

6. "Hezekiah was ill at the point of death. . . . He cried to God for mercy. God heard his prayer and granted him extra life. As a sign a shadow cast of the sun went back ten steps" (Is. 38:1-8). Today as Solomon goes for biopsy, Lord, we humbly but earnestly ask you, make the growth on Solomon's liver shrink ten times smaller so that the doctors know that You are great and nothing is impossible with You.

7. Solomon, I am zero when it comes to medical knowledge. Most of the times, I find myself lost and confused . . . and . . . end up making all sorts of mistakes. In such times I take comfort in the fact that God is aware that I am a typical third-world child who has lived through all sorts of illnesses, fumbling through all sorts of theories, ideas, tips and testimonies. Hence I have developed what I call the prayer of a third-world child in which I . . . acknowledge that the only reason I am still alive is because of God's divine love and . . . I can face today and tomorrow in a world full of strange diseases. . . . [We] need [to have] . . . faith in a God of the third-world child. This God is the only one who makes sense where nothing else does. Be assured that . . . I (believe this) . . . for you . . . that God's divine love will continue to sustain the third-world child in you . . . until you fulfill what God has kept you for all these years.

8. "Do not be afraid, Daniel, since the first day that you set your mind to gain understanding and to humble yourself before . . . God, your words were heard, and I have come in response to

them. But the prince of the Persian Kingdom resisted me twenty-one days. Then Michael came to help me" (Dan. 10:12-13). 30 March 1999 is the twenty-first day since the body of Christ started praying for Solomon. Today, Solomon is healed!

9. This is the day of the accomplishment of the miracle. It is done.

10. God created you and God knows each part of your body. . . . [T]he same God can mend it. God isn't confused regarding your condition. God is willing to heal. In Matt. 8:2-3 Jesus' reply was "I am willing." There is no doubt that God is willing to heal you. By the stripes of Jesus, you are healed. Thank God it is His/Her will to heal you.

11. "By your faith you are healed. You have pleased God with your faith" (Heb. 11:1-6).

12. God is the most available powerful weapon and in Jesus' name we claim healing in your body and spirit. What people have failed, God cannot fail.

13. I will restore health to you and heal your wounds. . . . [T]he winter is past, the rain is over, the flowers appear. . . . [The] time of singing has come.

14. Solomon is healed and he will live in Jesus' name!

The evening of Thursday, 22 April 1999, Solomon passed into eternity. When Solomon announced "I want to go home," I knew that I needed the encouragement and solidarity of other Christians. I needed the presence of those with faith for healing to stand against the inevitable. Solomon's death shook my faith. I felt so betrayed that I needed my faith to be strengthened by threading it together with those who had not yet given up. Just prior to his death, a couple came and prayed with us both for an hour or so, reciting the words of Psalm 23: "The Lord is my shepherd. . . . I will fear no evil." Soon after they had left, Solomon died. I did not understand how his friends could leave at that particular time. They later explained that they had seen a vision of brilliant blue light that covered Solomon's chest and the top of our house, accompanied by the beautiful angelic singing about Jesus' victory and heavenly glory that gave them a foresight into Solomon's immanent departure.

When Solomon died, I prayed to Jesus that he would raise Solomon from the dead just as he had done with Lazarus. I spoke life into his ears and hoped that he would rise. Even after the doctor confirmed his death and his bodily remains were finally carried away, I still hoped that some Christians were praying for the resurrection of his body. Though I felt betrayed when I saw them assist those taking his body away, I still hoped that just like me, not wanting to create unnecessary drama, they were silently trusting God for such a miracle. However, his body did not resurrect.

REFLECTIONS

The Phenomenon of Health

According to Leslie D. Weatherhead, physical health is the complete and successful functioning of every part of the human body in harmonious relationship with every other part of that body and with its particular and relevant environment. While anthropological studies have shown that disease and healing should be conceived within their own religio-cultural environment, Solomon's cancer was regarded as a mystery by the faith-based community—an infliction from the devil probably through witchcraft.[5] In our case, a cure was conceived in the context of what may be called "faith-healing" involving prayer and ritual. Here I use ritual as a community prescribed symbolic and formal act whose important element is in its being a symbol of important beliefs—especially the ritual surrounding prayers of healing.[6]

Prayer is conceived as a process through which human beings explore the divine cosmos in their search for answers to issues that are beyond their conception. My conception of prayer is echoed by that of Untenberger, who states that prayer "often changes the one who prays rather than persuades an omniscient God" (1996, 223). Going beyond this, prayer also assists the intercessor with accepting God's answer in case it is contrary to what is expected. I further submit that the personal transformation that comes as a result of prayer is in a sense a preparation for the intercessor to be partly constituted into the being of God as an agent of divine intervention. In this case, the agents of God's intervention include family members, friends in the faith-based communities, and faith healers. Sometimes the prayers offered included symbolic actions such as the anointing of oil for the sick (James 5:14), and "Christianized" religio-cultural scattering of grains of salt in the patient's room as a sign of purification, meaning, the chasing away of evil spirits.

Some may raise the objection that a person can never be absolute about God's meaning of healing unless we can be absolutely sure of God's supernatural activity in each case. As African women we are continuously burdened with care-giving roles to those who are sick in the family or community so it almost seems mandatory therefore to ritually advocate for health.

Faith-healing, as the term suggests, seems to weigh heavily on the predisposition of faith exhibited by those who seek healing. Medical research suggests that there is a vital relationship between one's attitude and the possibility of recovery or lack of it (Jackson 1981, 86). Exploring matters of faith, Hunt and Walker argue that for prayer to be effectively answered, eight divine principles should be demonstrated by the intercessor: 1) praying in the Spirit, 2) praying with the mind, 3) praying in Jesus' name, 4) praying while abiding in Christ, 5) praying in faith, 6) praying in humility, 7) praying in sincerity, and 8) praying with perseverance (Hunt and Walker 1997).

The first principle means that prayer is made in agreement with the Holy Spirit, the revealer of God's specific will and the spiritual enabler of the intercessor, to pray in ways that are in agreement with God's will and purpose. The messages written in the diary assume that the Holy Spirit is working through their prayers and intercessions. They even affirm that Solomon's healing was part of God's will and was therefore divinely given (messages 1, 7, 10, and 13). Praying in faith gives an assurance to the intercessor that what is being asked for will take place because of God's faithfulness (messages 3, 7, and 11), God's authority (message 12), God's power (messages 1, 5, and 8), and God's loving care (messages 2, 3, 6, and 7).

According to Jackson, the opposite of faith is fear and anxiety, both of which hinder divine answers to prayer (Jackson 1981). Although Solomon did not receive divine healing, the sampled messages generally reflected each of Hunt and Walker's eight principles of answered prayer. Following his death and after several years of painful reflection I sometimes wonder whether we really comprehend the mind of God. Even though God's nature is one of healing, what did this translate to in Solomon's case? Does divine healing depend totally on our faith as intercessors? What became of the promise that Solomon would not die but live to declare the works of the Lord (Ps. 118:17)? Did we not display sufficient faith? Were those women and men of God misled in their faith? Or did God betray us? Could it be that all of us did not fully understand the meaning of health? (see Moyo 2002, 399). Could it be that God's promise of divine healing was more of an eschatological hope for the future than merely physical healing within the present?

Eschatological Hope as a Midwife of New Beginnings

When it has to do with expectation of a better life, women never say "never"; what they say is "not yet." For them, an eschatology that resonates with their desire for empowerment is a theology of hope. Women give of themselves because they believe that such giving ensures and preserves the life-force, face, and dignity of others (Oduyoye 2001, 112-13).[7]

For Moltmann, Christianity, founded on the saving work of Christ, offers an eschatology of hope. For him, there is an enduring connection between the possibility of a transformable world and the promised celestial future. This is possible because Christ, who victoriously destroyed the encompassing power of evil out of his love and daily transformational work through us, suffers with us on the road of hope. This realized *eschaton* "is aroused by the promise whose fulfillment can only come from God's eschatological action transcending all the possibilities of history, since it involves the end of all evil, suffering, death in the glory of the divine presence indwelling in all things" (McGrath 2001, 639).

My conception of eschatological hope as healing has two primary facets. First is my conception of physical death. For my husband Solomon, death was what Jeremy Taylor would refer to as a transition from pain and suffering into a world of felicities more wonderful, in the company of angels and saints (McGrath 2001, 627). For women and men who have otherwise been socialized to be independent decision makers, peaceful death becomes an escapist form of healing from the pain and loss of human dignity, through conditions of complete helpless dependence on the caregivers (see Oduyoye 2001, 90-109).

The healing of the body from pain through death is not perceived in the conception of Origen, who understands that death rescues the soul from the imprisonment of the body (McGrath 2001, 616). I rather view the body as a divine sanctuary and feel that the multiple experiences of life shadow that which is to come. Echoing Pope Benedict XII, I believe that Solomon graduated into celestial paradise with Christ where he met God face to face (McGrath 2001, 623). In acknowledging that this eschatological hope is foretasted in this present physical life, I refer to the diary's first biblical text from Romans, which is not included above: "We know that all things work together for good for those who love God, who are called according to his purpose" (Rom. 8:28). God's constant working in everything that happens for good in the life of the Christian could mean that nothing ever takes place outside the scope of God's providential care. Is it possible that the definition of the "good" that God is birthing is to be understood from God's perspective? It seems, in the face of disappointment in prayer, that we should remember that God is wiser than any human person. This realization should help us to accept the limitations in our conception of God's will, especially within the mysteries of death and dying, and to believe in not only the undying hope of an immanent resurrection but also in the divine midwife's intervention for new beginnings for those hurting.

The second facet of my understanding of healing as eschatological hope promises us new beginnings in which new life is discerned dualistically. New life for Solomon means he can still influence the life of his earthly family through our memories of him and as our ancestor;[8] for the bereaved, his new life also offers hope for new beginnings. Moltmann argues that through eschatology Christian theology provides a vision of hope through the transforming work of God. As such, I refuse to accommodate the status quo of suffering, loneliness, and hopelessness—for this hope consists not only in the *parousia* (future event) nor "as something which has already taken place in the confrontation of the believer with *kerygma* (proclamation)" (McGrath 2001, 632). It consists rather in our calling and mission to transform for the world. This hope encourages us to find new meanings and expressions in life even after bereavement.[9] Each disappointment in prayer should be a challenge to develop new and deeper insights as we work to discern why God's answer contradicted our own (Hunt and Walker 1997, 145). Another aspect of that hope might be our ability to create safe spaces for the expression of emotional frustrations, whether to God or those who are therapeutically journeying with us.

Three attributes of God enhance this theology of hope. The first is God's unconditional love, coupled with God's justice, whereby through Her/His infinite wisdom, God brings interventions into our lives that seek out the best in a situation. These nullify possible misconceptions implied by simplistic Christian explanations of particular crises, such as "Sister, accept this as God's will." These rejoinders are sometimes insensitive and almost always escapist, resembling Marx's statement that faith (religion) is the opiate of the people.[10] Supposedly aimed at easing our sense of loss or halting any critique of our faith or belief in God brought on through desperation or wrought in anger and pain, it often results in the three-fold crisis of depression, denial, and spiritual fatigue. If God is what Christians theologize about, then why should any wise human being feel pressurized to defend Her/Him?

CONCLUSION

Unfortunately, because of the lack of professional counseling services in most Christian communities, such prayer casualties are seldom pastorally and theologically guided back to spiritual wholeness and health. Common explanations such as "You needed more faith" seem to contradict the very nature of God's love and God's preferential option for the oppressed. According to Oduyoye, Jesus "never accepted deprivation as the destiny of humanity; rather he demonstrated that suffering is not in the plan of God" (Oduyoye 2001, 57). Does Christianity have any room for such an egocentric god who is preoccupied with the selfish fulfillment of Her/His own will at the expense of those whom God ostensibly loves? Does not God always work toward health, meeting all persons at their point of need?

The emphasis on believing faith on the part of the intercessor as a pre-requisite to divine healing (message 11) unnecessarily fabricates accusations about its lack, in the face of supposedly unanswered answers. It creates unnecessary guilt on the part of the caregivers on top of the usual grief caused by so many other unanswered questions.

Against such accusations and that of my own grief and pain, I have to remain a strong woman. But I am also a human being with care needs. The availability of sensitive pastoral care that deliberately involves the patient in decision-making instead of the "imposition" of prayers or "words of encouragement" would help even caregivers to hope for an eschatology that begins now. If we had "allowed" Solomon to decide what type of prayers to be offered and when, what course would his six-week period of illness have taken? Could it be that he wanted to have the serenity of his own sense of God's will about his life? Was he tired of us forcing our concept of healing into his life? I sometimes wonder![11]

NOTES

¹ I was Solomon's caregiver, together with other family members and friends, especially women.

² The CT scan results were highly suggestive of a large hepato-cellular carcinoma, but the confirmation through biopsy came a week *after* Solomon died.

³ The community expects me to be strong so as to carry the responsibilities of safeguarding the community's well-being without complaining or competing for power-sharing that, in my case, is in the hands of the patriarchs. I am expected to be emotionally expressive, a "jack of all trades" (see Proverbs 31:10-31) and superhuman, tirelessly enjoying all the work entrusted to me! (see Oduyoye 2002, 67-75).

⁴ Different versions of biblical texts were used, though not indicated. One reason for such an oversight is because this essay does not attempt any interpretation of such texts. Rather, I have tried to copy these messages verbatim, with some minimal editing but without altering their content or meaning other than making them gender inclusive. In order to maintain confidentiality, authors' names are not included.

⁵ During Solomon's six-week struggle with liver cancer, a friend suggested that we seek healing from a traditional healer (*ng'anga*) who used prayer to discern the right herbs for healing. After the consultation, however, we did not administer his herbs because we did not agree with how his prayers vacillated between Allah, Jesus, and general Ancestors, apart from his suggestion that Solomon was bewitched by his colleagues at his work place.

⁶ James Cox defines ritual as "a repeated and symbolic dramatization directing attention to a place where the sacred enters life thereby granting identity to participants in the drama, transforming them, communicating social meaning verbally and non-verbally, and offering a paradigm for how the world ought to be" (Cox 1998, x).

⁷ According to Oduyoye, women find meaning and empowerment in an eschatology of hope. (Oduyoye 2001, 112). As with Oduyoye, Moltmann's theology of hope connects the Christian eschatological hope of newness of life to the present enduring hope for justice, peace, and wholeness. As Richard J. Bauckham has shown, "Moltmann argued for the rediscovery of the corporate Christian conception of hope as a central motivation factor in the life and thought of the individual and the church" (McGrath 2001, 639).

⁸ Through physical death, it is African religio-cultural belief that Solomon has joined the living dead as an ancestor to his family. He can

therefore still influence the life of his family. Unfortunately, in my Christian Reformed theology such a belief seems idolatrous.

[9] In Tumbuka-Ngoni patriarchal communities, the favoring of widowers makes it easier for their birthing a new relationship despite the age and number of children. A widow's reality is exacerbated by age, children, and sometimes responsibility for her former husband's family.

[10] "Religion is the sigh of the oppressed creature, the heart of a heartless world, just as it is the spirit of a spiritless situation. It is the opium of the people" (quoted in Greely 1995, 4).

[11] In retrospect, I regret the fact that, together with others, we sometimes imposed our decisions regarding what to believe about ill-health on Solomon. We tended to overtake his own thoughts and overdose him with our passion for healing.

REFERENCES

Amoah, Elizabeth and P. Martin. 2001. *Heart, Mind and Tongue: A Heritage of Woven Words*. Accra: Sam-Woode Ltd.

Cahill, Lisa Sowle. 1996. *Sex, Gender and Christian Ethics*. Cambridge: Cambridge University Press.

Campbell, Susan S. 1998. *Called to Heal: Traditional Healing Meets Modern Medicine in South Africa*. Epping: Zebra Press.

Chopp, Rebecca S. 1990. *Liberation Theology and Pastoral Theology*. JPCP Monograph 2, Claremont, California: Journal of Pastoral Care Publication.

Chopp, Rebecca S., and Duane F. Parker. 1990. Monograph. "Liberation Theology and Pastoral Theology." Decatur, Georgia: *Journal of Pastoral Care Publications*.

Cox, J. L., ed. 1998. *Rites of Passage in Contemporary Africa*. Cardiff: Cardiff Academic Press.

Dale, David. 1989. *In His Hands: Towards a Theology of Healing*. London: Daybreak.

Feierman, Steven and John M. Janzen, eds. 1992. *The Social Basis of Health and Healing in Africa*. Berkeley: University of California Press.

Greely, Andrew M., ed. 1995. *Sociology and Religion*. Chicago: Harper Collins College Publishers.

Hancock, Trevor and Meredith Minkler. 2002. "Community Health Assessment or Healthy Community Assessment: Whose Community? Whose Health? Whose Assessment?" In *Community Organizing & Community Building for Health*. Edited by Meredith Minkler. New Brunswick, New Jersey: Rutgers University Press, 139-56.

Hardesty, Nancy. A. 1996. s.v. "Healing." In *Dictionary of Feminist Theologies.* Edited by Letty M. Russell and and J. Shannon Clarkson. Louisville, Kentucky: Westminster/John Knox.

Hunt, T. W. and Catherine Walker. 1997. *Walking in Fellowship with God: Disciple's Prayer Life.* Nashville: Life Way Press.

Jackson, Edgar N. 1981. *The Role of Faith in the Process of Healing.* Minneapolis, Minnesota: Winston Press.

Koenig, Harold G. 1999. *The Healing Power of Faith: Science Explores Medicine's Last Frontier.* New York: Simon and Schuster.

McGrath, Alistair E., ed. 2001. *The Christian Theology Reader.* Second Edition. Oxford: Blackwell.

Moyo, Fulata Lusungu. 2002. "Singing and Dancing Women's Liberation: My Story of Faith." In *Her-Stories: Hidden Histories of Women of Faith in Africa.* Edited by Isabel Apawo Phiri, Deverakshanam Betty Govinden, and Sarojini Nadar. Pietermaritzburg: Cluster Publications, 389-408.

———. 2003. "When the Telling Itself Is a Taboo: The Phoebe Practice." *Journal for Constructive Theology* 9 (2): 3-20.

———. 2004. "Religion, Spirituality and Being a Woman in Africa: Gender Construction within the African Religio-cultural Experiences." *Agenda* 61, 72-78.

Oduyoye, Mercy Amba and Elizabeth Amoah. 1990. "The Christ for African Women." In *With Passion and Compassion: Third World Women Doing Theology.* Edited by Mercy Amba Oduyoye and Virginia Fabella. Maryknoll, New York: Orbis Books.

———. 1995. *Daughters of Anowa: African Women and Patriarchy.* Maryknoll, New York: Orbis Books.

———. 1999. "Coming Home to Myself." In *Liberating Eschatology: Lectures in Honor of Letty Russell.* Edited by Margaret A. Farley and Serene Jones. Louisville, Kentucky: Westminster John Knox Press, 105-20.

———. 2001. *Introducing African Women Theology.* Sheffield: Sheffield Academic Press.

———. 2002. *Beads and Strands: Reflections of an African Woman on Christianity in Africa.* Carlisle: Paternoster Press (Akrpong-Akuapem, Ghana: Regnum Africa, 2004; Maryknoll, New York: Orbis Books, 2004).

———, and Musimbi R. A. Kanyoro, eds. 1991. *The Will to Arise.* Maryknoll, New York: Orbis Books.

Phiri, Isabel Apawo. 2004. "A Theological Analysis of the Voices of Teenage Girls on 'Men's Role in the Fight against HIV/AIDS' in KwaZulu-Natal, South Africa." *Journal of Theology for Southern Africa* 120: 34-54.

————, Deverakshanam Betty Govinden, Sarojini Nadar, eds. 2002. *Herstories: Hidden Histories of Women of Faith in Africa*. Pietermaritzburg: Cluster Publications.

Shorter, Aylward. 1985. *Jesus and the Witchdoctor: An Approach to Healing and Wholeness*. London/Maryknoll: Geoffrey Chapman/Orbis Books.

Unterberger, Gail L. 1996. s.v. "Prayer." In *Dictionary of Feminist Theologies*. Edited by Letty M. Russell and J. Shannon Clarkson. Louisville, Kentucky: Westminster/John Knox Press, 223-24.

Weatherhead, Lesley. D. 1959. *Psychology, Religion and Healing*. London: Hodder and Stoughton.

West, Gerald O. 2003. *The Academy of the Poor: Towards a Dialogical Reading of the Bible*. Pietermaritzburg: Cluster Publications.

Young, Iris Marion. 1990. *Justice and the Politics of Difference*. Princeton: Princeton University Press.

PART V

POSTSCRIPT

14

Daughters of Ethiopia

Constructing a Feminist Discourse in Ebony Strokes

Ogbu U. Kalu

NAMING THE THEME AND ITS BOUNDARIES

The Circle of Concerned African Women Theologians, which Mercy Amba Ewudziwa Oduyoye pioneered, has changed feminist discourse in African Christianity. It has achieved its first goal, which is to conduct research, write, and publish from African women's perspective. This reflection explores how the Circle could benefit from conversation between African and African American women theologians. It provides a male outsider's perspective. One recalls the enormous impact of the robust conversation with African Americans in Accra in 1977 (Appiah-Kubi and Torres 1978). It changed African theology.

Women constitute a core aspect of the explosion of Christianity in contemporary Africa. However, the story of black women reflects the impact of dispersion into the New World, which created new challenges and new environments in the ancient homeland. This reflection urges that black women should intentionally develop creative and sustained linkages as they reflect about God's relationship with women confronted by challenges in varied eco-systems. It is argued that these black women come from the same stock, are perceived as the same by non-black peoples, share the same intrinsic values and spirituality, and should bond together for survival. There is need for a long conversation. They bring different gifts to the table because there are differences that ema-nate from their different life experiences engendered by years of living in different cultures. Both affirm that their experiences set them apart from white women and their feminist causes. For some, this is because white women are oppressors. For others, the con-cerns are that white women presume that their condition is the norm; they paint negative images of the African woman as if they were mules and presume that African women need to be liber-ated from their hostile environment so as to be like white women. There is resentment about the patronizing, biased, exotic, and essentializing profiles of the condition of the African woman (Okume 2003, 67).

At the core, black women complain that cultural norms are deployed to construct and silence women. This has two implica-tions: there is no universal women's experience. The conversa-tion must be attentive to systemic and cultural differences. Con-textual theology must be built on adequate cultural mapping. The African social condition is very different from the North Ameri-can one. Homer Ashby has illustrated this with the example of marriage (Ashby 2003, 107). Moreover, African and African American women share the same frustration—that emergent the-ologies ignored female input. As Sheron Patterson sarcastically puts it: "Imagine this: A question is presented to you, but before you can answer it, an Anglo woman or man or an African Ameri-can man speaks on your behalf. Your opinions are not heard and do not matter" (Patterson 2000, 27-28).

The conversation may expose differences. First, African women differ in their images of womanhood: some emphasize invisibil-ity, others the autonomous achiever. Second, the celebration of the ebony kinship between African Americans and Africans has been informed by the nature of "discerning black identity." The battle between black nationalists and integrationists has been long drawn with no clear victor. W. E. B. DuBois elucidated it as the two souls of black folks—the Negro and the American—and the need to benefit from the dual cultural heritage. It is important for this conversation to understand the lay of the land on either shore of the great lake.

Third, rapid social and cultural changes continuously reshape feminist discourse, and doing feminist theology therefore requires a cultural map or in-depth anthropological data. African feminist literature images a strong force of externality in gender construction by arguing that colonialism and Christianity reshaped gender ideologies in contemporary African societies and churches by reinforcing the contested elements of patriarchy in the indigenous cultures, turning them into enduring structures that enervate other moderating influences. Put differently, modernizing cultural forces destroyed the salient values of indigenous communities without replacing them with adequate alternatives.

PLURALITY OF VOICES

A key aspect of the background to the conversation is that the women theologians do not come to the table with consensus. In fact, there are internal debates among African women theologians and among African American female scholars about the goals of the feminist struggle and even the terminology. Is it for the consolidation of elite women in powerful positions (that may be dubbed "femocracy")? Or are all sectors of womenfolk served? Should feminism privilege academic rigor or social engagement? There is no consensus about the diagnosis of the female predicament or the attitude to the past. Some urge a creative return to the past for inspiration from "our mothers' gardens"; others urge a radical discontinuity due to the exploitation of women by patriarchal ancestors and the traditions that they bequeathed. Mercy Oduyoye describes this as "women standing up, abandoning the crouched positions from which their life-breath stimulated the wood fires that burned under the earthenware pots of vegetables they had grown and harvested" (Oduyoye 1995, 2).

In *Beads and Strands*, Mercy Oduyoye urges a "departure from inflexibly ascribed positions whose hierarchical ordering was accepted as natural and permanent" (Oduyoye 2004, 4). Mercy Oduyoye's position is perhaps more subtle than her bald statements suggests. She uses the *art of remembrance* to do theology from the inside of an African religious worldview. The quest for salvation must be rooted in the indigenous language, cultural practices, and religious idioms of the people. For African Americans, the attitude to the slavery era is quite crucial. As Linda Thomas suggests, "the tasks of womanist theology are to claim history, to declare authority for ourselves, our men, our children, to learn from the experience of our forebears, to admit shortcomings and errors, and to improve our quality of life" (Thomas 2004, 38). This requires excavating the life stories of women, including the "empowering dimensions of conjuring and syncretistic black religiosity" and "doing roots." Cultural excavation can become empowering in the struggles of the present or in the task of regaining a sense of balance amidst the rapid changes of our times. The Jim Crow period is like the colonial moment in the African story.

On naming the movement, some African American women would rather abandon the term *feminism* to white women and articulate their peculiar experiences as *womanist*, a powerful word that emerges from the interior of black culture. To say that a girl child is *acting womanish* is to affirm that the person is beginning to exercise agency, act as a grown up, and show a creative, adult sense of initiative. As a result, Mitchem (2002) has examined the signal texts, the class and communal dimensions to the construction, and the pastoral and theological implications. Others demur for fear of abandoning the feminist turf to white women and thereby installing boundaries that enclose the black cause in conceptual ghettoes where people rummage through colored pain. Behind this debate are class factors, academic orientations, life experiences, the allure of separate development, and the challenge of fighting and winning from the inside of the dominant culture. As Oyewumi has argued, for Africans, *sister* is a more powerful metaphor because it denotes the knitting of a sustaining network that is non-kin-based, akin to such relationships as *ore* among the Yoruba or *chienjira/chemwali* among the women of southern Malawi. It enjoys confidence, intimacy, and reliability.

This sisterhood has been partially demonstrated through collective publishing. Members have published over thirty-two books in the last decade, focusing on the one hand on social problems such as poverty, family, violence, and health issues as these affect women, and on the other with theological discussions on reading the Bible from African women's perspectives; understanding God, Jesus Christ, and African women; African women's understanding of sin and salvation; on being human; on being church; and on eschatology (see Oduyoye 2001; Njoroge and Dube 2002).

Literary production by African American women has intensified too. But many perceive agency as an effective mobilization of women through projects that raise consciousness, demonstrate women's capability, and nurture a sense of worth. It is argued that when sisters share their experiences in environments of trust, they become empowered to reverse their vulnerable conditions (see Mitchem 2002, 85; Kalu 2003, 188-89).

On the theological level, methodology is the essence of all theologies. The questions asked and how they are answered determine the message and its impact. Both African and African American women theologians privilege *experience* as the framework for doing feminist theology. This harks back to the debates about contextualization and inculturation in doing post-colonial theology. It is attentive to the pilgrim and indigenous principles in the gospel's encounter with different cultures and communities, in other words, how local identities contest global processes. It touches the heart of theology as human reflection on God's relationship to human beings and the world of nature. For Delores Williams in her *Sisters in the Wilderness* (1993), there is need to see, affirm, and connect between academic reflection and community and the experiences of ordinary black women. Where one stands and what one experiences, therefore, become the starting point of doing theology. Having said this, there is perhaps an on-going fragmentation that underlies such a conversation. Individual experiences of the social and religious cultures vary, as do their quests for cultural fulfillment. Some women choose to be *rejectionist* by rejecting the Bible as canon; others are *radical reformers* who mine the radical elements within the gospel for empowerment; and still others have deployed biblicism as the mooring for *loyalist* postures. It should be added that the loyalist posture may be found prominently among Roman Catholics as well as among charismatic evangelical women. In spite of differences within each camp and among the camps, the protagonists urge intense dialogue as a method of doing feminist theology (see Kalu 2000, 161-93).

THE TIES THAT BIND

"Ties that bind" refers to the various strands of feminism that share a commonality. Academically, feminist discourses have benefited from the same intellectual tradition, especially deconstructive postmodernist discourse. Patriarchy, *the government of the fathers*, is color-blind and has operated in different social, political, cultural, and economic organizations throughout the centuries. It may have been stronger in pre-industrial and agricultural societies, but it retains its influence upon modern lifestyles and family structures. One of the Greek derivatives from the word "patriarchy" yielded the term *macho* to the English vocabulary, which conveys the image of violence, struggle, and force, and may explain its cultural register that includes violence against women and psychological pressures on children by fathers. Anti-patriarchy is a key platform in the feminist enterprise. It is beyond the protest against capitalism because underneath the broad oppression against those who do not control the means of production is the specific oppression of women. The register of feminist discourses, therefore, includes rebuilding the brokenness of women's psyche and self-image, regaining safe environments, removing the veil of invisibility, enhancing participation in politics and decision-making in the public spaces, recovering agency in making decisions about health, marital status, sexual orientation, job satisfaction, remuneration, and the organization of social structures that matter.

African and African American women, although divided continentally, have certain identical attitudes toward men: they want to build sustainable homes (in spite of the high level of unmarried adults in the African American black population), encourage the survival of the folk (ranging from the extended family to the community), partner with the men and succor them in responding to external forces that emasculate the men-folk, and be respected. It is common knowledge that women bear the brunt of the humiliation of their sons and husbands. This is often captured by the tendency to "stand by my man." Indeed, this can be quite risky. Attention should be paid to the fact that African and African women theologies have borrowed inspiration and discourses from broad international feminist groups. For instance, in spite of the quest for identity by African women's theologies, it has gained inspiration from the interventions of United Nation programs, new theological orientations within the World Council of Churches, and the development of Third World and Black theologies. This does not deny the impact of specific experiences in each ecosystem.

Nevertheless, feminist theologies have shifted emphases through time, and the causes and methods have benefited from broader social trends and multi-disciplinary resources. A distinction must be made between secular feminist scholarship and Christian feminist theology because they have different goals, assumptions, and methods. For instance, the negritude discourse has shaped African secular feminism, including a nuanced response to Diop's contention that originally African societies were matrilineal (Amadiume 1997, 176). The secular feminist enterprise has paid attention to matters of theory and yielded immense data on women in African indigenous communities.

In contrast, the Circle represents the mobilization of African women of faith who are "calling the church and religious communities to account." Mercy Oduyoye declares that she is writing as a Christian woman. Hers is a genre of Christian social ethics in which the Bible is central. The Exodus event is a basic paradigm for reflecting on women and patriarchy. She shares this passion with Linda Thomas because "the exodus story is a hermeneutical device used to draw a parallel between the oppressed Israelites and the oppressed African American community" (Thomas 2004, 38). Delores Williams concurs, but is intrigued with the story of Hagar in the wilderness. Others choose the ambiguous image of Esther. Women are aware of their demographic importance. *If it were not for the women*, perhaps churches would be empty. The numerical strength of women (which Linda Thomas estimates to be two-thirds) has an inverse ratio to their power in decision-making processes and exercise of ritual authority. The rationalization of this anomaly is made more intriguing by grounding gender ideology in certain exegesis of the canon, while, at the same time, sourcing the ethics operative within the ecclesia from the wider society. This is the argument in the three cycles of Oduyoye's *Daughters of Anowa* (1995). She explores how gender ideology in the language and proverbs and the cultural and socio-political practices of the Akan of Ghana and Yoruba of Nigeria inform the gender practices in the churches. Ironically, when liberal values spur a paradigm shift in the society, the ecclesia deploys the canon to insulate a conservative ethic that benefits men.

This tendency has determined the trend in feminist discourse. The first goal is to return to the canon and (since the Greek for *canon* means boundary) dissolve its enfolding boundaries by attacking its source: who wrote these scripts and with whose regnant bias? Admittedly, there have been some differing voices that seek to reconstruct the image and roles of women to show that these were broader than originally acknowledged. Others would rather discard the entire canon as irredeemable. Elizabeth Schüssler-Fiorenza has promoted the reconstructive genre, as best illustrated in her *Bread Not Stone* (1984).

The social sciences provide many tools for merging the erstwhile canon into new social realities and analysis and thereby open ecclesial boundaries to legitimize contemporary social values that seemingly affirm life. It is a long road and numerous wayfarers stop at many watering grounds along the route. As Richard B. Hays argues in *The Moral Vision of the New Testament* (1996), when one dissolves the canon, the conversation stops. Sometimes distinctions are made about the mode of reading the

Bible, whether from the hermeneutics of trust or the hermeneutics of suspicion. The core issue is whether to work from the inside, as the radical reformists do, or to attack the canon from the outside. Either option requires an elaborate engagement with biblical theology.

Two interesting aspects of African and African American women's theologies remain. First is the lack of adequate numbers of women theologians trained in the biblical disciplines. The situation is worse for Africans. African biblical scholarship has been generally weak. Knut Holter (2002) has demonstrated this with the study of African doctoral dissertations in the Old Testament.

Table 14-1. Decadenal Analysis of Number of African Old Testament Doctoral Dissertations

Decade	All Africa	Nigeria	Democratic Rep. of Congo
1960	3	1	—
1970	13	8	1
1980	28	10	2
1990	43	15	5
Totals	87	34	8

Two countries provided a half of the total for the continent. It should also be noted that the figures do not include South Africa. The statistics do not indicate the number written by women.

The second aspect is that most black female authors still believe in the church: they are mostly inside-combatants who prefer to use the short dagger; neither do they create a "women's church" that reads only the woman's Bible. Some attack the church's patriarchal ideology by urging women's ordination. They are accepted into seminaries in large numbers and sometimes change denominational affiliations to those places that ordain women. They also seek larger roles and stronger voices in ecclesial structures of power. There are more black women in seminaries in the United States than men, and this is going to be significant for the future. In 2004 alone, 60 percent of the student admissions into McCormick Theological Seminary, Chicago, were female, a trend that characterized the last seven years of the second millennium.

The situation in Africa is somewhat different: the percentage of female enrollment in Nigerian universities rose significantly in the period between 1980 and 1990, from 6,000 to 27,000. This trend reflects the high drop-out rate of males in secondary schools. Departments of religion/religious studies may enjoy high female enrollment figures, especially for the diploma courses, but female enrollment rates in postgraduate schools, seminaries, and Bible colleges are lower than would be the case in universities. Most female university graduates in religious studies become teachers and social welfare workers; few seek vocations in the church. However, the high visibility of women in Western theological education, with its attendant future implication upon church ministry, could prove useful in doing theology (Wright 2004, 22).

One index in reading a womanist is to watch where the author stands on womanists' relationship to men in the church. Some are so keen on designing an exclusive, identifiable theology that they become suspicious of men. Many, however, opt for partnership with men rather than engaging in the demonization of men. They reject the oppositional theology that pits men against women and they would subtly argue that patriarchy hurts all because it fails to mobilize all available resources for the building up of the whole. African women are wary about gender constructs that profile communities as if they were perpetually engaged in gender wars (Njoroge 1997, 2-13).

From this perspective, attention should be paid to the plurality of voices and the differences in the goals of the feminist struggles, their methods, nuances, strategies, and prescriptions. Changes in culture wars in America, the rise in education for women, and the growth of feminist and womanist literature have together engineered changes in theological discourse. These changes have a great impact on the rate and direction of change in gender status within African American churches. Recently, some American black churches have ordained women bishops.

In Africa, many denominations ordain women but conservatism is still rife. Can the changes among African American churches catalyze change on the African continent? Linkages are important.

CHARISMATICS AND GENDERED SPACE

In contemporary religious landscapes, charismatic influences predominate. But black religiosity has always been charismatic due to its indigenous charismatic worldview and religious practices. Those in the diaspora have retained a large dosage of this. Therefore, attention should be paid to the impact of charismatic practice upon feminist theology for at least seven reasons. First, there is much interest in religion and human sexuality; thus, it could be useful to examine the sexual agenda of different types of religiosity. The relationship between doctrinal affirmations, ecclesial heritage, and gender ideologies among churches is of great interest precisely because doctrines and ecclesial heritage legitimize polity and are expressed in liturgy and ethics.

A second factor is charismatic practice and religious space. Some have argued that the charismatic experience dissolves boundaries, creates freedom, and enlarges the space for women. Among many of its benefits, the criterion for accessing authority is based less on gender and more on possessing and exercising spiritual gifts or charismata. Thus, a woman who prophesies and performs miracles wins acceptance in spite of her gender.

Studies of the holiness movement and Pentecostalism have shown that women played an important role until the turn of the twentieth-century. John Wesley licensed women lay preachers as an "extraordinary calling." Many holiness groups ordained women or permitted their ministries. Some women became widely acclaimed evangelists, missionaries, and founding mothers of monasteries, prayer houses, and denominations. The women insisted that they had a calling as well as a mandate to preach and control over their voices and that Christ died for the whole people of God and not half. They published autobiographies and books. But, as fundamentalists attacked the trend, the leash was shortened. Only the Salvation Army survived the onslaught. Autobiographies and biographies are rich sources for doing feminist theology. Quite intriguing in the enterprise is to distinguish between white and black women precisely because the double jeopardy of race determined their varied experiences in church ministry. One must not miss the irony in the story of the "washer woman evangelist" Amanda Smith (d.1915) whose riveting autobiography, written in 1893, recounts how she was rejected by her black church and patronized by white churches! (Stanley 1993, 2002).

Third, there is a basketful of ironies: evangelical and charismatic spirituality fed on the freedom in Christ, but bred conservative ethics, biblicism, and the canonization of select Pauline "verses of terror," family values, and the submission of women. Even the Promise Keepers (a movement begun in the United States) of our times are alleged to have become a bastion of male chauvinist effort to restore non-liberal values about the status of women. The jury is still out on this assertion because some scholars are worried about the anti-male diatribe in feminist discourse that misses nuances such as in the activities of the Promise Keepers. In Africa, sociologists have argued that the Pentecostal environment is safe and protective of women. This explains female ardor.

Fourth, in Africa, the African indigenous churches were hailed as creative expressions of African religious genius at the interface of Christianity and culture. But a close look at their gender ideologies does not show that the status of women may have benefited from either the indigenous gender ideology or from the liberating aspects of pneumatic theology. In Nigeria, only one group ordains women. Menstrual taboos and other hurdles against women are placed at the doors of these churches.

Fifth is a resurgence of women's spirituality. This has arisen from contradictory sources such as the emphasis on the earth mother and goddesses in nature or ecological awareness, as well as from the intensification of Marian devotion and a proliferation of apparitions. The upsurge of interest in spirituality has been signaled by the growth of retreat centers and larger roles for women. In Protestant circles, the growth of sodalities such as Women's Aglow and many others encourage the mobilization and empowerment of women through prayer, pilgrimages, and devotional activities (Griffiths 1997). This trend explains the numerical strength of women's support for charismatic organizations.

It is related to a sixth factor, namely, a theological trend that could be dubbed the renaissance of Christology in feminist theology. Women find Jesus to be friendlier than those traditions held by churches and since the Holy Spirit glorifies Jesus, women have been at the forefront of the near hegemonic charismatic influence upon traditional mainline churches in the southern hemisphere. The trend is perceptible in Hisako Kinukawa's *Women and Jesus in Mark* (1994). In Africa, Christology is important in theology for a number of reasons: Jesus is a figure that needs to be inculturated into a worldview that is more theistic and charismatic. Theologians have debated through failed images whether he is an ancestor, guest, chief, or king.

The maleness of Jesus has been a contentious point in white feminism. This has triggered the insistence on inclusive language, which has no relevance to the structure of African languages. However, it is no longer acceptable to say that African languages are gender-neutral while writing the generic term "man" in English.

Liberation movements find in Jesus a champion of anti-structure, a revolutionary by which to model their struggles for social justice. Quite typical is Steve Biko in his enthusiasm over the sacking of the temple money-changers. The real robbers were not the hungry, petty pick-pockets in the streets; they were the merchants and bankers who operated within the temple walls! For Oduyoye, the salvation achieved by Jesus could be imaged from various stances in traditional Akan society. From a certain perspective, he is the *Osagyefo*, the liberator, a great friend and guarantor, *Adamfo Adu*. He is the *Ponfo Kese*, the one who pays the debt to redeem someone who may have been pawned into slavery (Oduyoye 2002).

Seventh, many have pointed to the *laicization* of churches, which reshapes power and authority at the infra-political zone. One dimension is that rapid growth has weakened the capacity of older institutions to control devotees as effectively. In addition, liturgical experimentations proliferate and the power of women's groups, such as the Mothers' Union, Women's Guild and other sororities within the churches, may have become stronger. Their financial capacity has increased the power of local congregations and competed against centralized church institutions. Among Protestants, the level of giving may have increased, but congregations prefer to spend their money. There has also been a definite power shift rooted in changing spirituality. Finally, womanist theology has emphasized the power of women in shifting attention from individual salvation to confrontation with structures of injustice—a practice of the theology of engagement. Black feminist theologies of various hues remember the contributions of women in the struggle for racial justice; they strive to be praxis-driven, thereby supporting pro-active efforts that confront structures that dehumanize women. Knowledge must be commitment.

CONCLUSION

In conclusion, there are a number of reasons for stimulating a long conversation between African American and African women theologians. The first is ideological. A survey of the literature shows that most collections of essays that engage the two-thirds women have been organized by white women. Some of these encourage them to produce data on the earth goddess, marine spirits, and other fertility goddesses in an effort to construct feminist spirituality. Rosemary Ruether can rightly point out that, while black women are castigating white feminists, some white women are the ones connecting into the wider transcontinental scene and mobilizing the two-thirds world women to do theology from pluralistic contexts.

The second reason is academic: emerging theologies need stronger and broader interpretative bases. Those who have done fieldwork in the African context have garnered data that enriched their understanding of religion and especially of Christianity. Moreover, each theology benefits from a plurality of voices when experiences are re-read from broader templates. A third reason is the need to engage global cultural and economic forces as they impact a variety of contexts. These forces create the contexts, challenges, and content of theology for the twenty-first century.

Fourth, Christian women must engage Muslim women because many such women live and breathe in religious pluralistic contexts. A dialogical theological method becomes imperative. Novels and activities of non-governmental organizations have produced enormous data on women under Muslim regimen, especially those under *sharia* law. A large proportion of contemporary Africa is Muslim and the growth of the Nation of Islam within the United States compels attention from scholars. The Circle has made a difference here through its African Muslim membership (see Oduyoye and Kanyoro 2001).

Fifth, African American and African women have paid attention to charismatic religiosity. Mercy Oduyoye, fondly acknowledged as "the mother of African Women Theologians," has provided solid leadership and has perhaps set the example. She was one of the founders of the charismatic Christian Union (CU) during her undergraduate days at the University of Ghana, Legon. Many of the leaders of contemporary Pentecostal movements in West Africa drank from the CU well. But she soon tired of it and preferred instead her Methodist roots. Other Circle members have written on charismatic religiosity as reflected in some articles in *Her Stories: Hidden Histories of Women of Faith in Africa* (Phiri, Govinden, and Nadar 2002).

Meanwhile, white sociologists have spawned theories concerning the significant impact that charismatic practice has had on women. As the theologian Cheryl Bridges Johns argues, if women's advocacy taps into the pneumatic resources extant within the Bible, they will discover that the "Pentecost story contains the story of the conscientization of women"; that the mission of Pentecost involves both men and women as co-laborers and joint heirs as members of God's new *ekklesia*. The Holy Spirit empowered many spirit-filled women to perform priestly, charismatic roles, to obey the call to move into mission fields without male or institutional support, and, in a revolutionary manner, to posture themselves in the line of God's eschatological design (Johns 1993, 161-65). More attention to this important facet is required due to its force in reshaping the religious landscape.

There has been a stunted tradition of researching only African independent churches. As observed earlier, charismatic spirituality may be offering more space for women. This opens a vast research potential. Finally, African American womanists would enrich their theology through the recovery of their African roots. This requires that they establish valid linkages and networks that obviate safari scholarship. It may require a conscious ideology of using the resources extant within their own environment to build lasting bridges with African women theologians. Scholars may borrow a leaf from some black churches that have excavated history and found that there was a period when African Americans pioneered the evangelization of Africa.

REFERENCES

Agumba, E. "The Search for My Place in Society." In *Transforming Power: Women in the Household of God*. Edited by Mercy Amba Oduyoye. Accra: Sam-Woode Ltd, 153-55.

Amadiume, I. 1987. *Male Daughters, Female Husbands: Gender and Sex in an African Society*. London: Zed Press.

———. 1997. *Reinventing Africa: Matriarchy, Religion and Culture*. London: Zed Books.

Appiah-Kubi, Kofi and Sergio Torres, eds. 1978. *African Theology Enroute*. Maryknoll, New York: Orbis Books.

Ashby, Homer U., Jr. 2003. *Our Home Is over Jordan: A Black Pastoral Theology*. St Louis: Chalice Press.

Getui, Mary and M. M. Theuri, eds. 2002. *Quest for Abundant Life in Africa*. Nairobi: Acton Publishers.

Griffiths, M. 1997. *God's Daughters: Evangelical Women and the Power of Submission*. Berkeley: University of California Press.

Hays, Richard B. 1996. *The Moral Vision of the New Testament—Community, Cross, New Creation: A Contemporary Introduction to New Testament Ethics*. San Francisco: Harper.

Hinga, Teresia M. 1998. "Christianity and Female Puberty Rites in Africa: The Agikuyu Case." In *Rites of Passage in Contemporary Africa*. Edited by J. L. Cox. Cardiff: Cardiff Academic Press, 129-45.

Holter, Knut. 2002. *Old Testament Research for Africa: A Critical Analysis and Annotated Bibliography of African Old Testament Dissertations, 1967-2000*. New York: Peter Lang.

Iyam, David U. 1995. *The Broken Hoe: Cultural Reconfiguration in Biase Southeast Nigeria*. Chicago: University of Chicago Press.

Johns, C. B. 1993. "Pentecostal Spirituality and Conscientization of Women." In *All Together in One Place*. Edited by H. D. Hunter and P. D. Hocken. Sheffield: Sheffield Academic Press, 161-65.

Kalu, Ogbu U. 1996. "Silent Victims: Violence Against Women in Nigerian Tertiary Institutions." Lagos: UNIFEM-UNDP Research.

———. 2000. *Power, Poverty and Prayer: The Challenges of Poverty and Pluralism in African Christianity, 1960-1996*. Frankfurt: Peter Lang.

———. 2001. *The Scourge of the Vandals: The Nature and Control of Cults in Nigerian Universities*. Enugu: University of Nigerian Press.

———. 2003. "Review of *Introducing Womanist Theology* by Stephanie Y. Mitchem." *Mission Studies: Journal of IAMS* 20: 188-89.

Kinukawa, Hisako. 1994. *Women and Jesus in Mark: A Japanese Feminist Perspective*. Maryknoll, New York: Orbis Books.

Mitchem, Stephanie Y. 2002. *Introducing Womanist Theology*. Maryknoll, New York: Orbis Books.

Njoroge, Nyambura J. 1997. "Resurrection People: Break the Chains of Injustice." *Reformed World* 47 (1): 2-13.

——— and Musa W. Dube, eds. 2001. *Talitha Cum! Theology of African Women*. Pietermaritzburg: Cluster Publications.

Oduyoye, Mercy Amba. 1995. *Daughters of Anowa: African Women and Patriarchy*. Maryknoll, New York: Orbis Books.

———. 2001. *Introducing African Women Theology*. Sheffield: Sheffield Academic Press.

———. 2004. *Beads and Strands: Reflections of an African Woman on Christianity in Africa*. Akropong-Akuapem: Regnum Africa; Maryknoll, New York: Orbis Books.

——— and Musimbi R. A. Kanyoro, eds. 2001. *The Will to Arise: African Women, Tradition, and the Church in Africa*. Maryknoll, New York: Orbis Books.

Okume, Oyeronke M. 1997. *The Invention of Women: Making an African Sense of Western Gender Discourses*. Minneapolis, Minnesota: University of Minnesota Press.

———. 2003. "What Women, Whose Development: A Critical Analysis on Reformist Evangelism on African Women." In *African Women and Feminism: Reflecting on the Politics of Sisterhood*. Edited by O. Oyewumi. Trenton, New Jersey: Africa World Press.

Patterson, Sheron C. 2000. *New Faith: A Black Christian Woman's Guide to Reformation, Re-Creation, Rediscovery, Renaissance, Resurrection, and Revival*. Minneapolis, Minnesota: Fortress Press.

Phiri, Isabel Apawo, Deverakshanam Betty Govinden, and Sarojini Nadar, eds. 2002. *Her-stories: Hidden Histories of Women of Faith in Africa*. Pietermaritzburg: Cluster Publications.

Ruether, Rosemary Radford. 2004. "A White Feminist Response to Black and Womanist Theologies." In *Living Stones in the Household of God: The Legacy and Future of Black Theology.* Edited by Linda E. Thomas. Minneapolis, Minnesota: Fortress Press.

Schüssler Fiorenza, Elisabeth. 1984. *Bread Not Stone: The Challenge of Feminist Biblical Interpretation.* Boston: Beacon Press.

Stanley, Susie C. 1993. *Feminist Pillar of Fire: The Life of Alma White.* Cleveland, Indiana: Pilgrim Press.

———. 2002. *Holy Boldness: Women Preachers' Autobiographies and the Sanctified Self.* Knoxville: University of Tennessee Press.

Thomas, Linda E., ed. 2004. *Living Stones in the Household of God: The Legacy and Future of Black Theology.* Minneapolis, Minnesota: Fortress Press.

Williams, Delores S. 1993. *Sisters in the Wilderness: The Challenge of Womanist God-talk.* Maryknoll, New York: Orbis Books.

Wright, J. A. 2004. "Doing Black Theology in the Black Church." In *Living Stones in the Household of God: the Legacy and Future of Black Theology.* Edited by Linda E. Thomas. Minneapolis, Minnesota: Fortress Press.

Contributors

Denise M. Ackermann, Ph.D. (South Africa) is Professor Emerita at the University of Stellenbosch, South Africa.

Dorcas Olubanke Akintunde, Ph.D. (Nigeria) is Senior Lecturer of New Testament in the Department of Religious Studies, University of Ibadan, Nigeria.

Dorothy B. E. A. Akoto (Ghana) is a Ph.D. student at Union Theological Seminary, New York and Lecturer in Old Testament at Trinity Theological Seminary, Legon, Ghana.

Elizabeth Amoah, Ph.D. (Ghana) is Professor of Religious Studies at the University of Ghana, Legon, Ghana.

Sophia Chirongoma (Zimbabwe) is a Ph.D. student in the Program of Theology and Development, University of KwaZulu-Natal, Pietermaritzburg, South Africa.

Musa W. Dube, Ph.D. (Botswana) is Associate Professor of New Testament at the University of Botswana.

Ogbu U. Kalu, Ph.D. (Nigeria) is the Henry Winters Luce Professor of World Christianity and Missions, McCormick Theological Seminary, Chicago, and the Director of the Chicago Center for Global Ministries, United States of America.

Musimbi R. A. Kanyoro, Ph.D. D.Min. (Kenya) is General Secretary of the World Young Women's Christian Association in Geneva, Switzerland.

M. Bernadette Mbuy Beya, Ph.D. (Democratic Republic of Congo) is a religious sister and Mother Superior of the Ursuline Sisters. She is also the Director of Bonne Espérance (Good Hope) based in Lumbumbashi, Democratic Republic of Congo.

Fulata Lusungo Moyo (Malawi) is a Ph.D. student in Systematic Theology at the University of KwaZulu-Natal and Lecturer in the Department of Theology and Religious Studies at the University of Malawi.

Sarojini Nadar, Ph.D. (South Africa) is Lecturer in Hebrew Bible at the University of KwaZulu-Natal, Pietermaritzburg, South Africa, and Coordinator of the International Network in Advanced Theological Education.

Nyambura J. Njoroge, Ph.D. (Kenya) is an ordained minister in the Presbyterian Church in Kenya and the Global Executive Secretary of the Ecumenical Theological Education Program of the World Council of Churches in Geneva, Switzerland.

Isabel Apawo Phiri, Ph.D. (Malawi) is the General Coordinator of the Circle of Concerned African Women Theologians and Professor of African Theology in the School of Theology, University of KwaZulu-Natal, Pietermaritzburg, South Africa.

Susan Rakoczy, IHM, Ph.D. (United States of America) is a religious sister and Professor of Spirituality and Systematic Theology at St. Joseph's Theological Institute, Cedara, Pietermaritzburg, South Africa.

Letty M. Russell, Ph.D. (United States of America) is Professor Emerita of Feminist Theology at Yale Divinity School, New Haven, and an ordained minister in the Presbyterian Church. She also serves as the Coordinator of the Doctor of Ministry Program with an international feminist emphasis at the San Francisco Theological Seminary, United States of America.